The Gospel that Jesus taught

THE KINGDOM GOSPEL

The Gospel that Jesus Taught
The Kingdom Gospel

Author: Sang Kwan Lee

First Published 2010

Translated by:

Sang Sur, Ph.D., Th.D.

Published by Prayer Tents Media
Old Tappan, NJ

ISBN 978-1-953167-99-6 (e-book)

ISBN 978-1-953167-98-9 (Softcover)

Words of Thanks

At one point, I asked myself, "why was I born on earth?." It was frustrating because I did not know the answer.

When the Lord told me to write this book, I saw the answer. Writing this one book is the reason why I was born. I learned that God had been planning from my birth and writing what would be the contents of this book in my heart. I was so grateful and thrilled that my mouth was hanging agape and I could not speak—only tears would flow. As I continued to read what He had put in my heart, I exclaimed, "there is no one on earth that is more loved than I am."

Beloved family that make up my flesh and blood:

Chun Jae Mo family that continuously lives as the body of Christ,

Elder Chul Joon Jung and Pastor Boo Young Huh that have helped me to get started in the Lord's work,

Deacon Seung Jah Lee that is always with working with me,

President Sang Hoon Han and wife Hae Joong Yoon supporting me to the end, bringing healing to me, and constantly being in communion with me,

My beloved wife and daughter Ha Young,

And all of you who are included in the blessings of God:

I sincerely hope that all of you too are able to stand before Jesus exclaiming "there is no one on earth that is more loved than I am!"

Seeds of unison are planted in this one book.

I hope that everyone we meet will be as happy as we are.

I am grateful to be born into this world.

2017. 4. 14.

Pastor Sang Kwan Lee

Translator Notes

You are about the take a journey to study the depth of the Gospel. This is Reverend Lee's life work to help us to understand the Gospel. He explains what we need to know and what we need to be able to explain to others who are interested in coming to know God.

As the President of *Prayer Tents*, a global Christian mission organization that seeks to connect neighbors to their local churches, I could not pass up an opportunity to take part in a book that comprehensively explains the Gospel (Find out more about Prayer Tents at *www.prayertents.com*).

I translated for Pastor Sang Kwan Lee because ever since I met him about eight years ago, he talked about a "heavenly gospel" that he claimed many Christians do not understand. When I looked further into his views, I found it hard to accept it as anything new because I thought this is how everyone already understood the Gospel. Then I began to learn that many so-called Christians, including ordained pastors and leadership in churches do not understand God and His work in the same way.

To test your knowledge, let me ask you if you understand the Gospel. Before you go further, try to explain the Gospel to yourself.

Now, was the Holy Spirit was included in your understanding of the Gospel? If not, I am glad you are reading this book. If you are able to explain how God's eternal plan of salvation incorporates the Spirit of God and how we should be raising hell (for Satan) as we live here on earth, this book will be a great reference for you to better strengthen your understanding on why you believe what you do. The Gospel tells us that our prayers are powerful, that we can heal the sick, cast out demons, and raise the dead.

Over the years, I observed God gifting Reverend Lee with wisdom and knowledge to expound on the one and true Gospel that is portrayed in the Bible. I am honored to bring this writing to English-speaking audiences.

Working with many young adults (ages 18-40), the missing people in the church today, they are longing for meaning and direction for greatest fulfillment in life. The Gospel tells us the meaning for which they are looking and from whom they can find the best direction for their lives. Knowing God and walking with Him is the way to fulfillment.

Additionally, understanding the Gospel will enable you to pray powerfully for others, because Christ is within you and is working to reveal Himself through you. Study this well, then let us go forth together make disciples of all peoples.

Child of God, Sang Sur

The Kingdom Gospel

Table of Contents

Prologue

For many years, I have been seeking spiritual growth studying more deeply about the Gospel both personally and from many scholars; however, I have not been able to fully understand the Gospel that Jesus taught.

Even though many spiritual gurus have shared the gospel with me, I do not think I was able to hear or understand it perhaps due to my lack of intelligence.

Until I was able to truly understand the Gospel, I knew as much as this: Jesus came to earth as the son of God and died to bring resolve to our sins. So He died on the cross, then rose again from the grave in three days to enter into heaven. After He completely took care of our sin problem (c.f. Hebrews 9:11-12), he sent us the Holy Spirit. Anyone who believes in these things would receive the Holy Spirit and be saved. Then this person should live in obedience to the Word of God to reign in blessings here on earth; he would also go to heaven when s/he would die. Depending on the person's actions, they would receive their due reward (c.f. Revelations 22:12). This was as much as I understood the gospel.

Even though my understanding was obviously lacking, it seemed I was holding a considerably successful ministry. I was recognized for casting out demons and healing the sick. Additionally, I traveled all over Korea and led many impactful seminars. I was considered very successful in eyes of many.

In fact, the church I started in 1988 in Kwang Joo was rapidly growing, and the church was at peace due to good members. Such success has even caused jealousy among several pastor peers.

Despite these seeming successes, I felt spiritually dry and felt trapped by various anxieties of the flesh. Even though God used me to cast out demons and demonstrated His power, I, my character and inner person, was personally not growing. I was held back with the desires of the flesh, lust of the eyes, and my personal pride.

On the exterior, I looked fine because of the title of a pastor and a busy lifestyle; however, my inner person was wandering in the dark being a slave to physical emotions.

Even though I gave sermons with my lips telling people to do good such as to love and forgive others; my heart still identified some people as *those I didn't like* and divided people as *those I didn't want to see.*

With my mouth, I talked about placing our hopes in the heavenly kingdom and proclaimed that we must live holy lives as the Bible teaches, and yet I was living as a slave of the flesh.

Jesus said this:

21"Not everyone who calls out to me, `Lord! Lord!' will enter the Kingdom of Heaven. Only those who actually do the will of my Father in heaven will enter. 22On judgment day many will say to me, `Lord! Lord! We prophesied in your name and cast out demons in your name and performed many miracles in your name.' 23But I will reply, `I never knew you. Get away from me, you who break God's laws.'

-Matthew 7:21-23

This message, which Jesus meant for false prophets, was clearly a message He was speaking to me.

Even though I played the role of a pastor and acted as though I was being obedient to the Word and doing the will of God outwardly; in reality, I was living a life so utterly despicable that words cannot describe it.

I struggled so hard to be free from this path of death. I sincerely desired to be a pastor approved by God. To achieve this, I fasted much and spent many days in tears. At times, I felt as if I was growing, but within days, I collapsed again back to my original state. Neither strength nor discipline was able to bring about change. To share what I was like back then:

20And when people escape from the wickedness of the world by knowing our Lord and Savior Jesus Christ and then get tangled up and enslaved by sin again, they are worse off than before. 21It would be better if they had never known the way to righteousness than to know it and then reject the command they were given to live a holy life. 22They prove the truth of this proverb: "A dog returns to its vomit." And another says, "A washed pig returns to the mud."

2 Peter 2:20-22

These words were exact description of my life.

I learned later that I did not really know the gospel that Jesus taught.

The reason is that I did not understand the Covenant that God the Father has promised and which the Christ the Son would accomplish. I learned later in my life that what God had promised *is* actually the Gospel of Jesus.

Not only have I fell for Satan's trick to believe that the "different kind" of Good News was from Jesus, but what is more surprising is that many pastors too believe this false news is the Gospel of Jesus.

Many people mistakenly believe a certain news is the Gospel that Jesus taught; and I write with sadness that the Lord is putting in my heart.

I also am regretful that I may not be able to express the Gospel of Jesus as beautifully as it really is because of my lack of knowledge.

New Living Translation is generally used for Scripture references in this book for easier understanding and readability; however, for clarification other translations may be used and will be marked as such.

Though we were on the way to death, God had a plan to save us through the Gospel:

Since God in his wisdom saw to it that the world would never know him through human wisdom, he has used our foolish preaching to save those who believe.
1 Corinthians 1:21

Since God has planned to save people through faith in the Gospel, we must therefore fully and clearly understand and believe in the Gospel.

Apostle Paul tells us that God intends to save even the gentiles through the Gospel:

3As I briefly wrote earlier, God himself revealed his mysterious plan to me. 4As you read what I have written, you will understand my insight into this plan regarding Christ. 5God did not reveal it to previous generations, but now by his Spirit he has revealed it to his holy apostles and prophets. 6And this is God's plan: Both Gentiles and Jews who believe the Good News share equally in the riches inherited by God's children. Both are part of the same body, and both enjoy the promise of blessings because they belong to Christ Jesus.
Ephesians 3:3-6

Likewise, God calls the gentiles with the salvation that he has planned:

13As for us, we can't help but thank God for you, dear brothers and sisters loved by the Lord. We are always thankful that God chose you to be among the first to experience salvation - a salvation that came through the Spirit who makes you holy and through your belief in the truth. 14He called you to salvation when we told you the Good News; now you can share in the glory of our Lord Jesus Christ.
2 Thessalonians 2:13-14

In that way, God calls those He will save and enables them to understand the Gospel. These people are born again and are considered children of God:

5which come from your confident hope of what God has reserved for you in heaven. You have had this expectation ever since you first heard the truth of the Good News. 6This same Good News that came to you is going out all over the world. It is bearing fruit everywhere by changing lives, just as it changed your lives from the day you first heard and understood the truth about God's wonderful grace.

Colossians 1:5-6

The "fruit" mentioned here refers to children of God.

Apostle Paul mentions this same truth:

For even if you had ten thousand others to teach you about Christ, you have only one spiritual father. For I became your father in Christ Jesus when I preached the Good News to you.

1Corinthians 4:15

In this way, God plans to save us and call us through the Gospel. He will help us understand it and cause us to be born again.

As a result, if one does not understand the Gospel, then this person has no relations with God.

Then what is this Gospel that Jesus has taught?

The core and most pervasive theme in Scriptures is the kingdom of God.

Whether it be Jesus or the Apostles, their main message has been regarding the kingdom of God.

If one does not have a clear understanding of the kingdom of God, s/he will not only forfeit the blessings in the kingdom of God, but s/he cannot receive God's mission and purpose for her/his life.

The Bible reveals the kingdom of God in perspectives of both present and future.

When Christians are asked why they believe in Jesus, many respond in the future perspective that the reason is "to go to heaven." So they share the message that "Jesus is the way to heaven." This is certainly correct.

However, Jesus taught the Gospel as the kingdom that is "near":

From then on Jesus began to preach, "Repent of your sins and turn to God, for the Kingdom of Heaven is near."

Matthew 4:17

This kingdom is not something that we look forward to seeing *in the future*, but rather, it is one that has come to find us and has already drawn near to us. In the traditional King James Version, it says to repent because kingdom of heaven is at a distance *reachable by hand*:

From that time Jesus began to preach, and to say, <u>Repent: for the kingdom of heaven is at hand.</u>

Matthew 4:17 (KJV)

Jesus was right there before them, and He declared that He Himself is the Kingdom of God that has arrived:

But if I am casting out demons by the Spirit of God, then the Kingdom of God has arrived among you.

Matthew 12:28

Here, the Holy Spirit was with Jesus, and Jesus Himself drew close to the people as the Kingdom of God. In this way, Jesus came to earth and declared Himself as the Kingdom of God.

Philip asked Jesus to show God to him:

8Philip said, "Lord, show us the Father, and we will be satisfied." 9Jesus replied, "Have I been with you all this time, Philip, and yet you still don't know who I am? Anyone who has seen me has seen the Father! So why are you asking me to show him to you? 10Don't you believe that I am in the Father and the Father is in me? The words I speak are not my own, but my Father who lives in me does his work through me. 11Just believe that I am in the Father and the Father is in me. Or at least believe because of the work you have seen me do.

John 14:8-11

Jesus declared God the Father is speaking and is working from within Him. In effect, He declared that He Himself is the Kingdom of God (and is God Himself).

23Jesus traveled throughout the region of Galilee, teaching in the synagogues and announcing the Good News about the Kingdom. And he healed every kind of disease and illness. 24News about him spread as far as Syria, and people soon began bringing to him all who were sick. And whatever their sickness or disease, or if they were demon possessed or epileptic or paralyzed - he healed them all. 25Large crowds followed him wherever he went - people from Galilee, the Ten Towns, Jerusalem, from all over Judea, and from east of the Jordan River.

Matthew 4:23-25

Jesus traveled through all the towns and villages of that area, teaching in the synagogues and announcing the Good News about the Kingdom. And he healed every kind of disease and illness.

Matthew 9:35

As Jesus healed many, He declared that He Himself is the Kingdom of God. He healed many because God the Father was in Him (c.f. John 14:10-11). As He healed all kinds of diseases, He continued to declare the Kingdom, or Himself, who was going to return back to earth through the Holy Spirit.

16And I will ask the Father, and he will give you another Advocate, who will never leave you. 17He is the Holy Spirit, who leads into all truth. The world cannot receive him, because it isn't looking for him and doesn't recognize him. But you know him, because he lives with you now and later will be in you. 18No, I will not abandon you as orphans?I will come to you. 19Soon the world will no longer see me, but you will see me. Since I live, you also will live. 20When I am raised to life again, you will know that I am in my Father, and you are in me, and I am in you.

John 14:16-20

Jesus declares that He will return through the Holy Spirit:

26But when the Father sends the Advocate as my representative—that is, the Holy Spirit—he will teach you everything and will remind you of everything I have told you. 27"I am leaving you with a gift?peace of mind and heart. And the peace I give is a gift the world cannot give. So don't be troubled or afraid. 28Remember what I told you: I am going away, but I will come back to you again. If you really loved me, you would be happy that I am going to the Father, who is greater than I am.

John 14:26-28

This way, Jesus has declared that He, who is the Kingdom of God, will return through the Holy Spirit.

13"You can enter God's Kingdom only through the narrow gate. The highway to hell is broad, and its gate is wide for the many who choose that way. 14But the gateway to life is very narrow and the road is difficult, and only a few ever find it.

Matthew 7:13-14

The door mentioned here can be clarified by the next verses:

7so he explained it to them: "I tell you the truth, I am the gate for the sheep...9Yes, I am the gate. Those who come in through me will be saved. They will come and go freely and will find good pastures.

John 10:7, 9

This narrow door refers to Jesus Himself who has drawn near to us through the Holy Spirit. We now ought to enter into Jesus who has returned to us as the narrow door.

Remain in me, and I will remain in you. For a branch cannot produce fruit if it is severed from the vine, and you cannot be fruitful unless you remain in me.

John 15:4

"Until John the Baptist, the law of Moses and the messages of the prophets were your guides. But now the Good News of the Kingdom of God is preached, and everyone is eager to get in.

Luke 16:16

The gospel that Jesus preached is one where people enter. This is where the secret of the Kingdom of God lies.

He replied, "You are permitted to understand the secrets of the Kingdom of God. But I use parables to teach the others so that the Scriptures might be fulfilled: `When they look, they won't really see. When they hear, they won't understand.'

Luke 8:10

If you do not understand the secrets of the Kingdom of God, then you have no salvation.

From here, let us examine through this book the amazing *secrets of the Kingdom of God.*

Chapter 1 – Significance of the Kingdom of Heaven

1-1. Heaven and Kingdom of God

(Kingdom of) Heaven and Kingdom of God share the same meaning and are used interchangeably in the Bible.

In Matthew 11:11 shows, "Kingdom of Heaven" as τῇ βαϐιλεία τῶν οὐρανῶν in original Greek.

I tell you the truth, of all who have ever lived, none is greater than John the Baptist. Yet even the least person in the Kingdom of Heaven is greater than he is!

Matthew 11:11

The parallel passage in Luke 7:28 says this passage but using the word "Kingdom of God": τῇ βαϐιλείᾳ τοὺ θεοὺ.

I tell you, of all who have ever lived, none is greater than John. Yet even the least person in the Kingdom of God is greater than he is!

Luke 7:28

In another place,

Matthew 13:11 uses the word "Kingdom of Heaven" (τῆς βαϐιλείας τῶν οὐρανῶν).

He replied, "You are permitted to understand the secrets of the Kingdom of Heaven, but others are not.

Matthew 13:11

Likewise, Luke tells the same message but using the words "Kingdom of God": τῆς βαϐιλείας τοὺ θεοὺ.

He replied, "You are permitted to understand the secrets of the Kingdom of God. But I use parables to teach the others so that the Scriptures might be fulfilled: `When they look, they won't really see. When they hear, they won't understand.'

Luke 8:10

And another,

Matthew 19:14 uses the term "Kingdom of Heaven" (ῆ βαϐιλεία τῶν οὐρανῶν).

But Jesus said, "Let the children come to me. Don't stop them! For the Kingdom of Heaven belongs to those who are like these children."

Matthew 19:14

The same passage in Mark shows Kingdom of God (ῆ βαϭιλεία τοὐ θεοὐ).

When Jesus saw what was happening, he was angry with his disciples. He said to them, "Let the children come to me. Don't stop them! For the Kingdom of God belongs to those who are like these children.

Mark 10:14

In that way, the "Kingdom of God" and "Kingdom of Heaven" are used interchangeably and share the same meaning.

Even in Matthew 19:23-24, equivalence in meaning can be seen:

23Then Jesus said to his disciples, "I tell you the truth, it is very hard for a rich person to enter the Kingdom of Heaven. 24I'll say it again - it is easier for a camel to go through the eye of a needle than for a rich person to enter the Kingdom of God!"

Matthew 19:23-24

This passage further demonstrates the equivalence of the terms "Kingdom of Heaven" and "Kingdom of God."

Note: Kingdom of heaven may be shortened as "heaven" going forward.

1-2. Significance of the Kingdom of Heaven, Part I
Jesus who came as a man

The Bible describes heaven as five major categories.

First, just as described thus far, heaven points to Jesus who came to earth. Another way of saying heaven is God's kingdom as previously mentioned.

Jesus came to earth as the Kingdom of Heaven, or said in another way, Kingdom of God. Put another way, Jesus came to earth as human (c.f. 1Timothy 2:5) as the sanctuary for the living God.

Jesus said the following:

19"All right," Jesus replied. "Destroy this temple, and in three days I will raise it up." 20"What!" they exclaimed. "It has taken forty-six years to build this Temple, and you can rebuild it in three days?" 21<u>But when Jesus said "this temple," he meant his own body.</u>

John 2:19-21

Jesus came to earth as a sanctuary for the living God and revealed Him during His life. Living this way as Jesus did is what it means to live as the Kingdom of God, or as heaven.

Philip asked Jesus to show God to him. Jesus replied:

8Philip said, "<u>Lord, show us the Father</u>, and we will be satisfied." 9Jesus replied, "Have I been with you all this time, Philip, and yet you still don't know who I am? <u>Anyone who has seen me has seen the Father!</u> So why are you asking me to show him to you? 10Don't you believe that <u>I am in the Father and the Father is in me</u>? The words I speak are not my own, but <u>my Father who lives in me does his work through me</u>.11Just believe that I am in the Father and <u>the Father is in me</u>. Or at least believe because of the work you have seen me do.

John 14:8-11

There needs to be an understanding of the term "in me."

As a plan for the fullness of time, <u>to unite all things in him</u>, things in heaven and things on earth.

Ephesians 1:10 (ESV)

to be put into effect when the times will have reached their fulfillment--<u>to bring all things in heaven and on earth together under one head</u>, even Christ.

Ephesians 1:10 NIV

Then, it is evident that "in me" means to "place as the head." Jesus lived "in the Father" (c.f. John 14:10-11) or with God as His head (c.f. 1Corinthians 11:3).

...head of Christ is God

1Corinthians 11:3

Jesus lived in the Father and placed Him as the head. Whatever the Father said, Jesus would live that out including in His thoughts and in His heart. By doing so, He revealed the Father by the way He lived.

God the Father was the "head" and the Son lived as the "body." This signifies that the body cannot do anything on its own, but it requires the thoughts and mind that the head gives (c.f. John 8:26-28).

To express this differently, the Father was the head of the body of Jesus. Jesus was able to live by the heart that the Father gave Him. The Father was able to form the body's heart according to His desires. Then, Jesus was able to reveal God through his body, but through the Father's life.

This is why Jesus responds the following to Philip:

9Jesus replied, "Have I been with you all this time, Philip, and yet you still don't know who I am? Anyone who has seen me has seen the Father! So why are you asking me to show him to you? 10Don't you believe that I am in the Father and the Father is in me? The words I speak are not my own, but my Father who lives in me does his work through me. 11Just believe that I am in the Father and the Father is in me. Or at least believe because of the work you have seen me do.

John 14:9-11

This is what it means to live as "heaven."

To summarize, Jesus came as the "Kingdom of Heaven," lived a life of "heaven," and shared the good news that people too can live as "heaven."

Jesus came to earth to demonstrate what heaven looks like:

From then on Jesus began to preach, "Repent of your sins and turn to God, for the Kingdom of Heaven is near."

Matthew 4:17

In King James Version, it reads

From that time Jesus began to preach, and to say, Repent: for the kingdom of heaven is at hand.

Matthew 4:17 (KJV)

It means to repent because heaven is at hand's reach.

Jesus has just declared in front of many people that He himself is heaven, and Jesus was right there within their hands' reach.

Jesus says this:

He replied, "You are permitted to understand the secrets of the Kingdom of Heaven, but others are not.

Matthew 13:11

Even here, Jesus is speaking of Himself as He refers to "Kingdom of Heaven."

It is for that reason,

But blessed are your eyes, because they see; and your ears, because they hear.

Matthew 13:16

The people around Jesus were seeing heaven's secrets then and there. Jesus was that secret of heaven! They were seeing and hearing him. This is why Jesus said their eyes and ears were blessed.

Jesus also said this:

But if I am casting out demons by the Spirit of God, then the Kingdom of God has arrived among you.

Matthew 12:28

Here, the Holy Spirit resided in Jesus and as a result, the Kingdom of God "has arrived" among them.

Jesus lived as heaven by being a sanctuary for God. As a result, Jesus healed all sickness and weaknesses by presenting and demonstrating God, who spoke and worked in Him.

Therefore, first important significance of heaven is that Jesus who came to earth as man *is* heaven Himself.

1-3. Significance of the Kingdom of Heaven, Part II Jesus who came in the Spirit

Second important significance of heaven is that Jesus came in the Spirit as the Kingdom of God at Pentecost.

Jesus said this:

And I tell you the truth, some standing here right now will not die before they see the Son of Man coming in his Kingdom."

Matthew 16:28

Jesus said to the people standing there listening to him that some of them will "not die before they see" Him "coming in His Kingdom." He was referring to when they will see Jesus returning in the Holy Spirit.

Luke says this little differently:

I tell you the truth, some standing here right now will not die before they see the Kingdom of God.

Luke 9:27

The difference is that Matthew says that *Jesus will come in His Kingdom* where Luke says that *Kingdom of God* is coming.

To clarify, Jesus brings the authority of the Kingdom and comes in the Holy Spirit. Jesus who is the Kingdom of God and heaven has come.

The law and prophets ended with John the Baptist. Now that the Good News of the Kingdom is preached, we must enter into this Kingdom.

Until John the Baptist, the law of Moses and the messages of the prophets were your guides. But now the Good News of the Kingdom of God is preached, and everyone is eager to get in.

Luke 16:16

This Kingdom of God that Jesus preached refers to Jesus who comes in the Spirit.

Jesus came as heaven, lived life of heaven, and shared the heaven's Gospel:

Jesus traveled throughout the region of Galilee, teaching in the synagogues and announcing the Good News about the Kingdom. And he healed every kind of disease and illness.

Matthew 4:23

Jesus traveled through all the towns and villages of that area, teaching in the synagogues and announcing the Good News about the Kingdom. And he healed every kind of disease and illness.

Matthew 9:35

Jesus preached the Good News about himself, the Kingdom of God, who will return in the Spirit.

However, Satan uses his minions to confuse and blind people from that truth about the Kingdom of God. He shares another kind of gospel that obscures the true Gospel.

Satan has abbreviated the Gospel to say that anyone that believes "Jesus died for our sins and raised from the dead in three days" will receive salvation.

Nonetheless, we must recognize the missing part from that statement, which is, Jesus came back to us as the Holy Spirit and as the Kingdom of God. Since the Pentecost, we receive salvation by accepting Jesus who came to us as the Holy Spirit (c.f. John 1:9-12).

We must accept Jesus who has come in the Spirit so that we may live in Christ.

In him we have redemption through his blood, the forgiveness of sins, in accordance with the riches of God's grace

Ephesians 1:7 NIV

13For he has rescued us from the kingdom of darkness and transferred us into the Kingdom of his dear Son, 14who purchased our freedom and forgave our sins.

Colossians 1:13-14

So I am willing to endure anything if it will bring salvation and eternal glory in Christ Jesus to those God has chosen.

2 Timothy 2:10

You have been taught the holy Scriptures from childhood, and they have given you the wisdom to receive the salvation that comes by trusting in Christ Jesus.

2 Timothy 3:15

As these verses show, all forgiveness and salvation occurs in Jesus Christ, the Kingdom of God.

It is required to be in Christ to be a new creation:

Therefore, if anyone is in Christ, he is a new creation; the old has gone, the new has come!
2 Corinthians 5:17 NIV

All of God's promises come true in Christ:

For all of God's promises have been fulfilled in Christ with a resounding "Yes!" And through Christ, our "Amen" (which means "Yes") ascends to God for his glory.
2 Corinthians 1:20

Even enablement occurs in Christ:

It is God who enables us, along with you, to stand firm for Christ. He has commissioned us,
2 Corinthians 1:21

Victories also occurs in Christ:

Now thanks be to God who always leads us in triumph in Christ, and through us diffuses the fragrance of His knowledge in every place.
2 Corinthians 2:14 NKJV

All blessings from heaven are given to us in Christ:

3Blessed be the God and Father of our Lord Jesus Christ, who has blessed us with every spiritual blessing in the heavenly places in Christ, 4just as He chose us in Him before the foundation of the world, that we should be holy and without blame before Him in love, 5having predestined us to adoption as sons by Jesus Christ to Himself, according to the good pleasure of His will, 6to the praise of the glory of His grace, by which He has made us accepted in the Beloved.
Ephesians 1:3-6 NKJV

Having peace is also in Christ:

I have told you all this so that you may have peace in me. Here on earth you will have many trials and sorrows. But take heart, because I have overcome the world."
John 16:33

Ability to do all things are also found in Christ:

For I can do everything through Christ, who gives me strength.

Philippians 4:13

Supplication of all of our needs are also found in Christ:

And this same God who takes care of me will supply all your needs from his glorious riches, which have been given to us in Christ Jesus.

Philippians 4:19

Even dying to our old self occurs in Christ.

I affirm, by the boasting in you which I have in Christ Jesus our Lord, I die daily.

1 Corinthians 15:31 NKJV

Just as we can see from above, living in Christ means (c.f. Ephesians 1:10) we live with Jesus as our head. When we live according to the Word (life), that is, the Head and live with the heart He gives us, Jesus works in us. His work will be revealed outwardly through our lives.

To say it differently, we too can live as heaven as Jesus is.

Life of Jesus was like this:

8Philip said, "Lord, show us the Father, and we will be satisfied." 9Jesus replied, "Have I been with you all this time, Philip, and yet you still don't know who I am? Anyone who has seen me has seen the Father! So why are you asking me to show him to you? 10Don't you believe that I am in the Father and the Father is in me? The words I speak are not my own, but my Father who lives in me does his work through me. 11Just believe that I am in the Father and the Father is in me. Or at least believe because of the work you have seen me do.

John 14:8-11

Like this, Jesus lived in the Father and the Father in Jesus.

This means that Jesus was in the Father and placed Him as the Head. Jesus lived with the heart that the Father gave and the Father worked in the Son. As a result, the Father was revealed in Jesus' life.

We too can live in Christ who came to us as the Kingdom of God by placing Him as the Head. If we live with the heart that He gives us then Jesus who is in us will work so that His life may be shown through ours.

This is why Jesus says this:

When I am raised to life again, you will know that I am in my Father, and you are in me, and I am in you.

John 14:20

This is what it means to live as heaven.

Then, how can we accept the Kingdom of Heaven, or Jesus, who has come to us?

9The one who is the true light, who gives light to everyone, was coming into the world.
10He came into the very world he created, but the world didn't recognize him. 11He
came to his own people, and even they rejected him. 12But to all who believed him and
accepted him, he gave the right to become children of God.

John 1:9-12

We must accept Jesus in order to be heaven and live in the Name of Jesus.

Now, how can we accept Jesus?

13They are reborn—not with a physical birth resulting from human passion or plan, but a birth that comes from God.

John 1:13

That is right. In order to accept Jesus who have come to us in the Spirit, we must hear and understand the Gospel through the Holy Spirit and be born again with the life that comes from God

11And this is what God has testified: He has given us eternal life, and this life is in his
Son. 12Whoever has the Son has life; whoever does not have God's Son does not have life.

1 John 5:11-12

As it says, Jesus *is* the life.

God's blessings begin from being 'born again' and this is where the secret lies.

Salvation is to be born again in the life that comes from God.

Only through that life are we able to live in Christ, place Him as the head, and live with the heart that Jesus gives us.

We will continue to look into this secret of being born again.

To conclude this section,

Forgiveness of sins and salvation only occurs in Christ, the Kingdom of God, who came to us in the Holy Spirit.

We must live in Christ from now on (c.f. Luke 16:16).

And so, the second important significance of heaven (Kingdom of God) is that Jesus came to us as heaven in the Holy Spirit.

Jesus, who is human, came as heaven to declare that He is heaven. This is the true Gospel that we must communicate to the world.

1-4. Significance of the Kingdom of Heaven, Part III Born Again Christian

As we have seen, heaven, kingdom of God and sanctuary of God are equivalent.

Don't you realize that all of you together are the temple of God and that the Spirit of God lives in you?
1 Corinthians 3:16

Don't you realize that your body is the temple of the Holy Spirit, who lives in you and was given to you by God? You do not belong to yourself,
1 Corinthians 6:19

And what union can there be between God's temple and idols? For we are the temple of the living God. As God said: "I will live in them and walk among them. I will be their God, and they will be my people.
2 Corinthians 6:16

And I am certain that God, who began the good work within you, will continue his work until it is finally finished on the day when Christ Jesus returns.
Philippians 1:6

For God is working in you, giving you the desire and the power to do what pleases him.
Philippians 2:13

Examine yourselves as to whether you are in the faith. Test yourselves. Do you not know yourselves, that Jesus Christ is in you?--unless indeed you are disqualified.
2 Corinthians 13:5 NKJV

Likewise, we need to be the sanctuary for God. Put another way, we need to live as heaven.

Jesus came as heaven and lived the life of heaven so that we too may live as heaven. During His time on earth, He preached the Good News that He will return in the Spirit.

He taught Philip that he lived as heaven (c.f. John 14:8-11) and revealed to us that we too can live as heaven:

Most assuredly, I say to you, he who believes in Me, the works that I do he will do also; and greater works than these he will do, because I go to My Father.
John 14:12

What was the purpose of Jesus going to the Father?

"Nevertheless I tell you the truth. It is to your advantage that I go away; for if I do not go away, the Helper will not come to you; but if I depart, I will send Him to you.
John 16:7

The reason why Jesus sent the Helper Holy Spirit is so that we may be born again with the life that comes from God. Then we may accept Jesus and live as a sanctuary for God (or heaven) in Christ (c.f. 1John 5:11-12).

The Holy Spirit enables us to live as heaven by teaching us all things and causing us to remember the Words Jesus has shared.

But when the Father sends the Advocate as my representative—that is, the Holy Spirit—he will teach you everything and will remind you of everything I have told you.
John 14:26

For it is not you who will be speaking - it will be the Spirit of your Father speaking through you.
Matthew 10:20

But when you are arrested and stand trial, don't worry in advance about what to say. Just say what God tells you at that time, for it is not you who will be speaking, but the Holy Spirit.
Mark 13:11

for the Holy Spirit will teach you at that time what needs to be said.
Luke 12:12

When we tell you these things, we do not use words that come from human wisdom. Instead, we speak words given to us by the Spirit, using the Spirit's words to explain spiritual truths.
1 Corinthians 2:13

21if indeed you have heard Him and have been taught by Him, as the truth is in Jesus: 22that you put off, concerning your former conduct, the old man which grows corrupt according to the deceitful lusts, 23and be renewed in the spirit of your mind, 24and that you put on the new man which was created according to God, in true righteousness and holiness.

Ephesians 4:21-24 NKJV

A new man refers to those that believe in and have accepted Jesus. They are born again in the life that comes from God. They live as heaven just as Jesus is (c.f. 1John 5:20). They are in Christ and are taught by Him.

Jesus said this:

21Again he said, "Peace be with you. As the Father has sent me, so I am sending you." 22Then he breathed on them and said, "Receive the Holy Spirit."

John 20:21-22

Just as Jesus lived in the Father with the life that comes from Him, we are to receive the Holy Spirit and be born again with the life that comes from Him. By accepting Jesus this way, we can live in Christ.

The Bible clearly says this:

10God, for whom and through whom everything was made, chose to bring many children into glory. And it was only right that he should make Jesus, through his suffering, a perfect leader, fit to bring them into their salvation. 11So now Jesus and the ones he makes holy have the same Father. That is why Jesus is not ashamed to call them his brothers and sisters.

Hebrews 2:10-11

Jesus and we are born of the same life and are therefore brothers; Jesus is the eldest brother (c.f. Romans 8:29).

We too ought to live as heaven just as our eldest brother did. We must live as God's holy nation:

But you are not like that, for you are a chosen people. You are royal priests, a holy nation, God's very own possession. As a result, you can show others the goodness of God, for he called you out of the darkness into his wonderful light.

1 Peter 2:9

5and from Jesus Christ. He is the faithful witness to these things, the first to rise from the dead, and the ruler of all the kings of the world. All glory to him who loves us and has freed us from our sins by shedding his blood for us. 6He has made us a Kingdom of priests for God his Father. All glory and power to him forever and ever! Amen.

Revelation 1:5-6

9And they sang a new song with these words: "You are worthy to take the scroll and break its seals and open it. For you were slaughtered, and your blood has ransomed people for God from every tribe and language and people and nation. 10And you have caused them to become a Kingdom of priests for our God. And they will reign on the earth."

Revelation 5:9-10

We too must live as the Kingdom (nation) of God. We must live as heaven.

We will soon look into how we can live as heaven by accepting Jesus and being born again in the life that comes from God.

I hope that by the time you finish reading this book that you will see yourself living as heaven.

To reiterate, if you are living in Christ, place Him as your head, and live with the heart that He gives you. Then Jesus who lives in you will work to show His life through yours.

My old self has been crucified with Christ. It is no longer I who live, but Christ lives in me. So I live in this earthly body by trusting in the Son of God, who loved me and gave himself for me.

Galatians 2:20

26For you are all children of God through faith in Christ Jesus. 27And all who have been united with Christ in baptism have put on Christ, like putting on new clothes.

Galatians 3:26-27

1-5. Jesus Who Lives in Me

Kingdom of God, or Jesus who has come in the Spirit, now lives in us.

One day the Pharisees asked Jesus, "When will the Kingdom of God come?" Jesus replied, "The Kingdom of God can't be detected by visible signs. (to be visible by our physical eyes)

Luke 17:20

You won't be able to say, `Here it is!' or `It's over there!' For the Kingdom of God is already among you.

Luke 17:21

My old self has been crucified with Christ. It is no longer I who live, but Christ lives in me. So I live in this earthly body by trusting in the Son of God, who loved me and gave himself for me.

Galatians 2:20

To be born again as a child of God, it is a new life that starts with accepting Jesus and living in Him.

11And this is what God has testified: He has given us eternal life, and this life is in his Son.12Whoever has the Son has life; whoever does not have God's Son does not have life.

1 John 5:11-12

Children of God are those that are born again in Christ that place Him as their head and hear His voice:

My sheep listen to my voice; I know them, and they follow me.

John 10:27

For that reason, the Bible clearly says this:

Examine yourselves as to whether you are in the faith. Test yourselves. Do you not know yourselves, that Jesus Christ is in you?—unless indeed you are disqualified.

2 Corinthians 13:5 NKJV

Note that is asks "Do you not know yourselves?" This means each person is able to clearly hear His voice and able to see with the eyes of their heart. Instead, many people recognize that the Holy Spirit/Jesus resides in him/her because someone like a pastor told him/her to believe in this—this should not be the case.

This is why Jesus says this:

16And I will ask the Father, and he will give you another Advocate, who will never leave you. 17He is the Holy Spirit, who leads into all truth. The world cannot receive him, because it isn't looking for him and doesn't recognize him. But you know him, because he lives with you now and later will be in you. 18No, I will not abandon you as orphans—I will come to you. 19Soon the world will no longer see me, but you will see me. Since I live, you also will live. 20When I am raised to life again, you will know that I am in my Father, and you are in me, and I am in you.

John 14:16-20

We must be able to see Jesus that lives in us. Not by our physical eyes, but by the eyes of the heart (c.f. Ephesians 1:18).

If you are unable to see the resurrected Jesus that has come in the Spirit, you are still of the world (c.f. John 14:19).

We are people that live by the will of God; His greatest will for us is to see Jesus, then believe in Him so that we may obtain eternal life.

For it is my Father's will that all who see his Son and believe in him should have eternal life. I will raise them up at the last day.

John 6:40

"The last day" mentioned here refers to a time from Jesus' birth to His resurrection and even to now (c.f. 1 Peter 1:20, 5-7). We are to see and believe in the Son so that we may receive the life that comes from God (be born again).

In order for us to be born again with the life that comes from God, Christ must be formed in us (c.f. Galatians 4:19). Picture of being born again may be similar to that of being born by a human mother: The baby receives the mother's characteristics. Character of Christ is to be a sanctuary for the living God (c.f. John 2:19-21).

In order for us to be formed in Christ's likeness, we must begin with seeing Jesus through the Holy Spirit (c.f. John 6:40, 2 Corinthians 3:18). Then we can be transformed to be a sanctuary for God (Kingdom of Heaven or Kingdom of God). This way we will be able to accept Jesus into our hearts.

Jesus said this clearly:

Teach these new disciples to obey all the commands I have given you. And be sure of this: I am with you always, even to the end of the age.

Matthew 28:20

In some Bible versions such the the English Standard Version (ESV), this verse uses the word "behold." This means to see.

Like this, we ought to see Spirit Jesus that is in us, and listen to His voice. This is the Law of the Spirit of Life.

And so, only through the Law of the Spirit of Life, the problem of sin and death can be resolved and we are able to live lives that fulfill the requirements of the law.

2And because you belong to him, the power of the life-giving Spirit has freed you from the power of sin that leads to death. 3The law of Moses was unable to save us because of the weakness of our sinful nature. So God did what the law could not do. He sent his own Son in a body like the bodies we sinners have. And in that body God declared an end to sin's control over us by giving his Son as a sacrifice for our sins. 4He did this so that the just requirement of the law would be fully satisfied for us, who no longer follow our sinful nature but instead follow the Spirit.

Romans 8:2-4

How Jesus lived on earth as heaven, as sanctuary for the living God, is the law of the Spirit Jesus.

Just as all living creatures can only live according to the abilities within them, Jesus too lived only by the Law of the Spirit of Life.

Jesus lived seeing God the Father working from in Him through the Law of the Spirit of Life.

19So Jesus explained, "I tell you the truth, the Son can do nothing by himself. He does only what he sees the Father doing. Whatever the Father does, the Son also does. 20For the Father loves the Son and shows him everything he is doing. In fact, the Father will show him how to do even greater works than healing this man. Then you will truly be astonished.

John 5:19-20

The eldest son Jesus saw the Father in Him and lived through His Father (c.f. John 14:8-11).

We too must live through and abide by the Law of the Spirit of Life as we see Jesus (c.f. John 14:16-21).

We will go deeper in this topic.

1-6. Significance of the Kingdom of Heaven, Part IV Thousand Year Reign

Jesus declared the Gospel and the message was that He is heaven. He also declared about a kingdom in the future where He will reign for thousand years (c.f. Revelation 20:4-6).

Unfortunately, the Bible does not provide much detail regarding this kingdom. Let's break down what is available to us.

The Gospel is joyful news about Jesus Himself.

2God promised this Good News long ago through his prophets in the holy Scriptures.
3The Good News is about his Son. In his earthly life he was born into King David's
family line, 4and he was shown to be the Son of God when he was raised from the dead
by the power of the Holy Spirit. He is Jesus Christ our Lord.

Romans 1:2-4

This Gospel is about Jesus Christ. Salvation is about Jesus Himself. All forgiveness of sin and salvation can only occur in Christ (c.f. Ephesians 1:7, 2 Timothy 2:10).

This salvation appears in three different forms because of what Jesus did in the past, our ability to overcome Satan's attacks by continued salvation as we live as a sanctuary for God, and a coming salvation to enter the Kingdom where we can reign with Jesus for thousand years.

First Form of Salvation: Ability to Live as Heaven (because of what Jesus Christ has done)

4But God is so rich in mercy, and he loved us so much, 5that even though we were dead because of our sins, he gave us life when he raised Christ from the dead. (It is only by God's grace that you have been saved!) 6For he raised us from the dead along with Christ and seated us with him in the heavenly realms because we are united with Christ Jesus. 7So God can point to us in all future ages as examples of the incredible wealth of his grace and kindness toward us, as shown in all he has done for us who are united with Christ Jesus. 8God (has) saved you by his grace when you believed. And you can't take credit for this; it is a gift from God. 9Salvation is not a reward for the good things we have done, so none of us can boast about it. 10For we are God's masterpiece. He has created us anew in Christ Jesus, so we can do the good things he planned for us long ago.

Ephesians 2:4-10

As it says in these verses, our salvation has nothing to do with our good works, but it is only given by faith. It is solely because of His grace that we are born again in the life that comes from God and receive salvation in Christ (c.f. 1 John 5:11-12).

For by grace you have been saved through faith, and that not of yourselves; it is the gift of God

Ephesians 2:8 NKJV

In New King James Version, verse 8 says, "you have been saved through faith." Note that this is in ***present perfect*** tense. This means that this has started in the past, but it is continuing. In other words, salvation has *already occurred* and therefore, we *are already* in status of not going to hell.

It refers to the status where we are born again with the life that comes from God because, through the Holy Spirit, we were able to understand the Gospel and believe (c.f. Colossians 1:5-6). This salvation has *already been given* and *it is not changed regardless of circumstances.*

This is like a child being born. A child has done no good works as s/he was born. The parents give birth out of their grace, it is a gift to the child. Once the child is born, the relationship between the parents and her/him can never be changed regardless of circumstances.

Then what would it look like to believe in Jesus and be born again in the life that comes from God?

Just as we have studied in earlier chapters, we are brothers with Jesus (Hebrews 2:10-11). Just as Jesus appeared as heaven when He was born in the Spirit, we too, who are born again, appear as heaven, that is in Christ's likeness.

We will later look further into how we may be born again as heaven and live in Christ's likeness.

Second Form of Salvation: Living as Heaven (as Sanctuary for the Living God) in the Present for the Coming Salvation

Therefore, my beloved, as you have always obeyed, not as in my presence only, but now much more in my absence, work out your own salvation with fear and trembling
Philippians 2:12 NKJV

In this verse, note "(you) work out your own salvation" is in ***present*** tense in ***active*** voice. "You" is implied. This means you ought to *continue* to work out your salvation.

Just because we have been born again with the life that comes from God (heaven), it does not mean we can be passive. Satan continues to prowl around like a roaring lion:

Stay alert! Watch out for your great enemy, the devil. He prowls around like a roaring lion, looking for someone to devour.
1 Peter 5:8

Even though you are a born again child of God, we must *continue* to live in His life so that we may be saved from the attacks of the roaring lion.

For the sin of this one man, Adam, caused death to rule over many. But even greater is God's wonderful grace and his gift of righteousness, for all who receive it will live in triumph over sin and death through this one man, Jesus Christ.
Romans 5:17

12Therefore, my beloved, as you have always obeyed, not as in my presence only, but now much more in my absence, work out your own salvation with fear and trembling; 13for it is God who works in you both to will and to do for His good pleasure.
Philippians 2:12-13 NKJV

For the law of the Spirit of life in Christ Jesus has made me free from the law of sin and death.
Romans 8:2

Now thanks be to God who always leads us in triumph in Christ, and through us diffuses the fragrance of His knowledge in every place.
2 Corinthians 2:14 NKJV

8Stay alert! Watch out for your great enemy, the devil. He prowls around like a roaring lion, looking for someone to devour. 9Stand firm against him, and be strong in your faith. Remember that your Christian brothers and sisters all over the world are going through the same kind of suffering you are. 10In his kindness God called you to share in his eternal glory by means of Christ Jesus. So after you have suffered a little while, he will restore, support, and strengthen you, and he will place you on a firm foundation. 11All power to him forever! Amen.

1 Peter 5:8-11

The only way to overcome Satan's attacks is to be firm in our faith and live according to the Law of the Spirit of Life. When we do, God who is working in us (1 John 5:20) will enable us to be victorious.

But you belong to God, my dear children. You have already won a victory over those people, because the Spirit who lives in you is greater than the spirit who lives in the world.

1 John 4:4

We are to live as a sanctuary for the Living God (heaven) so that we may be saved from Satan's attacks.

Now let us look at the third form of Salvation that is found in Jesus Christ.

Third Form of Salvation: Salvation that is yet to be received

17But the Lord stood by me and gave me strength, so that through me the message might be fully proclaimed and all the Gentiles might hear it. So I was rescued from the lion's mouth. 18The Lord will rescue me from every evil attack and save me for his heavenly kingdom. To him be the glory forever and ever. Amen.

2 Timothy 4:17-18 (NRSV)

Verse 18 here says "will rescue … and save." This is a ***simple future*** tense, which means it will surely happen at some time in the future. It is about the coming salvation.

Apostle Paul has already received salvation (c.f. Ephesians 2:8) and has been living a life working out his salvation (c.f. Philippians 2:12-13).

However, Apostle Paul says in verse 18 that the "Lord will rescue … and save" him. He was referring to the future salvation that is needed to enter into a certain heaven. He was referring to the heaven where Jesus will reign with *certain* Christians for thousand years.

4Then I saw thrones, and the people sitting on them had been given the authority to judge. And I saw the souls of those who had been beheaded for their testimony about Jesus and for proclaiming the word of God. They had not worshiped the beast or his statue, nor accepted his mark on their forehead or their hands. They all came to life again, and they reigned with Christ for a thousand years. 5This is the first resurrection. (The rest of the dead did not come back to life until the thousand years had ended.)
6Blessed and holy are those who share in the first resurrection. For them the second death holds no power, but they will be priests of God and of Christ and will reign with him a thousand years.

Revelation 20:4-6

Just because one believes in Jesus does not mean that s/he will participate in the first resurrection. There is an order to the people who will be resurrected, and not all that received salvation in Christ will be resurrected at the same time.

22Just as everyone dies because we all belong to Adam, everyone who belongs to Christ will be given new life. 23But there is an order to this resurrection: Christ was raised as the first of the harvest; then all who belong to Christ will be raised when he comes back.
24After that the end will come, when he will turn the Kingdom over to God the Father, having destroyed every ruler and authority and power.

1 Corinthians 15:22-24

It says that there is certainly an order of resurrection. First is Jesus, then *those who belong to Jesus.* Who are those that belong to Jesus?

4Remain in me, and I will remain in you. For a branch cannot produce fruit if it is severed from the vine, and you cannot be fruitful unless you remain in me. 5"Yes, I am the vine; you are the branches. Those who remain in me, and I in them, will produce much fruit. For apart from me you can do nothing.

John 15:4-5

Jesus is the tree and we are the branches that are connected to the tree. As the tree provides for the branches that belong to it, we belong to Christ only if we are nourished by what He provides. We are the ones that belong to Him only if we eat the Word of God as He speaks to us from within us.

27But you have received the Holy Spirit, and he lives within you, so you don't need anyone to teach you what is true. For the Spirit teaches you everything you need to know, and what he teaches is true - it is not a lie. So just as he has taught you, remain in fellowship with Christ. 28And now, dear children, remain in fellowship with Christ so that when he returns, you will be full of courage and not shrink back from him in shame.

1 John 2:27-28

Those that remain in fellowship with Christ following the teachings of the Holy Spirit and nourished by the Word that is spoken to them will participate in the first resurrection when Jesus returns.

Those that did not partake in the first resurrection will receive judgment before the great white throne (c.f. Revelation 20:11-15). Some will enter the lake of fire; some will receive eternal resurrection.

22Just as everyone dies because we all belong to Adam, everyone who belongs to Christ will be given new life. 23But there is an order to this resurrection: Christ was raised as the first of the harvest; then all who belong to Christ will be raised when he comes back. 24After that the end will come, ***when he will turn the Kingdom over to God the Father****, having destroyed every ruler and authority and power.*

1 Corinthians 15:22-23

This is the first resurrection. (The rest of the dead did not come back to life until the thousand years had ended.)

Revelation 20:5

The fourth significance of heaven refers to the kingdom that Jesus and some of His believers will reign for thousand years. Not everyone that has received the life that comes from God will partake in this kingdom. Only those that are continually nourished by Jesus and measure up to the full and complete standard of Christ will take part in the first resurrection when Jesus returns. They will receive the crown and they will reign with Jesus for thousand years. This is one of the rewards given to His followers. This reward is what we call the *salvation that we have yet to receive.*

To summarize, the fourth important significance of heaven (c.f. 2 Timothy 4:18) refers to the thousand years we will reign together with Jesus.

1-7. Significance of the Kingdom of Heaven, Part V Eternal Kingdom of God

Fifth significance of heaven is the eternal life that children of God will experience. This occurs after the judgment at the great white throne, which follows the thousand-year reign.

For this reason, there is no person yet, other than Jesus, who has entered into this heaven.

Jesus said this to the robber that was on the cross next to Him:

And Jesus replied, "I assure you, today you will be with me in paradise."

Luke 23:43

Jesus went to this paradise as He said.

Then in three days, he resurrected and told Mary Magdalene to not "cling to Him" because He has not gone to the Father yet:

"Don't cling to me," Jesus said, "for I haven't yet ascended to the Father. But go find my brothers and tell them, `I am ascending to my Father and your Father, to my God and your God.'"

John 20:17

The place where the Father is, as referenced in the passage above, is the heaven we will reside eternally after the judgment at the great white throne.

Jesus has come from this heaven and He is the only one that has been there:

No one has ever gone to heaven and returned. But the Son of Man has come down from heaven.

John 3:13

If heaven is not available to us now, where do you believe the believers in Christ will go once they die? Whether they were from Old Testament times or believers in the New Testament that has been born again through the Holy Spirit, what happens to them when they decease?

The Bible says they are with Abraham:

"Finally, the poor man died and was carried by the angels to be with Abraham. The rich man also died and was buried

Luke 16:22

The reason they are with Abraham is that the promise God made with Abraham has not been fully fulfilled in Jesus Christ yet.

The order of fulfillment of the Covenant goes as follows:

1. Jesus resurrects
2. Jesus reigns for thousand years
3. Jesus judges at the great white throne (Revelation 20:11-15)
4. Satan, his demons, and false prophets are sent to the eternal lake of fire
5. The children of God will then go to the place where the Father is. The eternal heaven, the eternal kingdom of God.

For this reason, there is no person that has entered heaven yet. The same goes for hell for the same reason. They are waiting for the fulfillment of the Covenant.

Fifth important significance of the Kingdom of God refers to the eternal place where children of God will be with the Father.

Only the children of God, those that have the life that comes from God, are able to see and enter into the Kingdom of God. (John 3:1-16)

So far we have uncovered five types of heaven. This heaven can only be seen by and entered by those that have the life that comes from God.

> *3Jesus replied, "I tell you the truth, unless you are born again, you cannot see the Kingdom of God." 4"What do you mean?" exclaimed Nicodemus. "How can an old man go back into his mother's womb and be born again?" 5Jesus replied, "I assure you, no one can enter the Kingdom of God without being born of water and the Spirit."*
>
> *John 3:3-5*

The passage above applies to the five types of heaven we have seen thus far.

Then, we have one concern based on the timeline. Is there salvation for those that lived before time of Jesus?

Consider the order of how Jesus gave us right to be children of God:

1. Jesus took upon all of our sins as He died on the cross, then
2. Jesus resurrected from His grave in three days, then
3. Jesus stayed on earth for forty days before ascending to heaven to be in the "perfect Tabernacle" (c.f. Hebrews 9:11-12), then
4. The Holy Spirit is sent so that we too can be children of God by receiving the life that comes from God

How does that sequence apply to those that lived before Jesus' time? Are they not allowed into heaven because they did not have Jesus to believe in during their lifetime?

The short answer is that they too can enter heaven as we can today. Now, let me explain:

What was God's original Covenant and when did He make it? God's Covenant is actually revealed to the first man and woman He created in Genesis 3:15 and 21. This is theologically called the Original Covenant or the Original Gospel.

15And I will cause hostility between you and the woman, and between your offspring and her offspring. He will strike your head, and you will strike his heel." 21And the LORD God made clothing from animal skins for Adam and his wife.

Genesis 3:15, 21

Who can this "woman's offspring" be referring to?

Obviously, this reference is about Jesus.

The "woman" mentioned here refers to Jesus' earthly mother Mary, and in the spiritual sense, the Holy Spirit.

Jesus was born by the Holy Spirit:

18This is how Jesus the Messiah was born. His mother, Mary, was engaged to be married to Joseph. But before the marriage took place, while she was still a virgin, she became pregnant through the power of the Holy Spirit. 19Joseph, her fiance, was a good man and did not want to disgrace her publicly, so he decided to break the engagement quietly. 20As he considered this, an angel of the Lord appeared to him in a dream. "Joseph, son of David," the angel said, "do not be afraid to take Mary as your wife. For the child within her was conceived by the Holy Spirit.

Matthew 1:18-20

Jesus was born of a woman but also of the Holy Spirit. Additionally, the Scriptures tell us that of those born of the Spirit, He was the firstborn, or our eldest brother:

For God knew his people in advance, and he chose them to become like his Son, so that his Son would be the firstborn among many brothers and sisters.

Romans 8:29

Jesus is the firstborn of the Holy Spirit. The Bible tells us that the Holy Spirit is also our mother.

But the other woman, Sarah, represents the heavenly Jerusalem. She is the free woman, and she is our mother. 29But you are now being persecuted by those who want you to keep the law, just as Ishmael, the child born by human effort, persecuted Isaac, the child born by the power of the Spirit. 31So, dear brothers and sisters, we are not children of the slave woman; we are children of the free woman.

Galatians 4:26, 29, 31

As it says above, the Holy Spirit is mentioned as the woman; those that are born again children of God are called offspring of the woman.

To say it differently, Jesus is the firstborn of many children that will be borne by the "woman," or the Holy Spirit. Everyone born of the Spirit are called brothers (and sisters) of Jesus.

10God, for whom and through whom everything was made, chose to bring many children into glory. And it was only right that he should make Jesus, through his suffering, a perfect leader, fit to bring them into their salvation.11So now Jesus and the ones he makes holy have the same Father. That is why Jesus is not ashamed to call them his brothers and sisters.

Hebrews 2:10-11

We are children of the woman and are born again as a brother (or sister) of Jesus. "Woman's offspring" in Genesis 3:15 refers to coming births of children of God.

God has now elaborated further on the promise He made with Abraham:

What's more, the Scriptures looked forward to this time when God would declare the Gentiles to be righteous because of their faith. God proclaimed this good news to Abraham long ago when he said, "All nations will be blessed through you."

Galatians 3:8

God fulfilled His Covenant by ensuring Jesus was in the heritage of Abraham:

> *14Through Christ Jesus, God has blessed the Gentiles with the same blessing he promised to Abraham, so that we who are believers might receive the promised Holy Spirit through faith. 15Dear brothers and sisters, here's an example from everyday life. Just as no one can set aside or amend an irrevocable agreement, so it is in this case. 16God gave the promises to Abraham and his child. And notice that the Scripture doesn't say "to his children," as if it meant many descendants. Rather, it says "to his child"—and that, of course, means Christ.*
>
> *Galatian 3:14-16*

The plan of God's salvation existed from the first man and woman (Genesis 3:15, 21). The saints of the Old Testament looked forward to be born again as children of God by fulfillment of this promise. God fulfilled this promise by sending Jesus Christ, a descendant of Abraham.

This is why Jesus says this:

> *You search the Scriptures because you think they give you eternal life. But the Scriptures point to me!*
>
> *John 5:39*

Remember, above "Scriptures" refer to the Old Testament.

God who is the Alpha and Omega, the beginning and the end considered believers in the Old Testament His children no differently from those that will come after fulfillment of the Covenant through Jesus Christ.

The reason is that they looked forward to and believed that God will send a seed of Abraham, a Messiah or Christ, to save them from their sins so that they may have eternal life.

> *22Then you will tell him, 'This is what the LORD says: Israel is my firstborn son. 23I commanded you, "Let my son go, so he can worship me." But since you have refused, I will now kill your firstborn son!"'*
>
> *Exodus 4:22-23*

> *12For when you die and are buried with your ancestors, I will raise up one of your descendants, your own offspring, and I will make his kingdom strong. 13He is the one who will build a house - a temple - for my name. And I will secure his royal throne forever. 14I will be his father, and he will be my son. If he sins, I will correct and discipline him with the rod, like any father would do. 15But my favor will not be taken from him as I took it from Saul, whom I removed from your sight.*
>
> *2 Samuel 7:12-15*

5 "Do not be afraid, for I am with you. I will gather you and your children from east and west. 6I will say to the north and south, 'Bring my sons and daughters back to Israel from the distant corners of the earth. 7Bring all who claim me as their God, for I have made them for my glory. It was I who created them.'"

Isaiah 43:5-7

Before fulfillment of Jesus' death on the cross, they have not received forgiveness of sins yet. Without the resurrection and sending of the Holy Spirit, they have not been born again with the life that comes from God. Then, why did God call them "children?"

The only reason is that they looked forward to and believed in the salvation from sins and promise of eternal life because of the Covenant that God has already made.

All believers, whether from before time of Christ or after, are considered children of God in view of God, who considers from perspective of eternity.

This is why God says the following through Daniel:

Many of those whose bodies lie dead and buried will rise up, some to everlasting life and some to shame and everlasting disgrace.

Daniel 12:2

This was the same faith of Abraham.

Jesus said this:

There will be weeping and gnashing of teeth, for you will see Abraham, Isaac, Jacob, and all the prophets in the Kingdom of God, but you will be thrown out.

Luke 13:28

To enter into the Kingdom of God, rebirth through the Holy Spirit is required. For Abraham, Isaac, and Jacob to be included in this Kingdom, it must mean that they too are born again with the life that comes from God.

To reiterate, no one can enter the Kingdom of God without the life that comes from God.

And anyone whose name was not found recorded in the Book of Life was thrown into the lake of fire.

Revelation 20:15

Nothing evil will be allowed to enter, nor anyone who practices shameful idolatry and dishonesty - but only those whose names are written in the Lamb's Book of Life.

Revelation 21:27

Only the children of God, those that have the life that comes from God, are able to enter and live in the Kingdom of God (c.f. John 3:3-10).

Additionally, we can only accept, see, and live in Jesus when we are born again with the life that comes from God. This can only happen through the work of the Spirit, through whom Jesus came back to be with us.

Until John the Baptist, the law of Moses and the messages of the prophets were your guides. But now the Good News of the Kingdom of God is preached, and everyone is eager to get in.

Luke 16:16

16And I will ask the Father, and he will give you another Advocate, who will never leave you. 17He is the Holy Spirit, who leads into all truth. The world cannot receive him, because it isn't looking for him and doesn't recognize him. But you know him, because he lives with you now and later will be in you. 18No, I will not abandon you as orphans—I will come to you. 19Soon the world will no longer see me, but you will see me. Since I live, you also will live. 20When I am raised to life again, you will know that I am in my Father, and you are in me, and I am in you.

John 14:16-20

Verse 20 says "When I am raised to life again." This is referring to the day when we will see Jesus through the Spirit.

Chapter 2 – Life of Jesus, The One Who Came to Us as Heaven

2-1. Ministry of Jesus on Earth

Jesus is God Himself, the only true God.

And we know that the Son of God has come, and he has given us understanding so that we can know the true God. And now we live in fellowship with the true God because we live in fellowship with his Son, Jesus Christ. He is the only true God, and he is eternal life.

1 John 5:20

Jesus created all things in heavens and the earth.

15Christ is the visible image of the invisible God. He existed before anything was created and is supreme over all creation, 16for through him God created everything in the heavenly realms and on earth. He made the things we can see and the things we can't see—such as thrones, kingdoms, rulers, and authorities in the unseen world. Everything was created through him and for him. 17He existed before anything else, and he holds all creation together.

Colossians 1:15-17

Jesus has created all things, including the things we cannot see, the Spiritual realm. When He created them, He followed a certain order:

By faith we understand that the entire universe was formed at God's command, that what we now see did not come from anything that can be seen.

Hebrews 11:3

The Bible says that the things that we see today has come from what is not seen. What we know of creation in Genesis 1 and 2, the heavens and the earth, have all come from an invisible realm.

Then we can conclude that the things that happen in the physical realm has occurred due to what happened at a realm that we cannot see or touch.

The Bible reveals some information about this spiritual realm. Spiritual beings revealed in the Bible can be essentially described as three kinds:

First, God is Spirit.

For God is Spirit, so those who worship him must worship in spirit and in truth.

John 4:24

Second, angels are spiritual beings.

Therefore, angels are only servants - spirits sent to care for people who will inherit salvation.

Hebrews: 1:14

The fallen angels are Satan and his demons.

This great dragon - the ancient serpent called the devil, or Satan, the one deceiving the whole world - was thrown down to the earth with all his angels.

Revelation 12:9

Third, humans are also spiritual beings.

For then the dust will return to the earth, and the spirit will return to God who gave it.

Ecclesiastes 12:7

This message concerning the fate of Israel came from the Lord: "This message is from the Lord, who stretched out the heavens, laid the foundations of the earth, and formed the human spirit.

Zechariah 12:1

Angels do not have physical bodies, but humans do.

Spiritual beings live forever. This means you and I will live forever even after our physical bodies expire on earth.

You are eternal whether you believe in Jesus or not.

When our flesh dies in the Lord, our spirit lives eternally in Christ.

And I heard a voice from heaven saying, "Write this down: Blessed are those who die in the Lord from now on. Yes, says the Spirit, they are blessed indeed, for they will rest from their hard work; for their good deeds follow them!"

Revelation 14:13

This means when we physically die outside of Christ, our spirits live eternally without Him. The spiritual realm where Jesus does not reside is called grave (or Sheol from original Hebrew), abyss, or hell according to the Bible.

The Bible describes three kinds of realms for spiritual beings:

First is the spiritual realm described in Genesis 3:

This is the story of Adam and Eve committing sin.

Their sin was not committed out of their own motives without external influence. They were persuaded by someone outside of them—Satan, who spoke through the serpent. Satan was not someone Adam and Eve were able to visibly see.

But when people keep on sinning, it shows that they belong to the devil, who has been sinning since the beginning. But the Son of God came to destroy the works of the devil.

1 John 3:8

This great dragon - the ancient serpent called the devil, or Satan, the one deceiving the whole world - was thrown down to the earth with all his angels.

Revelation 12:9

We can see that Adam and Eve only committed sin because of the influence of the invisible being Satan.

The Bible tells us that Cain was the first murderer. He killed his own brother Abel. Some great emotional strife must have caused Cain to go forward and kill his own brother.

The Bible tells us that Satan put this mind and emotion in Cain to cause the murder:

We must not be like Cain, who belonged to the evil one and killed his brother. And why did he kill him? Because Cain had been doing what was evil, and his brother had been doing what was righteous.

1 John 3:12

This is why Jesus called Satan the "murderer from the beginning," not Cain (c.f. John 8:44).

Satan continues to seek people to devour:

Stay alert! Watch out for your great enemy, the devil. He prowls around like a roaring lion, looking for someone to devour.

1 Peter 5:8

We can see that what appears in front of our eyes is a result of things that happen in another realm that we cannot see.

All activities that occurred in the Bible happened because of God or Satan.

1One day Samuel said to Saul, "It was the LORD who told me to anoint you as king of his people, Israel. Now listen to this message from the LORD! 2This is what the LORD of Heaven's Armies has declared: I have decided to settle accounts with the nation of Amalek for opposing Israel when they came from Egypt. 3Now go and completely destroy the entire Amalekite nation - men, women, children, babies, cattle, sheep, goats, camels, and donkeys."

1 Samuel 15:1-3

Verse 3 shows God of Love (c.f. 1 John 4:8) directing Saul to kill all men, women, children, and even babies.

How can God who is love demand such a violent act?

The reason is that God saw that the people of Amalek were *in Satan.*

The fact that the people of Amalek were siding with Satan was not visible to anyone in a physical sense, and this is why God had to declare the truth that humans could not discern.

Going to hell is no different.

Then the King will turn to those on the left and say, `Away with you, you cursed ones, into the eternal fire prepared for the devil and his demons.

Matthew 25:41

The Bible reveals that Satan is the ruler and authority of the unseen world.

For we are not fighting against flesh-and-blood enemies, but against evil rulers and authorities of the unseen world, against mighty powers in this dark world, and against evil spirits in the heavenly places.

Ephesians 6:12

For he has rescued us from the kingdom of darkness and transferred us into the Kingdom of his dear Son

Colossians 1:13

The Bible tells us that this world is of darkness and the ruler of the dark world is the devil.

Jesus even described Satan as the ruler of this world:

The time for judging this world has come, when Satan, the ruler of this world, will be cast out.

John 12:31

I don't have much more time to talk to you, because the ruler of this world approaches. He has no power over me

John 14:30

All people living in this world are ruled by the prince of darkness. As a result, they cannot know or even see the eternal spiritual realm without help. Many are are tricked into following the false-father, the devil, (c.f. John 8:44) and they are unable to see the Truth.

Jesus came to this world of darkness as the light to show us the concealed spiritual realm.

The one who is the true light, who gives light to everyone, was coming into the world.

John 1:9

I have come as a light to shine in this dark world, so that all who put their trust in me will no longer remain in the dark.

John 12:46

It was especially through Jesus' ministry of healing that He revealed the spiritual realm to us.

Consider when Jesus healed the mute:

32When they left, a demon-possessed man who couldn't speak was brought to Jesus. 33So Jesus cast out the demon, and then the man began to speak. The crowds were amazed. "Nothing like this has ever happened in Israel!" they exclaimed.

Matthew 9:32-33

In order to heal the physically visible sickness of being mute, Jesus cast out the spirit that cannot be seen by physical eyes.

Then a demon-possessed man, who was blind and couldn't speak, was brought to Jesus. He healed the man so that he could both speak and see.

Matthew 12:22

To heal someone who is blind and mute, Jesus revealed that it was due to an invisible spirit.

14At the foot of the mountain, a large crowd was waiting for them. A man came and knelt before Jesus and said, 15"Lord, have mercy on my son. He has seizures and suffers terribly. He often falls into the fire or into the water. 16So I brought him to your disciples, but they couldn't heal him." 17Jesus said, "You faithless and corrupt people! How long must I be with you? How long must I put up with you? Bring the boy here to me." 18Then Jesus rebuked the demon in the boy, and it left him. From that moment the boy was well.

Matthew 17:14-18

The same goes for seizures.

38After leaving the synagogue that day, Jesus went to Simon's home, where he found Simon's mother-in-law very sick with a high fever. "Please heal her," everyone begged. 39Standing at her bedside, he rebuked the fever, and it left her. And she got up at once and prepared a meal for them. 40As the sun went down that evening, people throughout the village brought sick family members to Jesus. No matter what their diseases were, the touch of his hand healed every one. 41Many were possessed by demons; and the demons came out at his command, shouting, "You are the Son of God!" But because they knew he was the Messiah, he rebuked them and refused to let them speak.

Luke 4:38-41

Verse 39 shows that even simple fevers are acts of Satan in the invisible spiritual realm.

To summarize, one of Jesus' key activities while on earth has been to reveal the concealed spiritual realm that is in the darkness of this world.

And you know that God anointed Jesus of Nazareth with the Holy Spirit and with power. Then Jesus went around doing good and healing all who were oppressed by the devil, for God was with him.

Acts 10:38

But when people keep on sinning, it shows that they belong to the devil, who has been sinning since the beginning. But the Son of God came to destroy the works of the devil.

1 John 3:8

So then, all things that we can see here on earth are a result of activities in the spiritual realm that we cannot see.

The ruler of the spiritual realm is our king Jesus.

33Then Pilate went back into his headquarters and called for Jesus to be brought to him.
"Are you the king of the Jews?" he asked him. 34Jesus replied, "Is this your own
question, or did others tell you about me?" 35"Am I a Jew?" Pilate retorted. "Your own
people and their leading priests brought you to me for trial. Why? What have you done?"
36Jesus answered, "My Kingdom is not an earthly kingdom. If it were, my followers
would fight to keep me from being handed over to the Jewish leaders. But my Kingdom is
not of this world." 37Pilate said, "So you are a king?" Jesus responded, "You say I am
a king. Actually, I was born and came into the world to testify to the truth. All who love
the truth recognize that what I say is true." 38"What is truth?" Pilate asked. Then he
went out again to the people and told them, "He is not guilty of any crime.

John 18:33-38

Verse 36 says that the spiritual realm is Jesus' kingdom.

The reason why people face ruin in their lives is that they do not know this truth.

Events that happen in the physical realm occur because of activities in the invisible spiritual realm.

The Good News is that Jesus is the king of this spiritual realm. This is the truth as referred in verses 37 and 38.

And you will know the truth, and the truth will set you free

John 8:32

2-2. Life of Jesus, the One Who Came to Us as Heaven

In God's view, a person that lives a wholesome life is one that knows their purpose and mission.

A person that does not know his/her purpose and mission is called a "sinner" according to the Bible.

Sin, according to the Bible is written in Greek as αμαϱτίβα (pronounced Amar-tee-ba). Its meaning is similar to having to hit the mark on the bull's eye. Then to miss this mark is to be off course from the purpose of one's life.

Many Christians fail in their Christian living because they do not know the reason and purpose for their lives. As a result, they live the wrong lives in the eyes of God.

We can learn about the purpose and mission of our lives by examining the life of the man Jesus.

For there is only one God and one Mediator who can reconcile God and humanity - the man Christ Jesus.

1 Timothy 2:5

What kind of life did Jesus the man live?

One day, Phillip asked Jesus to show him the Father. This was Jesus' response:

8Philip said, "Lord, show us the Father, and we will be satisfied." 9Jesus replied, "Have I been with you all this time, Philip, and yet you still don't know who I am? Anyone who has seen me has seen the Father! So why are you asking me to show him to you? 10Don't you believe that I am in the Father and the Father is in me? The words I speak are not my own, but my Father who lives in me does his work through me. 11Just believe that I am in the Father and the Father is in me. Or at least believe because of the work you have seen me do.

John 14:8-11

Jesus says that it is the Father doing the work in Him, that is, the Father is living in Him as Jesus takes the role of a sanctuary where the Father dwells. He then adds that those that have seen Him has seen the Father.

Bible says the following about God:

Since God in his wisdom saw to it that the world would never know him through human wisdom, he has used our foolish preaching to save those who believe.

1 Corinthians 1:21

He alone can never die, and he lives in light so brilliant that no human can approach him. No human eye has ever seen him, nor ever will. All honor and power to him forever! Amen.

1 Timothy 6:16

God is not someone that can be made known or visible by the wisdom of the world. However, the man Jesus revealed God through how He lived.

Yes. The reason and purpose for a person, each of us, is to reveal God to the world, the One that cannot be made known or visible by the wisdom of the world.

When the Jews asked Jesus who He was, Jesus responded like this:

25"Who are you?" they demanded. Jesus replied, "The one I have always claimed to be. 26I have much to say about you and much to condemn, but I won't. For I say only what I have heard from the one who sent me, and he is completely truthful." 27But they still didn't understand that he was talking about his Father. 28So Jesus said, "When you have lifted up the Son of Man on the cross, then you will understand that I AM he. I do nothing on my own but say only what the Father taught me.

John 8:25-28

Jesus did nothing on His own and only spoke and acted as taught as the Father living in Him has shared with Him.

Jesus lived as the Kingdom of Heaven by living with the Father as His head.

A body cannot live without the head. It is unable to think or persist without one.

To put in another way, Jesus did not live on His own. He lived with the heart of the Father because His Father was the head of His life and He was fully led by every Word of the Father. Jesus revealed the Father by the way He lived because the Father continued to work in Him. This was readily revealed to those around Him.

But Jesus told him, "No! The Scriptures say, `People do not live by bread alone, but by every word that comes from the mouth of God.'"

Matthew 4:4

49I don't speak on my own authority. The Father who sent me has commanded me what to say and how to say it. 50And I know his commands lead to eternal life; so I say whatever the Father tells me to say."

John 12:49-50

Anyone who doesn't love me will not obey me. And remember, my words are not my own. What I am telling you is from the Father who sent me.

John 14:24

The man Jesus lived as a sanctuary for the Living God. He followed every command the Father spoke and revealed God by how He lived.

23Then Jesus got into the boat and started across the lake with his disciples.
24Suddenly, a fierce storm struck the lake, with waves breaking into the boat. But Jesus was sleeping. 25The disciples went and woke him up, shouting, "Lord, save us! We're going to drown!" 26Jesus responded, "Why are you afraid? You have so little faith!" Then he got up and rebuked the wind and waves, and suddenly there was a great calm.
27The disciples were amazed. "Who is this man?" they asked. "Even the winds and waves obey him!"

Matthew 8:23-27

We can see that Jesus listened to the voice of God and was obedient even in this event.

When Jesus speaks:

- Sickness that persisted for 38 years disappears (c.f. John 5:2-8)
- Paralyzed person gets healed (c.f. Matthew 9:1-8)
- Bleeding that persisted for 12 years gets healed (c.f. Matthew 9:20-22)
- Dead daughter of synagogue leader Jairus is raised to life (c.f. Mark 5:35-43)
- Dead Lazarus is raised to life (c.f. John 11:1-44)
- Peter catches a fish with a coin sufficient to pay for temple taxes as mandated by law (c.f. Matthew 17:24-27)

Yes, even fishes hear and obey Jesus.

All of creation listened to and obeyed the word of the man Jesus. Only reason why this man was able to do this was that he lived as a sanctuary for the living God. The Father in Him was working to reveal Himself through this man.

No one has ever seen God. But the unique One, who is himself God, is near to the Father's heart. He has revealed God to us.

John 1:18

Even when the man Jesus died on the cross, it was a holy act to demonstrate the desire and love of the Father in Him.

To say conclusively, the reason a man lives and his purpose is to reveal the Father who cannot be seen or known by human wisdom to the dark world.

Your wife must be able to see God through you.

Your husband must be able to see God through you.

Your children must be able to see God through you.

Your neighbors must be able to see God through you.

Your enemies must be able to see God through you.

This is what the Bible says about that:

So now we can tell who are children of God and who are children of the devil. Anyone who does not live righteously and does not love other believers does not belong to God.
1 John 3:10

If we do not live demonstrating the God of love (1 John 4:8), then we do not belong to God.

26For you are all children of God through faith in Christ Jesus. 27And all who have been united with Christ in baptism <u>have put on Christ, like putting on new clothes.</u>
Galatians 3:26-27

To "put on Christ like new clothes" means that one is living to demonstrate the Jesus, who is God (1 John 5:20).

The man Jesus came to earth as heaven and lived to show the living God, who could not be seen or known by human eyes in this dark world.

2-3. Life of Heaven (Life of Jesus)

In Scriptures, we see plural form of heaven such as the "heavens."

Look, the highest heavens and the earth and everything in it all belong to the LORD your God.

Deuteronomy 10:14

But will God really live on earth? Why, even the highest heavens cannot contain you. How much less this Temple I have built!

1 Kings 8:27

Sing to the one who rides across the ancient heavens, his mighty voice thundering from the sky.

Psalms 68:33

There are many heavens, but the third one is called the paradise.

2I was caught up to the third heaven fourteen years ago. Whether I was in my body or out of my body, I don't know—only God knows. 3Yes, only God knows whether I was in my body or outside my body. But I do know 4that I was caught up to paradise and heard things so astounding that they cannot be expressed in words, things no human is allowed to tell.

2 Corinthians 12:2-4

Paradise is called the third heaven, but there is another heaven where God resides.

Abraham, Lazarus and other believers are already in this paradise.

Jesus said to the robber on his right when being hung on the cross:

42Then he said, "Jesus, remember me when you come into your Kingdom." 43And Jesus replied, "I assure you, today you will be with me in paradise."

Luke 23:42-43

It was after Jesus entered the paradise (v. 43) that He resurrected. Then He went to Mary Magdalene and said:

"Don't cling to me," Jesus said, "for I haven't yet ascended to the Father. But go find my brothers and tell them, 'I am ascending to my Father and your Father, to my God and your God.'"

John 20:17

The third heaven, or paradise, is not where God the Father resides. Where God resides is where we will reside with Him forever.

Satan, or the devil, (c.f. Revelation 12:9) sought to attack God and take over this heaven where God resides.

12"How you are fallen from heaven, O shining star, son of the morning! You have been thrown down to the earth, you who destroyed the nations of the world. 13For you said to yourself, 'I will ascend to heaven and set my throne above God's stars. I will preside on the mountain of the gods far away in the north. 14I will climb to the highest heavens and be like the Most High.' 15Instead, you will be brought down to the place of the dead, down to its lowest depths.

Isaiah 14:12-15

Lead angel of this rebellion was named Lucifer. God cast down and eternally bound Lucifer and his followers to Sheol (a finite place of darkness) for a set amount of time.

And I remind you of the angels who did not stay within the limits of authority God gave them but left the place where they belonged. God has kept them securely chained in prisons of darkness, waiting for the great day of judgment.

Jude 1:6

Satan has been eternally bound to darkness and cannot escape Sheol. Since his fate is sealed, he prowls around like a roaring lion looking for someone to devour (1 Peter 5:8). Jesus came to destroy Satan's work (1 John 3:8).

And yes, this place called Sheol, or darkness, is the world that we currently live in.

Since terminology may get confusing, let us define some for the rest of the book:

The eternal heaven where God resides, we shall call that the "eternal world," and

The place where Satan is bound forever, we shall call that the "finite world."

God created this finite world (c.f. Genesis 1:1-31).

8God called the space "sky." And evening passed and morning came, marking the second day. 13And evening passed and morning came, marking the third day. 19And evening passed and morning came, marking the fourth day. 23And evening passed and morning came, marking the fifth day. 31Then God looked over all he had made, and he saw that it was very good! And evening passed and morning came, marking the sixth day.

Genesis 1:8, 13, 19, 23, 31

God has created this *finite world* within finite time and space.

One might even say that God created a finite three-dimensional world in an infinite four-dimensional world.

In this finite world, heavens also exist:

1Come here and listen, O nations of the earth. Let the world and everything in it hear my words. 2For the Lord is enraged against the nations. His fury is against all their armies. He will completely destroy them, dooming them to slaughter. 3Their dead will be left unburied, and the stench of rotting bodies will fill the land. The mountains will flow with their blood. 4The heavens above will melt away and disappear like a rolled-up scroll. The stars will fall from the sky like withered leaves from a grapevine, or shriveled figs from a fig tree.

Isaiah 34:1-4

"Immediately after the anguish of those days, the sun will be darkened, the moon will give no light, the stars will fall from the sky, and the powers in the heavens will be shaken.

Matthew 24:29

10But the day of the Lord will come as unexpectedly as a thief. Then the heavens will pass away with a terrible noise, and the very elements themselves will disappear in fire, and the earth and everything on it will be found to deserve judgment. 11Since everything around us is going to be destroyed like this, what holy and godly lives you should live, 12looking forward to the day of God and hurrying it along. On that day, he will set the heavens on fire, and the elements will melt away in the flames.

2 Peter 3:10-12

(Also see correlation in Revelation 6:12-14)

As above, our current finite world will turn into hell.

This is why in 2 Peter 2:4, there is a reference to equivalence of darkness (c.f. Jude 1:6) and hell. This earth will become hell.

For God did not spare even the angels who sinned. He threw them into hell, in gloomy pits of darkness, where they are being held until the day of judgment.

2 Peter 2:4

This *finite world* can so then be referenced as coming hell. However, His children, those that have the life that comes from God, will live in the New Heaven and New Earth eternally.

10But the day of the Lord will come as unexpectedly as a thief. Then the heavens will pass away with a terrible noise, and the very elements themselves will disappear in fire, and the earth and everything on it will be found to deserve judgment. 11Since everything around us is going to be destroyed like this, what holy and godly lives you should live, 12looking forward to the day of God and hurrying it along. On that day, he will set the heavens on fire, and the elements will melt away in the flames. 13But we are looking forward to the new heavens and new earth he has promised, a world filled with God's righteousness.

2 Peter 3:10-13

God has created the *finite world* from the *eternal world.*

Now, what is important is how and with what He created the finite world.

God created all things with the Word that came from his mouth. "God said" something and it came to be.

3Then God said, "Let there be light," and there was light.

6Then God said, "Let there be a space between the waters, to separate the waters of the heavens from the waters of the earth."

9Then God said, "Let the waters beneath the sky flow together into one place, so dry ground may appear." And that is what happened.

14Then God said, "Let lights appear in the sky to separate the day from the night. Let them be signs to mark the seasons, days, and years.

20Then God said, "Let the waters swarm with fish and other life. Let the skies be filled with birds of every kind."

24Then God said, "Let the earth produce every sort of animal, each producing offspring of the same kind - livestock, small animals that scurry along the ground, and wild animals." And that is what happened.

26Then God said, "Let us make human beings in our image, to be like us. They will reign over the fish in the sea, the birds in the sky, the livestock, all the wild animals on the earth, and the small animals that scurry along the ground."

29Then God said, "Look! I have given you every seed-bearing plant throughout the earth and all the fruit trees for your food.

Genesis 1:3, 6, 9, 14, 20, 24, 26, 29

God created all things in the *finite world* through His Word.

The reason why everything in the *finite world* was created through His Word is so that everything in the *finite world* would listen to and obey the voice of God, its Creator.

This is the simply how the Bible unfolded throughout history.

The reason why Joshua was able to stop the sun and moon from moving (c.f. Joshua 10:12-13), the Red Sea separated to make paths for God's people, the Jordan river dried up, and walls of Jericho collapsed was simply because all things on earth obey the voice of its Maker.

So then, all of God's creation in this *finite world* has ears to hear the voice of their Originator.

31When the Lord spoke, flies descended on the Egyptians, and gnats swarmed across Egypt. 32He sent them hail instead of rain, and lightning flashed over the land. 33He ruined their grapevines and fig trees and shattered all the trees. 34He spoke, and hordes of locusts came - young locusts beyond number. 35They ate up everything green in the land, destroying all the crops in their fields.

Psalms 105:31-35

Even the flies can hear the voice of God and even the locusts obey God. It is because God created all things through His Word.

6In that day the wolf and the lamb will live together; the leopard will lie down with the baby goat. The calf and the yearling will be safe with the lion, and a little child will lead them all. 7The cow will graze near the bear. The cub and the calf will lie down together. The lion will eat hay like a cow. 8The baby will play safely near the hole of a cobra. Yes, a little child will put its hand in a nest of deadly snakes without harm. 9Nothing will hurt or destroy in all my holy mountain, for as the waters fill the sea, so the earth will be filled with people who know the Lord.

Isaiah 11:6-9

All creatures on earth are able to live at peace because they receive instructions from God. This is why God says He will make a Covenant with animals and birds at His time:

On that day I will make a Covenant with all the wild animals and the birds of the sky and the animals that scurry along the ground so they will not harm you. I will remove all weapons of war from the land, all swords and bows, so you can live unafraid in peace and safety.

Hosea 2:18

All creatures that live in the *finite world* are given the ability to hear from their Creator and obey His Word because they were created by His Word.

In the Old Testament, many prophets declared the Word of God.

Most clear message where a prophet spoke to the creation appears in Ezekiel 37:

*1The Lord took hold of me, and I was carried away by the Spirit of the Lord to a valley filled with bones. 2He led me all around among the bones that covered the valley floor. They were scattered everywhere across the ground and were completely dried out. 3Then he asked me, "Son of man, can these bones become living people again?" "O Sovereign Lord," I replied, "you alone know the answer to that." 4Then he said to me, "**Speak** a prophetic message to these bones and say, 'Dry bones, listen to the word of the Lord! 5This is what the Sovereign Lord says: Look! I am going to put breath into you and make you live again! 6I will put flesh and muscles on you and cover you with skin. I will put breath into you, and you will come to life. Then you will know that I am the Lord.'" 7So I **spoke** this message, just as he told me. Suddenly as I **spoke**, there was a rattling noise all across the valley. The bones of each body came together and attached themselves as complete skeletons. 8Then as I watched, muscles and flesh formed over the bones. Then skin formed to cover their bodies, but they still had no breath in them. 9Then he said to me, "**Speak** a prophetic message to the winds, son of man. **Speak** a prophetic message and say, 'This is what the Sovereign Lord says: Come, O breath, from the four winds! Breathe into these dead bodies so they may live again.'" 10So I **spoke** the message as he commanded me, and breath came into their bodies. They all came to life and stood up on their feet - a great army. 11Then he said to me, "Son of man, these bones represent the people of Israel. They are saying, 'We have become old, dry bones - all hope is gone. Our nation is finished.' 12Therefore, **prophesy** to them and **say**, 'This is what the Sovereign Lord says: O my people, I will open your graves of exile and cause you to rise again. Then I will bring you back to the land of Israel. 13When this happens, O my people, you will know that I am the Lord. 14I will put my Spirit in you, and you will live again and return home to your own land. Then you will know that I, the Lord, have spoken, and I have done what I said. Yes, the Lord has spoken!'"*

Ezekiel 37:1-14

We know that the prophesied Word of God has been fulfilled throughout history.

Testimony of Jesus is the spirit of prophecy:

And I fell at his feet to worship him. But he said to me, "See that you do not do that! I am your fellow servant, and of your brethren who have the testimony of Jesus. Worship God! For the testimony of Jesus is the spirit of prophecy."

Revelation 19:10 NKJV

Jesus came as man, spoke as the Father revealed to Him and showed the Father through the way He lived.

If I hadn't done such miraculous signs among them that no one else could do, they would not be guilty. But as it is, they have seen everything I did, yet they still hate me and my Father.

John 15:24

Even when there was a dangerous storm, Jesus simply spoke and the waves calmed (c.f. Matthew 8:23-27).

Jesus healed a woman that has been bleeding for twelve years (c.f. Matthew 9:20-22), raised the dead daughter of a synagogue leader (c.f. Matthew 9:18-26), walked on water (c.f. Matthew 14:22-33), caught a fish with money that was needed (c.f. Matthew 17:24-27), healed the person that was paralyzed for 38 years (c.f. John 5:1-9), fed five thousand men with two fishes and five loaves of bread (c.f. John 6:1-15), and even healed the ear of a servant by putting it back on him (c.f. Luke 22:50-51).

These are certainly not the whole list of all miracles that Jesus performed, as the number of His miracles would not fit in a book. He was able to do these things because He was speaking what the Father, who was in Him, was doing. As He spoke the Word of God, He revealed God.

49I don't speak on my own authority. The Father who sent me has commanded me what to say and how to say it. 50And I know his commands lead to eternal life; so I say whatever the Father tells me to say."

John 12:49-50

Anyone who doesn't love me will not obey me. And remember, my words are not my own. What I am telling you is from the Father who sent me.

John 14:24

Jesus listened for the voice of the Father from within Him and spoke what the Father said. When the Creator's words were spoken, all of creation would listen and obey the command.

Let us look at what happened when Jesus came out of Bethany:

12The next morning as they were leaving Bethany, Jesus was hungry. 13He noticed a fig tree in full leaf a little way off, so he went over to see if he could find any figs. But there were only leaves because it was too early in the season for fruit. 14Then Jesus said to the tree, "May no one ever eat your fruit again!" And the disciples heard him say it.

Mark 11:12-14

The fig tree here represents the law-abiding Israel. God had given them the law through Moses.

What Jesus was declaring here is that He will no longer seek fruit from the laws of Moses.

However, in this passage, there is another message that all of God's creation obey at the Word of God. Since the tree did not obey the expectation of Jesus, He rebuked it in front of His disciples.

Then He entered the temple:

15When they arrived back in Jerusalem, Jesus entered the Temple and began to drive out the people buying and selling animals for sacrifices. He knocked over the tables of the money changers and the chairs of those selling doves, 16and he stopped everyone from using the Temple as a marketplace. 17He said to them, "The Scriptures declare, `My Temple will be called a house of prayer for all nations,' but you have turned it into a den of thieves."

Mark 11:15-17

Jesus uses Scriptures to declare that His "Temple will be called a house of prayer." Then on the next morning, Peter asks Jesus:

19That evening Jesus and the disciples left the city. 20The next morning as they passed by the fig tree he had cursed, the disciples noticed it had withered from the roots up. 21Peter remembered what Jesus had said to the tree on the previous day and exclaimed, "Look, Rabbi! The fig tree you cursed has withered and died!" 22Then ***Jesus said to the disciples, "Have faith in God.***

Mark 11:19-22

Jesus' response is a bit queer. Why did Jesus, out of nowhere, say to have in faith in God?

It is because when Jesus rebuked the fig tree, it was not on His own accord. It was coming from the voice of the Father who dwelled in Him as a sanctuary (c.f. John 8:25-28). Jesus was telling the disciples to believe the Word of God that the Father had spoken.

This is why Jesus says this:

22Then Jesus said to the disciples, "Have faith in God. 23I tell you the truth, you can say to this mountain, `May you be lifted up and thrown into the sea,' and it will happen. But you must really believe it will happen and have no doubt in your heart. 24I tell you, you can pray for anything, and if you believe that you've received it, it will be yours.

Mark 11:22-24

Verse 24 says, "you can pray for anything" and to "believe that you've received it." This is referring to after conversing with God (prayer) then speaking the Word of God spoken by Him. Then we should believe in what God has done as if we have received it.

To say it again, Jesus lived His life listening to the voice of God that was in Him. As He heard from God, He acted in obedience and the Word came to life.

> *So the Word became human and made his home among us. He was full of unfailing love and faithfulness. And we have seen his glory, the glory of the Father's one and only Son.*
> *John 1:14*

"Word became human" means that God who was speaking from within Jesus was revealed through the life of Jesus.

This lifestyle is of the man Jesus. For those of us who are born again by the Spirit and has the life of Jesus, this too ought to be our lifestyle.

The reason why we live and our purpose in life are to be a sanctuary (heaven) for the living God. We are to show the living God through the way we live.

Children of God are those in Christ that lives with the heart that God supplies and as a result, reveals Him who is working in them.

Chapter 3 – The Name of God the Father

3-1. The Name of God the Father, Part I

The man Jesus lived a life revealing God by being a sanctuary for the living God (also known as the Kingdom of God) (c.f. John 14:8-11). He placed God as His head and acted in accordance with the heart, mind and the instructions God provided.

While the man Jesus lived on earth, He says He guarded them in the *Father's Name* (c.f. John 17:12).

Jesus replied, "I have already told you, and you don't believe me. The proof is the work I do in my Father's name.

John 10:25

Jesus said that He is one with the Father by the Name of the Father (c.f. John 17:11).

Jesus revealed the Father through His life (c.f. John 1:18), but even as He revealed the Father, He declares He has done it through the Name of the Father (c.f. John 17:6).

What does it mean to reveal the Father by the Name of the Father?

To talk about the topic of the Father's Name would be too vast to cover, and so we will only discuss the Father's Name as it pertains to the secrets of the Kingdom of Heaven in this book.

Jesus who came as the Kingdom of God (also known as "heaven") came to earth in the Father's Name, lived in the Father's Name, and revealed the Father's Name through His life.

For I have come to you in my Father's name, and you have rejected me. Yet if others come in their own name, you gladly welcome them.

John 5:43

Jesus replied, "I have already told you, and you don't believe me. The proof is the work I do in my Father's name.

John 10:25

I have made your name known to those whom you gave me from the world. They were yours, and you gave them to me, and they have kept your word.

John 17:6 (NRSV)

Jesus came in the Name of the Father, lived in His Name, and revealed His Name through His life.

Jesus came as the Christ (also known as Messiah) to cast away demons by the Name of the Father that had been given to Him (c.f. Acts 10:38); he also ruined the works of the devil (c.f. 1 John 3:8), calmed the waves, fed five thousand, raised the dead, and healed all kinds of sicknesses by the Father's Name (c.f. Matthew 4:23-24, 9:35).

During my time here, I protected them by the power of the name you gave me. I guarded them so that not one was lost, except the one headed for destruction, as the Scriptures foretold.

John 17:12

Jesus was one with God by the Name of the Father that was given to Him.

Now I am departing from the world; they are staying in this world, but I am coming to you. Holy Father, you have given me your name; now protect them by the power of your name so that they will be united just as we are.

John 17:11

To reiterate, Jesus did not live on His own accords; rather, He lived to complete the work that the Father gave Him and gave glory to the Father by His obedience.

I brought glory to you here on earth by completing the work you gave me to do.

John 17:4

What do you think is the work the Father wanted Jesus to do?

I have made your name known to those whom you gave me from the world. They were yours, and you gave them to me, and they have kept your word.

John 17:6 (NRSV)

Jesus worked to make the Name of the Father known to the world. In all that He did, He submitted before the Name of the Father. Jesus said this:

I have revealed you to them, and I will continue to do so. Then your love for me will be in them, and I will be in them.

John 17:26

This verse reveals to us that those that know the Name of God the Father will receive the same love that Jesus receives from the Father. Jesus will dwell in the persons that know the Name of God the Father

Said conversely, it means that we do not receive the love of God because we *do not know* the Name of God the Father. We are not fully one with Jesus because we *do not know* the Name of God the Father.

We must, then, know and understand the Name of God the Father. What Name did the Father give to the Son?

Joseph and Mary did not hold a discussion to name their child. God had sent an angel to Joseph and Mary and had given the child his Name even before their child was born. The angel said to Joseph:

And she will have a son, and you are to name him Jesus, for he will save his people from their sins.

Matthew 1:21

The angel said to Mary:

You will conceive and give birth to a son, and you will name him Jesus.

Luke 1:31

God gave His Son the Name of Jesus as He sent Him to earth. The Bible says that the Son is far greater than the angels because He has received a Name that is greater.

This shows that the Son is far greater than the angels, just as the name God gave him is greater than their names.

Hebrews 1:4

Yes.

Even though Satan is the king of this dark world, Jesus has the authority given by the Father to ruin Satan's work. God had sent His Son with His own Name. Jesus lived fulfilling the Father's will and showed the Father to the world through the way He lived.

The Father promised to send the Holy Spirit in the Name of Jesus:

But the Helper, the Holy Spirit, whom the Father will send in My name, He will teach you all things, and bring to your remembrance all things that I said to you.

John 14:26 NKJV

Let us take a moment to ensure we understand this.

Jesus came to earth with the Name given by the Father, the Name "Jesus." The Name of Jesus is therefore the Name of the Father.

The Holy Spirit was to be sent in the Name of Jesus, which is the Name of the Father. Then it is:

Jesus is the Name of the Father

Jesus is the Name of the Son

Jesus is the Name of the Holy Spirit

The Father, Son, and Holy Spirit are one.

Now I am departing from the world; they are staying in this world, but I am coming to you. Holy Father, you have given me your name; now protect them by the power of your name so that they will be united just as we are.

John 17:11

And Jesus said to His disciples:

Therefore, go and make disciples of all the nations, baptizing them in the name of the Father and the Son and the Holy Spirit.

Matthew 28:19

Notice that the command here is to baptize *in the name of the Father, the Son, and Holy Spirit.* Did you know Jesus' disciples baptized only in the Name of Jesus after Jesus departed from them? They were not being disobedient, as the Name of Jesus *is* the Name of the Father, Son, and Holy Spirit.

The Holy Spirit had not yet come upon any of them, for they had only been baptized in the name of the Lord Jesus.

Acts 8:16

As soon as they heard this, they were baptized in the name of the Lord Jesus.

Acts 19:5

In Zechariah 14, it says that the Name of the Lord will be centralized into One Name.

8On that day living waters shall flow out from Jerusalem, half of them to the eastern sea and half of them to the western sea. It shall continue in summer as in winter. 9And the LORD will be king over all the earth. On that day the LORD will be one and his name one.

Zechariah 14:8-9 (ESV)

"Jerusalem" in verse 8 refers to the Holy Spirit (c.f. Galatians 4:26, 29), and the Holy Spirit supplies the living waters:

37On the last day of the feast, the great day, Jesus stood up and cried out, "If anyone thirsts, let him come to me and drink. 38Whoever believes in me, as the Scripture has said, 'Out of his heart will flow rivers of living water.'" 39Now this he said about the Spirit, whom those who believed in him were to receive, for as yet the Spirit had not been given, because Jesus was not yet glorified.

John 7:37-39

At the time when the Holy Spirit provides the rivers of living water through faith in Jesus, the Name of the Lord will be one.

Jesus came to earth as the King.

Pilate said, "So you are a king?" Jesus responded, "You say I am a king. Actually, I was born and came into the world to testify to the truth. All who love the truth recognize that what I say is true."

John 18:37

This is why once Jesus came to earth as the King, we no longer see any other *names of God* in Scriptures.

In the Old Testament, it says Jehovah God created the heavens and the earth.

In the beginning God created the heavens and the earth.

Genesis 1:1

This is what the Lord says - your Redeemer and Creator. 'I am the Lord, who made all things. I alone stretched out the heavens. Who was with me when I made the earth?

Isaiah 44:24

But in the New Testament, it says Jesus created the heavens and the earth.

1In the beginning the Word already existed The Word was with God, and the Word was God. 2He existed in the beginning with God. 3God created everything through him, and nothing was created except through him.

John 1:1-3

13For he has rescued us from the kingdom of darkness and transferred us into the Kingdom of his dear Son, 14who purchased our freedom and forgave our sins. 15Christ is the visible image of the invisible God. He existed before anything was created and is supreme over all creation, 16for through him God created everything in the heavenly realms and on earth. He made the things we can see and the things we can't see—such as thrones, kingdoms, rulers, and authorities in the unseen world. Everything was created through him and for him.

Colossians 1:13-16

So, we can see that Jehovah of the Old Testament and Jesus of the New are One. They have been working and are continuing to work together as One.

The Bible also says this:

10Yes, the Sovereign Lord is coming in power. He will rule with a powerful arm. See, he brings his reward with him as he comes. 11He will feed his flock like a shepherd. He will carry the lambs in his arms, holding them close to his heart. He will gently lead the mother sheep with their young.

Isaiah 40:10-11

I myself will tend my sheep and give them a place to lie down in peace, says the Sovereign Lord.

Ezekiel 34:15

We can hear the voice of God because the One that had promised to come Himself to be our shepherd has now come in the flesh as Jesus Christ.

My sheep listen to my voice; I know them, and they follow me.

John 10:27

And that is how the God of the Old Testament and Jesus of the New are the same.

The Name "Jehovah" signifies that He is the only true God (c.f. Isaiah 41:21-24, 45:20-23). "Jehovah" God is distinguished from any idols. This Name of "Jehovah" is the Name of Jesus Himself.

Let me explain that a bit more. Imagine an elephant, lion, tiger, deer, and other animals came up to you and said "I am human and my name is Sang Sur." No matter how much these animals want to claim to be human, they cannot be, or they would be counterfeits.

These idols, such as Baal, Asherah, Molech, Dangun, are nothing compared to the true God whose Name is "Jehovah." The Name "Jehovah" stands alone distinguished from anything else. This distinct Name of "Jehovah" is now being represented by the Name "Jesus." Note this passage from the Old Testament:

But everyone who calls on the name of the Lord will be saved… (Jehovah is translated as "Lord")

Joel 2:32

However, we know from Acts that there is no other name than the Name of Jesus that brings about salvation:

11For Jesus is the one referred to in the Scriptures, where it says, `The stone that you builders rejected has now become the cornerstone.' 12There is salvation in no one else! God has given no other name under heaven by which we must be saved."

Acts 4:11-12

So then, there is no other Name by which we can be saved other than the Name of Jehovah and the Name of Jesus. The reason why that can work is that the Name of Jehovah is also known as the Name of Jesus.

That is why now we must focus our attention to knowing the Name of Jesus more deeply.

To reiterate, in order for us to live as the Kingdom of God, we must understand the secrets of the Kingdom. Jesus specifically said those that do not know the secrets of the Kingdom will have no forgiveness of sins.

10When he was alone, those who were around him along with the twelve asked him about the parables. 11And he said to them, "To you has been given the secret of the kingdom of God, but for those outside, everything comes in parables; 12in order that 'they may indeed look, but not perceive, and may indeed listen, but not understand; so that they may not turn again and be forgiven.'"

Mark 4:10-12

Without understanding the secrets of the Kingdom, you would not receive forgiveness of sins.

46And he said, "Yes, it was written long ago that the Messiah would suffer and die and rise from the dead on the third day. 47It was also written that this message would be proclaimed in the authority of his name to all the nations, beginning in Jerusalem: 'There is forgiveness of sins for all who repent.'

Luke 24:46-47

Let us connect the dots. One passage says we need to know the secret of God in order to be forgiven. Then this passage says there is forgiveness of sins for all who repent under the authority of Jesus' Name. Then, the *secret of the Kingdom is the Name of Jesus.*

Even the disciples share this:

He is the one all the prophets testified about, saying that everyone who believes in him will have their sins forgiven through his name.

Acts 10:43

I remind you, my dear children: Your sins are forgiven in Jesus' name.

1 John 2:12 (MSG)

Secret of the Kingdom is the Name of Jesus, and we must understand His Name correctly to be forgiven from our sins.

If we do not know the Name of Jesus, there is no forgiveness and salvation. The reason is simple: If one does not know the secret of the Kingdom of God, which is the Name of Jesus, they cannot become the Kingdom of God.

Therefore, it is important for us to know deeply about the Name of Jesus. It is the Name of God the Father has given to the Son.

What kind of secret exists in the Name of Jesus with which Jesus protected his disciples through it? (c.f. John 17:12)

What kind of secret exists in the Name of Jesus by which God the Father and the Son are One? (c.f. John 17:11)

What kind of secret exists in the Name of Jesus that the waves obey, the dead come back to life, the evil spirits are cast away, all kinds of sickness is healed, five thousand men are fed with few fishes and loaves, and Jesus walks on water?

We must absolutely learn and understand the secrets of the Name of God the Father.

As Philip shared the Good News about the Kingdom of God, He also shared the Good News about the Name of Jesus:

But now the people believed Philip's message of Good News concerning the Kingdom of God and the name of Jesus Christ. As a result, many men and women were baptized.
Acts 8:12

The Bible clearly tells us that by the power of His Name, we can be born again and live with the life that comes from God:

30The disciples saw Jesus do many other miraculous signs in addition to the ones recorded in this book. 31But these are written so that you may continue to believe that Jesus is the Messiah, the Son of God, and that by believing in him you will have life by the power of his name.
John 20:30-31

Chapter two in Hebrews explains the reason and purpose for why God intended to bear many children. We can also see Jesus declaring to His brothers and sisters about the power of His Name:

10God, for whom and through whom everything was made, chose to bring many children into glory. And it was only right that he should make Jesus, through his suffering, a perfect leader, fit to bring them into their salvation. 11So now Jesus and the ones he makes holy have the same Father. That is why Jesus is not ashamed to call them his brothers and sisters. 12For he said to God, "I will proclaim your name to my brothers and sisters. I will praise you among your assembled people."
Hebrews 2:10-12

In verse 12, the word "proclaim" can mean to "declare" or "make known." This verse means that Jesus will reveal to us the secrets of heaven. He will show us and teach us how to live as heaven as He reveals the power of His Name. Then we too will be able to live with the Name of the Father as our banner just as Jesus lived.

We must know about His Name with certainty.

If we do not know the secret of heaven, the Name of Jesus, then there is no forgiveness of sins or salvation. We cannot live in unity with Jesus (c.f. John 17:11).

Name of Jesus is the focus for children of God. For that reason, we must fully know and believe in the Name of Jesus, which is the secret of heaven.

3-2. Where did the Name of the Father, also known as Jesus, reside in the Old Testament?

When we survey the history of Israel in the Old Testament, we can see the nation of Israel being made. Along the way, Israel comes to settle in the land of Egypt with Jacob and Joseph. Then Moses becomes the leader of an exodus, and they go through the Red Sea after the Lord split the waters to provide safe passage. Then God reveals the sanctuary in heaven to Moses and asks him to build a replica (c.f. Hebrews 8:5).

Then they pass over the Jordan River and enter the land of Canaan to build this temple. Though initially, they served the Lord wholeheartedly, they eventually turn away from the Lord. As a result, the temple is destroyed and they are taken into exile. Then they came to their senses and repented (turned back to the Lord). They returned to Canaan that was in ruins, and they began to reconstruct the temple. This is how the history of Israel concludes in the Old Testament.

It may be possible to summarize that building this temple was the history of Israel. We can also see that God's focus had been on the land of Canaan.

> *11Rather, the land you will soon take over is a land of hills and <u>valleys with plenty of rain - 12a land that the LORD your God cares for. He watches over it through each season of the year!</u>*
>
> *Deuteronomy 11:11-12*

Canaan was unique in that when it rained plentifully, they had an abundance of water to use; however, when the skies produced no rain, there would be a drought.

This uniqueness was so that God's people could only subsist by the grace of God.

The reason why God's focus was on the land of Canaan was that He intended to build a sanctuary there (c.f. 1 Kings 9:1-3)

Then what was God's purpose and reason for building this temple?

1Then Solomon prayed, "O LORD, you have said that you would live in a thick cloud of darkness. 2Now I have built a glorious Temple for you, a place where you can live forever!" 3Then the king turned around to the entire community of Israel standing before him and gave this blessing. 4"Praise the LORD, the God of Israel, who has kept the promise he made to my father, David. For he told my father, 5'From the day I brought my people out of the land of Egypt, I have never chosen a city among any of the tribes of Israel as the place where a Temple should be built to honor my name. Nor have I chosen a king to lead my people Israel. 6But now I have chosen Jerusalem as the place for my name to be honored, and I have chosen David to be king over my people Israel.'" 7Then Solomon said, "My father, David, wanted to build this Temple to honor the name of the LORD, the God of Israel. 8But the LORD told him, 'You wanted to build the Temple to honor my name. Your intention is good, 9but you are not the one to do it. One of your own sons will build the Temple to honor me.' 10"And now the LORD has fulfilled the promise he made, for I have become king in my father's place, and now I sit on the throne of Israel, just as the LORD promised. I have built this Temple to honor the name of the LORD, the God of Israel.

2 Chronicles 6:1-10

The temple of God was to be built as a place to honor the Name of Jehovah (Jesus).

Then where in the temple is the Name of Jehovah (Jesus)?

There I have placed the Ark, which contains the Covenant that the LORD made with the people of Israel."

2 Chronicles 6:11

God placed the Covenant that He made with the people of Israel inside the Ark.

Though we will dive into this further, to help understand this for now, let me reveal briefly about a future topic. The "Covenant" is the second one made with the people of Israel in the land of Moab (c.f. Deuteronomy 29:1-30:20). In this Covenant, God made two promises:

First, God promised to "circumcise" our and our children's hearts so that we may be able to love God with all our hearts and souls and enable us to truly live (c.f Deuteronomy 30:6). What does it mean to "truly live?" It means He will enable us to live as the Kingdom of God (heaven) (c.f. Deuteronomy 30:11-14).

Second, God promised to give us His life.

And in this fellowship we enjoy the eternal life he promised us.

1 John 2:25

The Ark of God that preserved the Covenant of God contained the Name of the Jehovah Lord.

> *He led them to Baalah of Judah to bring back the Ark of God, which bears the name of the LORD of Heaven's Armies, who is enthroned between the cherubim.*
>
> *2 Samuel 6:2*

As we reviewed before, the Name of Jehovah is the same as the Name of Jesus.

> *But everyone who calls on the name of the Lord will be saved*
>
> *Joel 2:32*

"The Name of the Lord" is the Name of Jesus because we know that there is no other Name by which we can be saved other than the Name of Jesus (c.f. Acts 4:10-12).

Therefore, the Name of the Ark that holds the Covenant of God is Jesus. In another words, Jesus holds the Covenant of life.

The Name of the Lord of "Heaven's Armies" is Jesus, and inside this ark (or in Him) is the Covenant that provides way to life. The way to this life is Jesus.

We can see that these three hold the same meaning:

- Living in the life that comes from God
  (here, life = the Covenant that is in the ark)
- Living in the name of the ark
- Living in the Name of Jesus

The Bible says that there is no name under heaven by which we can be saved (c.f. Acts 4:12). It is only by the Name of Jesus that we can be saved. It is only by the Name of Jesus that we can receive life (the promise of the Covenant).

The Father gave His Name to the Son, and this Name is Jesus. The Father and Son are one through this Name. This unison was evident through the way Jesus lived (c.f. John 17:11).

The Name of the Father, Son, and Holy Spirit can be used interchangeably because they all share the same life.

Wherever the Ark of God goes, the Jordan River dries up providing safe passage (c.f. Joshua 3:14-17).

Wherever the Ark of God goes, the Walls of Jericho fall (c.f. Joshua 6:12-21)

Wherever the Ark of God goes, the statue of Dagon falls apart (c.f. 1 Samuel 5:1-5)

Wherever the Ark of God goes, the hand of the Lord is there and the enemies are terrified and flee (c.f. 1 Samuel 5:6-12).

These things happen to show all things in heaven and on earth and under the earth kneel down before the life of God (life that comes from God, also known as the Name of the ark, or the Name of Jesus) (c.f. Philippians 2:10).

The life that the Father has given to the Son is a life that is lived in the Father.

To say that differently, when we place the Father as the head and listen to the Word (Life) of the Father, then the result of our lives would show others the heart of the Father.

Therefore, we ought to show the Name of the Father (Jesus) to the world. We can do this by living lives showing the Father's heart by remaining in the Father and with the life of the Father.

The following are equivalent:

- The Father
- Life that comes from the Father (Father's Life)
- Heart of the Father (Father's Heart)
- Name of the Father

Additionally, the Name of the Father *is* the Name of Jesus. In that Name, the Father, Son, and the Holy Spirit are always working together in unison.

Here is a passage that shows that Jesus, the Son of the Living Father, lived with the life that came from the Father and lived in the Father. His life showed the Father to others:

> *8Philip said, "Lord, show us the Father, and we will be satisfied." 9Jesus replied, "Have I been with you all this time, Philip, and yet you still don't know who I am? <u>Anyone who has seen me has seen the Father! So why are you asking me to show him to you?</u> 10Don't you believe that <u>I am in the Father</u> and the Father is in me? The words I speak are not my own, but <u>my Father who lives in me does his work through me</u>. 11Just believe that <u>I am in the Father</u> and the Father is in me. Or at least believe because of the work you have seen me do.*
>
> *John 14:8-11*

Jesus showed His Father through the way He lived.

No one has ever seen God. But the unique One, who is himself God, is near to the Father's heart. He has revealed God to us.

John 1:18

How did Jesus show the Father?

I have revealed you to the ones you gave me from this world. They were always yours. You gave them to me, and they have kept your word.

John 17:6

Jesus showed the Father by revealing the Father's Name. He did this by living with the life that comes from the Father (c.f. John 14:10-11), placing the Father as His head (c.f. 1 Corinthians 11:3), and by receiving the heart of the Father. That is why all things in heaven and on earth and under the earth would bow before His Name (c.f. Philippians 2:10).

The Bible equates the Father Himself and His Name. This can be evidenced by the following passages:

Those who know your name trust in you, for you, O LORD, do not abandon those who search for you

Psalms 9:10

The name of the Lord is a strong fortress; the godly run to him and are safe.

Proverbs 18:10

I made known to them your name, and I will continue to make it known, that the love with which you have loved me may be in them, and I in them."

John 17:26 (ESV)

Yet to all who received him, to those who believed in his name, he gave the right to become children of God.

John 1:12

and that repentance and forgiveness of sins should be proclaimed in his name to all nations, beginning from Jerusalem.

Luke 24:47 (ESV)

He is the one all the prophets testified about, saying that everyone who believes in him will have their sins forgiven through his name.

Acts 10:43

I remind you, my dear children: Your sins are forgiven in Jesus' name.
1 John 2:12 (MSG)

Verse above says sins are forgiven through His Name; however, another verse says that forgiveness is through Jesus:

"Brothers, listen! We are here to proclaim that through this man Jesus there is forgiveness for your sins.
Acts 13:38

Jesus and *His Name* are therefore *equivalent.*

Therefore, we too ought to reveal Jesus (or His Name) through our lives.

The focus for the children of God, those that have received the life that comes from God, is the Name of Jesus (glory, life, and heart of God) (c.f. Hebrews 1:4). Their purpose and mission is to reveal the living Father through their lives.

16Let the word of Christ dwell in you richly as you teach and admonish one another with all wisdom, and as you sing psalms, hymns and spiritual songs with gratitude in your hearts to God. 17And whatever you do, whether in word or deed, do it all in the name of the Lord Jesus, giving thanks to God the Father through him.
Colossians 3:16-17 NIV

30Jesus did many other miraculous signs in the presence of his disciples, which are not recorded in this book. 31But these are written that you may believe that Jesus is the Christ, the Son of God, and that by believing you may have life in his name.
John 20:30-31

Fear the Lord if you are wise! His voice calls to everyone in Jerusalem. "The armies of destruction are coming; the Lord is sending them.
Micah 6:9

12What can I offer the Lord for all he has done for me? 13I will lift up the cup of salvation and praise the Lord's name for saving me.
Psalms 116:12-13

To recap: to live in the Name (Life) of Jesus, we must live in Christ by placing Him as our head and living with the heart that He gives us.

This is how we can live as heaven. We will look further about this way of living.

3-3. The Name of the Father, Part II

The Name of the Father is the Name of Jesus.

Name of Jesus is the Name of the life of the Father (Father's life). From the Father's life comes the heart of God.

To live in the Name of Jesus means to live as a sanctuary for the living God, place Jesus as the head, and live with the heart that Jesus gives (c.f. Colossians 3:17).

Name of the Ark of God is Jesus (c.f. 2 Samuel 6:2), and in that Ark is the Father's life enclosed as a Covenant.

The Ark of God that we can see with our physical eyes is named Jesus. However, in Jesus (the Ark) is the Life (Covenant) that we cannot see with our physical eyes and hearts.

Salvation is the enablement to see the Life that cannot be seen physically with our eyes or hearts. This word salvation is synonymous with the Ark of God and the Name of Jesus (Jesus = Salvation = enablement to see the Life).

It is through salvation, also known as the Ark of God and the Name of Jesus, we are given the ability to see using the eyes of our hearts what we cannot with our physical eyes (c.f. Ephesians 1:18). The heart and might of Christ that come from the life of God are what we call salvation.

Let the same mind be in you that was in Christ Jesus
Philippians 2:5 (NRSV)

This "same mind" is always with those that are born again, but even to them, their physical eyes or hearts cannot see or discern this.

In order to see and discern, we need to work with the Holy Spirit in us that continually speaks and teaches about Jesus (c.f. John 14:26). Through that, we are able to see the glory of God (c.f. John 16:13-14). Then through the power of the amazing Life of God, the heart of Christ that is in you overflows. This is how you can have the heart of Christ.

This heart of Christ is what can flow out of those that are born again. This heart is also synonymous with the Name of Jesus.

God's work will be revealed when we act in the Name of Jesus:

5You must have the same attitude that Christ Jesus had. 6Though he was God, he did not think of equality with God as something to cling to. 7Instead, he gave up his divine privileges; he took the humble position of a slave and was born as a human being. When he appeared in human form, 8he humbled himself in obedience to God and died a criminal's death on a cross. 9Therefore ***(after having acted with the mind of Jesus)****, God* *elevated him to the place of highest honor and gave him the name above all other names, 10that at the name of Jesus* *every knee should bow, in heaven and on earth and under the earth, 11and every tongue confess that Jesus Christ is Lord, to the glory of God the Father.*

Philippians 2:5-11

Let us look at this passage a little deeper.

God is light.

This is the message we heard from Jesus and now declare to you: God is light, and there is no darkness in him at all.

1 John 1:5

In this light, there is life (c.f. John 1:4).

In this light, there is God's glory.

This glory is in the life of God and contains the might, power, character, knowledge, and wisdom of God

In the life of God, there is abundance of the glory of God.

However, the glory that is in the life of God cannot be seen.

The glory that cannot be seen is made visible through the Holy Spirit. By being in Christ, we will be able to see using the eyes of our hearts. This is what it means to have the heart of Christ or the Name of Jesus.

As we operate in this Name, all things in heaven and on earth or under the earth bows. The results are demons being cast away and sicknesses being healed.

To help you understand, let us consider a beautiful tree. This beautiful tree was actually contained in the single seed that eventually grows into this tree. The small seed included what would become the tree and the red, yellow, and blue flowers it would bloom too. However, these that are included in this seed are not physically visible while it is a seed.

Regardless, people intuitively know that the seed contains the beautiful tree, flowers, and maybe even fruits. Just because people know does not make the process of the tree growth any faster. People know this fact and in faith in what they know, they take the action to plant the seed and gives it water and sunshine.

Like this, the Life of God, which can be compared to the seed, includes the glory of God, which is filled with God's authority, power, character, wisdom, and knowledge.

However, just by looking at the seed (the invisible Life of God), we cannot see or discern the glory of God included in the Life.

Only through faith and through the Holy Spirit are we able to drink the living water that only Jesus (the Rock) gives. We will then be led by the Truth that is inside of us (God's Life). The glory of God will appear as the heart of Christ in us. Then with this heart, we will be able to hear His voice, the voice of Christ.

This is what it means to put on Christ and to live in the image of Christ.

Jesus came to us as heaven, as kingdom of God, and as the sanctuary for the living God. Everything that was of God were filled with glory in the life of Jesus.

Jesus did nothing on His own accord (c.f. John 5:30). Instead, He did everything that the Father in Him spoke and taught Him. As the Father was showing Him, He saw the glory of God (c.f. John 5:19-20).

Then the heart of God appeared in Jesus' life, and Jesus was able to live with that heart. Living this way is to live:

- in the Name of the Father, and
- revealing the Name of the Father, and
- showing the Father

This is why in order to show the glory of God, it must begin with the mind of Christ. When Jesus performed all miracles, He did them in the Name of the Father. To do it in the Name of the Father meant He had to first listen to the speaking and teaching of the Father and operate with the heart that the Father gave Him. We too must live this way like Jesus.

Children of God that are born again with the life of Christ have all the glory of God within them.

> *I have given them the glory you gave me, so they may be one as we are one.*
> *John 17:22*

To reiterate, in the life of God, there is glory that has abundance of His might, power, character, knowledge, and wisdom.

Though it may not be visible yet, the Name of Jesus (or the heart of Jesus) has Life.

> *14Then if my people who are called by my name will humble themselves and pray and seek my face and turn from their wicked ways, I will hear from heaven and will forgive their sins and restore their land. 15My eyes will be open and my ears attentive to every prayer made in this place. 16For I have chosen this Temple and set it apart to be holy - a place where my name will be honored forever. I will always watch over it, for it is dear to my heart.*
>
> *2 Chronicles 7:14-16*

If we are truly the sanctuary for the living God and have been born again through the life that comes from God, it is pertinent that the source of Life within our hearts is the Name of Jesus.

However, we will not be able to see it.

Now we must live demonstrating the unseen Name of Jesus (that has the glory) that is in the Life of the Father.

Then how shall we live?

How shall we live so that we can show the Name of Jesus (that has the glory) that is in the Life of the Father?

We shall find out more…

Chapter 4 – The Covenant of God

4-1. The Covenant of God

Let me begin this chapter sharing about my experience as I wrote this book.

I had first published this book in 2010; however, the Covenant of God was not fully clear to me at that time. As a result, I could not fully live out my life as heaven. I praise and thank God for leading me thus far.

We will take a brief look at the nature of sin.

We can express sin in three ways. Sin is:

1. Living according to one's accord
2. Living with the thoughts and mind of the flesh
3. Not living with the Spirit of God

These three actually mean the exact same thing.

When God created people, He intended them to live within God's planned order.

But there is one thing I want you to know: The head of every man is Christ, the head of woman is man, and the head of Christ is God.

1 Corinthians 11:3

Let us take a deeper look into this verse:

It says the head of a woman is man; head of man is Jesus; and the head of Jesus is God.

However, Eve did not listen to her head Adam and lived according to her own accords. Adam too failed to follow the Word of God and lived according to his own accords. Both of them became slaves to Satan and were led to ruin.

What should Adam and Eve have done instead? They should have eaten from the tree of life to be born again with new life. Then they would have been in Christ, placed Jesus as their head and be able to live with the thoughts and mind that comes from Christ. Even for them, they should have lived in the Name of Jesus.

Adam listened to Eve (and therefore became her slave - see Romans 6:16), who had completely fallen into Satan's trap (see Genesis 3:6, which is equivalent to the message in 1 John 2:15-16). Eve was a slave of Satan and so was Adam. They were heading toward the path of a curse, to their deaths, following Satan (c.f. Matthew 25:41).

God created a plan to save them.

This plan is called "Law of Faith" (c.f. Romans 3:27).

The Law of Faith is something that God initiated. When we believe in this Covenant, God saves us by fulfilling the Covenant.

This Law of Faith is the only plan of salvation that the almighty God prepared for us – it is the wisdom of God.

There is no other way that sinners can be forgiven from their sins.

The only way is for the sinner to hear and believe in the Covenant that God has promised (c.f. Galatians 3:2,5). Salvation is complete by the fulfillment of this Covenant.

The Covenant of God is called the Gospel (Good News) according to the Bible. We must believe in this Gospel.

For I am not ashamed of this Good News about Christ. It is the power of God at work, saving everyone who believes-the Jew first and also the Gentile.
Romans 1:16

In the verse above, it says only those who believe are saved.

This Good News tells us how God makes us right in his sight. This is accomplished from start to finish by faith. As the Scriptures say, "It is through faith that a righteous person has life."

The righteous person lives believing in what God will fulfill.

4-2. The Plan of God, Part I
God Creates Us in His Image

Before we dive into the Covenant of God, let us examine the plan of God so that we can better understand the former.

The key reason is that the plan of God becomes the Covenant of God, the Gospel.

Plan of God refers to what God intended to accomplish from the start.

God had purposed to fulfill this plan through Jesus Christ even before God created the heavens and the earth,

This plan has been to bear children of God that lives like Jesus.

10God, for whom and through whom everything was made, chose to bring many children into glory. And it was only right that he should make Jesus, through his suffering, a perfect leader, fit to bring them into their salvation. 11So now Jesus and the ones he makes holy have the same Father. That is why Jesus is not ashamed to call them his brothers and sisters. 12For he said to God, "I will proclaim your name to my brothers and sisters. I will praise you among your assembled people."

Hebrews 2:10-12

Jesus, who is our brother, lived as heaven by being a sanctuary for the living God and placing God as His head (c.f. 1 Corinthians 11:3). By doing so, He revealed the Father in His living, speaking the Word that God spoke to Him. As a result, He was able to reign over all creation with the Name of Jesus, the Name that the Father had given Him.

The reason why God created us in His image is that He desired us to live like Jesus and be His children.

The word "image" holds two meanings:

First, it refers to the physical form.

You must not make for yourself an idol of any kind or an image of anything in the heavens or on the earth or in the sea.

Exodus 20:4

The verse above refers to the physical form of this image and that is why it says to "not make"…"image of anything."

33Each of the six branches will have three lamp cups shaped like almond blossoms, complete with buds and petals. 34Craft the center stem of the lampstand with four lamp cups shaped like almond blossoms, complete with buds and petals.
Exodus 25:33-34

The word "shaped" above refers to the physical form as intended in the word "image."

So you must make images of your tumors and images of your mice that ravage the land, and give glory to the God of Israel. Perhaps he will lighten his hand from off you and your gods and your land.
1 Samuel 6:5

Above is another verse that uses the word "image" to refer to its physical form.

5He paneled the main room of the Temple with cypress wood, overlaid it with fine gold, and decorated it with carvings of palm trees and chains. 10He made two figures shaped like cherubim, overlaid them with gold, and placed them in the Most Holy Place. 14Across the entrance of the Most Holy Place he hung a curtain made of fine linen, decorated with blue, purple, and scarlet thread and embroidered with figures of cherubim.
2 Chronicles 3:5, 10, 14

Above is another verse that shows reference to a physical form.

Second, the word "image" refers to likeness of character of God.

Satan, who is the god of this world, has blinded the minds of those who don't believe. They are unable to see the glorious light of the Good News. They don't understand this message about the glory of Christ, who is the exact likeness of God.
2 Corinthians 4:4

In the verse above, the image refers to Jesus who is in likeness of God in character.

And He is the image of the invisible God, the first-born of all creation.
Colossians 1:15

Again, the verse above associates image with character likeness.

Long ago God spoke many times and in many ways to our ancestors through the prophets. 2And now in these final days, he has spoken to us through his Son. God promised everything to the Son as an inheritance, and through the Son he created the universe. 3The Son radiates God's own glory and expresses the very character of God, and he sustains everything by the mighty power of his command. When he had cleansed us from our sins, he sat down in the place of honor at the right hand of the majestic God in heaven.

Hebrews 1:1-3

As verses above show, Scriptures use the word "image" to mean both physical form and likeness of character.

Jesus has the character likeness of God.

However, when God created man in His "image," it was in the physical form, not in likeness with God.

If God created man in God's character likeness like Jesus, then Adam and Eve would not have been able to sin and become a slave to Satan (c.f. Hebrews 4:15).

Then God said, "Let us make human beings in our image, to be like us. They will reign over the fish in the sea, the birds in the sky, the livestock, all the wild animals on the earth, and the small animals that scurry along the ground."

Genesis 1:26

Why do you think He created you and me in His image?

To answer that question, consider why clothes are made in the form of a person. It is so that a person can fit into it and wear them.

Gloves too are made in the form of human hands so that humans can place their hands inside the gloves.

The reason why God created us in His form is too so that God may "fit" and dwell in a person.

Rephrasing, God created us in His form so that Christ, who is the Kingdom of Heaven, may dwell in us. When He does, we will be able to demonstrate the living God through our lives.

God created us in His image so that we may be able to live in the Name of the Father, now known as the Name of Jesus.

4-3. The Plan of God, Part II
The Church

The plan God intended to accomplish through Jesus Christ is to bear many children that are like Jesus (c.f. Hebrews 2:10-11). For those children, God has specific inheritance prepared for them in the Father's kingdom.

3All praise to God, the Father of our Lord Jesus Christ. It is by his great mercy that we have been born again, because God raised Jesus Christ from the dead. Now we live with great expectation, 4and we have a priceless inheritance - an inheritance that is kept in heaven for you, pure and undefiled, beyond the reach of change and decay.

1Peter 1:3-4

The world we live in is just one of the models and a shadow of what is to come.

In reality, God has prepared for His children an inheritance that can never perish, spoil or fade away. His children are those who are in Christ and are a church because they place Jesus as their Head.

9I was chosen to explain to everyone this mysterious plan that God, the Creator of all things, had kept secret from the beginning. 10God's purpose in all this was to use the church to display his wisdom in its rich variety to all the unseen rulers and authorities in the heavenly places.

Ephesians 3:9-10

The church is the body of Christ.

22God has put all things under the authority of Christ and has made him head over all things for the benefit of the church. 23And the church is his body; it is made full and complete by Christ, who fills all things everywhere with himself.

Ephesians 1:22-23

The verses above show that God desired to bear children that belong to Him, those that are in Christ and place Him as their Head. Such children of God are also known as the Church. His plan is for the Church to come to know the various wisdom of God through the powers in the heavens.

When we are born again in the life that comes from God, we are reborn as the Church (c.f. 1 John 5:11-12). That is the plan that God will definitely accomplish on earth: to build that body of Christ. This is why Jesus said after hearing the testimony of Peter that He "will build (His) Church".

16Simon Peter answered, "You are the Messiah, the Son of the living God." 17Jesus replied, "You are blessed, Simon son of John, because my Father in heaven has revealed this to you. You did not learn this from any human being. 18Now I say to you that you are Peter (which means `rock'), and upon this rock I will build my church, and all the powers of hell will not conquer it.

Matthew 16:16-18

Jesus built His Church and gave the keys of the Kingdom to it.

And I will give you the keys of the Kingdom of Heaven. Whatever you forbid on earth will be forbidden in heaven, and whatever you permit on earth will be permitted in heaven.

Matthew 16:19

The Church places Christ as their head. They speak with the heart that Christ provides. This heart of Christ is the Life that comes from God, also known as the Name of Jesus.

Connecting the dots, the keys of the Kingdom of Heaven that was given to the Church is the Name of Jesus.

Church places Christ as their head and lives as His body. Those that live with Christ as the Head are said to live *in Christ.*

He might gather together in one all things in Christ, both which are in heaven and which are on earth—in Him.

Ephesians 1:10 NKJV

10to be put into effect when the times will have reached their fulfillment—to bring all things in heaven and on earth together under one head, even Christ.

Ephesians 1:10 NIV

Note that the Good News Translation translates "in Christ" as "with Christ as head."

Therefore, these words have the same meaning:

- To live as the Church
- To live in Christ

- To live with Christ as the head
- To listen to and obey the Word of Christ
- To live with the heart that comes from Christ
- To live in the Name of Jesus

God had planned all these things with intent to fulfill them in Christ:

9I was chosen to explain to everyone this mysterious plan that God, the Creator of all things, had kept secret from the beginning. 10God's purpose in all this was to use the church to display his wisdom in its rich variety to all the unseen rulers and authorities in the heavenly places. 11This was his eternal plan, which he carried out through Christ Jesus our Lord.

Ephesians 3:9-11

In order to raise the Church of Jesus Christ, God created humans with one Spirit. The reason for the creation is so that God may bear children that are holy (c.f. Malachi 2:15, 1 Timothy 4:6-10). That is the reason why God created only one person, Adam; then while Adam was sleeping, took a bone from him to form the woman, Eve.

God created one person, then split this one person and made two.

That is why God called the woman and said this:

This explains why a man leaves his father and mother and is joined to his wife, and the two are united into one.

Genesis 2:24

However, do you see something peculiar?

God created one person and then separated them to be two. Then God asks them to unite again to be one.

Why did God create people this way?

This is where we will find another secret about God.

God intended Adam and Eve to eat from the Tree of Life so that they would be born again to have the life that comes from God. They would be in Christ, place Jesus as their head, and live with the heart that Christ gives. They would be united, or one, with Christ.

11And this is what God has testified: He has given us eternal life, and this life is in his Son. 12Whoever has the Son has life; whoever does not have God's Son does not have life.

1 John 5:11-12

The Son refers to Jesus Christ in the verse above (see also Matthew 16:16).

Therefore, as God created the heavens, the earth and the humans in it, he already had the plan for them to be born again through the life that comes from God. They would be in Christ, place Christ as their head, have the heart that Christ provides, be united in the Name of Jesus and live as the body of Christ.

That's why the Bible says this:

30And we are members of his body. 31As the Scriptures say, "A man leaves his father and mother and is joined to his wife, and the two are united into one." 32This is a great mystery, but it is an illustration of the way Christ and the church are one.

Ephesians 5:30-32

The "secret" alluded from Genesis 2:24 is now made clear. From the time of creation, God intended to build the Church that places Jesus as their head so that they (the Church) may live as the body. The secret is simply that the Church had always been the plan of God even before humans were created.

That is why Apostle Paul uses the expression "churches in Christ" (c.f. Galatians 1:22) and people made "holy by means of Christ Jesus" (c.f. 1 Corinthians 1:2).

How can we be one? Can anything in this world enable us to unite?

No. Only those that are born again from the life that comes from God and place Christ as their head can have the heart of Christ that enables them to be one. Therefore, only when Christ is placed as our head:

- A husband and wife can be one
- Brothers (and sisters) can be one
- Families can be one
- We can be one even with our enemies

To reemphasize, we can be one only through the Name of Jesus.

Now I am departing from the world; they are staying in this world, but I am coming to you. Holy Father, you have given me your name; now protect them by the power of your name so that they will be united just as we are.

John 17:11

Happiness comes from living in unity.

Happiness comes from living in the Name of Jesus.

Even from the time God created the human race, He had already intended for them to be born again through the life that comes from God. Such people would live in Christ, place Christ as their head, live with the heart that Christ gives, live in unity in the Name of Jesus (c.f. John 17:11), and ultimately, live as the Church.

4-4. The Original Covenant Gospel Revealed for the First Time

As we have seen earlier, Adam and Eve listened to the advice of Satan and committed sin. As a result, they became Satan's slaves and were on their way to eternal hell (c.f. Matthew 25:41).

Sin in Greek form is αμαρτία (Amartia). It means to miss the mark. So sin is "missing" or not meeting the purpose of one's creation. To say Adam and Eve have sinned means they have missed their purpose for their lives.

Let us review – to be within the purpose of God, we are to be people that are born again with the life that comes from God. Then we would be in Christ, place Christ as our head, have the heart that Christ gives, live in the Name of Jesus, and then demonstrate the living God through the way we live. Those that do not do this are called sinners.

God has established a plan to save such sinners. Salvation, then, occurs when God's original plan would be fulfilled for these people.

This plan is called the Law of Faith (c.f. Romans 3:27).

The law of faith is something God initiated as a Covenant. If we respond to and believe in this Covenant, God will fulfill His end of the Covenant, which is to bring about salvation for us who believe.

This Covenant was established from beginning of time and it is called the "Original Covenant."

And I will cause hostility between you and the woman, and between your offspring and her offspring. He will strike your head, and you will strike his heel."

Genesis 3:15

The "woman" here refers to the Holy Spirit.

26But the other woman, Sarah, represents the heavenly Jerusalem. <u>She is the free woman, and she is our mother</u>. 29But you are now being persecuted by those who want you to keep the law, just as Ishmael, the child born by human effort, persecuted Isaac, the <u>child born by the power of the Spirit</u>. 31So, dear brothers and sisters, we are not children of the slave woman; <u>we are children of the free woman</u>.

Galatians 4:26, 29, 31

As the verses above show, the Bible tells us that those born of the Spirit are children of the free woman. The eldest brother of them all is Jesus Christ (c.f. Romans 8:29).

God's Original Covenant is revealed to us in Genesis 3:15 and 21. God has fulfilled this Covenant by sending His Son Jesus and He continues to bring about salvation for those who believes even today.

> *26For you are all children of God through faith in Christ Jesus. 27And all who have been united with Christ in baptism have put on Christ, like putting on new clothes.*
> *Galatians 3:26-27*

Putting on Christ like new clothes means that Christ lives in us, and as a result, we are able to demonstrate Christ in our lives.

To clarify:

The Original Covenant, which is the contents of the Gospel, is that Christ will be sent through a woman to demolish the work of Satan (c.f. 1 John 3:8). Christ will give us new life (we would be considered to be "born by a woman") and save us from Satan's schemes. Then we would live in Christ, place Christ as our head, be the living Church (c.f. Ephesians 1:22-23), listen to the Words of Christ and have the heart of Christ.

God's promise is that, just as the eldest son Jesus lived as the Kingdom of Heaven, we too would be born again and be able to live in Christ, in the Name of Jesus. This promise is called the Original Covenant, which is also called the Kingdom Gospel. The Kingdom Gospel is living the life of the Kingdom just as Jesus did (c.f. Matthew 24:14).

This Covenant is the plan of God that He had in mind from the beginning of time to resolve the sin issue for people like Adam and Eve. Anyone that has become a slave of Satan would be restored through Christ that has come from a woman.

In reference to Abel's offering written in Genesis 4:1-5:

> *It was by faith that Abel brought a more acceptable offering to God than Cain did. Abel's offering gave evidence that he was a righteous man, and God showed his approval of his gifts. Although Abel is long dead, he still speaks to us by his example of faith.*
> *Hebrews 11:4*

Abel believed in the Original Covenant (also known as the Kingdom Gospel) and gave his sacrifice.

Enoch also believed in the Covenant and lived by faith:

It was by faith that Enoch was taken up to heaven without dying - "he disappeared, because God took him." For before he was taken up, he was known as a person who pleased God.

Hebrews 11:5

Likewise, Noah believed in this Covenant and built the ark by faith:

It was by faith that Noah built a large boat to save his family from the flood. He obeyed God, who warned him about things that had never happened before. By his faith Noah condemned the rest of the world, and he received the righteousness that comes by faith.

Hebrews 11:7

Abraham too believed in the promise and obeyed when God called:

It was by faith that Abraham obeyed when God called him to leave home and go to another land that God would give him as his inheritance. He went without knowing where he was going.

Hebrews 11:8

4-5. Abraham, the Father of Faith

The Original Covenant (the Gospel) is the promise that people can be born again with the life that comes from God so that they may live in Christ, wear Christ (demonstrating Him in their lives), and live as heaven (as the Kingdom of God).

In order to fulfill this Covenant, God calls a person who believed in this promise, Abraham, from Ur of the Chaldeans.

The LORD had said to Abram, "Leave your native country, your relatives, and your father's family, and go to the land that I will show you. 2I will make you into a great nation. I will bless you and make you famous, and you will be a blessing to others. 3I will bless those who bless you and curse those who treat you with contempt. All the families on earth will be blessed through you." 4So Abram departed as the LORD had instructed, and Lot went with him. Abram was seventy-five years old when he left Haran.

Genesis 12:1-4

"Abram departed as the Lord has instructed" is transliterated as "Abraham obeyed" in Hebrews 11:8.

When we put Genesis 12:1-4, Hebrews 11:8 and Galatians 3:8 together, we will find that Abraham, Abel, Enoch and Noah all believed the Original Covenant (the Gospel). They simply obeyed in faith the promise that God will bless all families through Abraham.

What's more, the Scriptures looked forward to this time when God would declare the Gentiles to be righteous because of their faith. God proclaimed this good news to Abraham long ago when he said, "All nations will be blessed through you."

Galatians 3:8

It was by faith that Abraham obeyed when God called him to leave home and go to another land that God would give him as his inheritance. He went without knowing where he was going.

Hebrews 11:8

As verses above show, Abraham believed that God will fulfill His promise. By faith, He listened to God's instructions and simply obeyed.

In order to fulfill the promise He made to Abraham, God promised him a son in Genesis 15, which was actually alluding to the Son Jesus according to Galatians 3:16. Abraham simply believed in this promise, and God considered him righteous because of his faith (c.f. Genesis 15:6).

4Then the LORD said to him, "No, your servant will not be your heir, for you will have a son of your own who will be your heir." 5Then the LORD took Abram outside and said to him, "Look up into the sky and count the stars if you can. That's how many descendants you will have!" 6And Abram believed the LORD, and the LORD counted him as righteous because of his faith.

Genesis 15:4-6

God also promises the land where Abraham's children would reside in the verses that follow (v. 8-11, 17). This Promised Land, the land of Canaan, is a shadow of entering into Christ, the Kingdom of God.

Unfortunately, Abraham got impatient and could not wait for God to fulfill His promise for a son. So he listens to Sarai, a person, and goes to have a child Ishmael with Hagar (c.f. Genesis 16:1-16).

The Bible describes this act as "having followed the flesh" (the thought and mind of the flesh):

22For it is written that Abraham had two sons, one by a slave woman and one by a free woman. 23But the son of the slave was born according to the flesh, while the son of the free woman was born through promise.

Galatians 4:22-23 (ESV)

Therefore, when there is a great plan from God, but we operate from our own understanding, it is called *living in the flesh.*

We can see that this failure continues on the heritage of Ishmael. His descendants continue to live in enmity with God even to this day.

6For to set the mind on the flesh is death, but to set the mind on the Spirit is life and peace. 7For the mind that is set on the flesh is hostile to God, for it does not submit to God's law; indeed, it cannot. 8Those who are in the flesh cannot please God.

Romans 8:6-8

Key point to note in the verses above is that, if we listen only to the words of other people, even though it began as a promise from God, you can become an enemy to God.

We can see from Scriptures that the written law has led toward this direction:

6He has enabled us to be ministers of his new Covenant. This is a Covenant not of written laws, but of the Spirit. The old written Covenant ends in death; but under the new Covenant, the Spirit gives life. 7The old way, with laws etched in stone, led to death, though it began with such glory that the people of Israel could not bear to look at Moses' face. For his face shone with the glory of God, even though the brightness was already fading away

2 Corinthians 3:6-7

The lesson here is that if you *ONLY* hear the Scriptures from *other people* or try to follow the words of Scriptures on your *own understanding*, you may live according to the flesh and as a slave to Satan.

He did this by ending the system of law with its commandments and regulations. He made peace between Jews and Gentiles by creating in himself one new people from the two groups.

Ephesians 2:15

God does not change what is written in Scriptures (c.f. 1 Corinthians 4:6); however, one cannot solely attempt to live on the written Word of God to consider themselves as true children of God.

We need both the Word of God that is written in Scriptures AND the teachings of the Holy Spirit so that we may have the heart that Jesus gives and live in His Name.

Abraham listened to Sarai, a person, and tried to fulfill the promise God had made on his own abilities. As a result, Abraham was in rebellion to God and became God's enemy. As a result, God was silent with Abraham for 13 years.

4-6. The Covenant Established with Abraham

Just as Abel, Enoch, and Noah did, Abraham believed in the promise (the Original Covenant, which is the Gospel) from when he lived in Ur of the Chaldeans (c.f. Hebrews 11:4, 5, 7, 8). Abraham believed and accepted that all nations would be blessed through him and he obeyed in faith.

The LORD had said to Abram, "Leave your native country, your relatives, and your father's family, and go to the land that I will show you. 2I will make you into a great nation. I will bless you and make you famous, and you will be a blessing to others. 3I will bless those who bless you and curse those who treat you with contempt. All the families on earth will be blessed through you." 4So Abram departed as the LORD had instructed, and Lot went with him. Abram was seventy-five years old when he left Haran.

Genesis 12:1-4

What's more, the Scriptures looked forward to this time when God would declare the Gentiles to be righteous because of their faith. God proclaimed this good news to Abraham long ago when he said, "All nations will be blessed through you.

Galatians 3:8

God promised Abraham a child. Abraham believed, and God considered his faith as righteous (c.f. Genesis 15:6).

However, Abraham was weak in faith and could not wait for God's timing, and without faith, listened to a person (Sarai) to bear the child Ishmael with human thinking and mind.

Abraham's problem is that he lacked faith

God was silent toward Abraham for 13 years because of this.

Genesis 17 begins with God appearing for the first time to Abraham in 13 years. His first words were "I am God Almighty." Then He says "walk before me and be blameless."

When Abram was ninety-nine years old the LORD appeared to Abram and said to him, "I am God Almighty; walk before me, and be blameless,

Genesis 17:1 (ESV)

When God said to "be blameless," He did not intend Abraham to do it on his own; but rather, He meant: "since I will make you whole, just live blamelessly in my presence. This can be seen in the following verses:

13But you must be blameless before the LORD your God. 15Moses continued, "The LORD your God will raise up for you a prophet like me from among your fellow Israelites. You must listen to him. 18I will raise up a prophet like you from among their fellow Israelites. I will put my words in his mouth, and he will tell the people everything I command him. 19 I will personally deal with anyone who will not listen to the messages the prophet proclaims on my behalf.

Deuteronomy 18:13, 15, 18, 19

To live blamelessly means to listen to the prophet that God is sending. Similar message appears in book of Acts:

22Moses said, `The LORD your God will raise up for you a **Prophet like me** from among your own people. Listen carefully to everything he tells you.' 23Then Moses said, `Anyone who will not listen to that Prophet will be completely cut off from God's people.' 24"Starting with Samuel, every prophet spoke about what is happening today. 25You are the children of those prophets, and you are included in the Covenant God promised to your ancestors. For God said to Abraham, `Through your descendants all the families on earth will be blessed.' 26When God raised up his servant, Jesus, he sent him first to you people of Israel, to bless you by turning each of you back from your sinful ways."

Acts 3:22-26

It says "Prophet like me" (v. 22), which refers to Jesus Christ.

To be blameless means to listen to Christ whom God has sent and to live according to Him.

So we tell others about Christ, warning everyone and teaching everyone with all the wisdom God has given us. We want to present them to God, perfect in their relationship to Christ.

Colossians 1:28

Let us analyze the passages so far. God will enable us to be blameless before Him. He will give us the faith (promise of the Original Covenant) so that we can be born again as children of God and live in Christ.

However, we need this blameless faith like that of Abraham so that we may be truly blameless in Christ.

This blameless faith was required so that God would send His Son, the Christ, who will carry out the promise of God (c.f. Galatians 3:16).

For that reason, God establishes a revised, or new, Covenant with Abraham.

A new Covenant was not to replace the Original Covenant; rather, it simply added provisions to enable Abraham to have that faith so that the Kingdom Gospel may be fulfilled.

Therefore, God provided the blameless faith to Abraham so that through this faith, the child Jesus may be borne. It was through this faith that God was able to fulfill the Kingdom Gospel.

This faith came because of the Covenant of Circumcision:

God also gave Abraham the Covenant of circumcision at that time. So when Abraham became the father of Isaac, he circumcised him on the eighth day. And the practice was continued when Isaac became the father of Jacob, and when Jacob became the father of the twelve patriarchs of the Israelite nation.

Acts 7:8

It is through the Covenant of Circumcision that Abraham was able to have unwavering faith, and as a result, Isaac (lineage from where Jesus was born, c.f. Galatians 3:16) was born.

We too can trust in this Covenant of Circumcision and rely on God to give us unwavering blameless faith. Only with that unwavering faith can the Original Covenant be fulfilled in us. This is why Abraham is called the Father of faith.

Now, only children of Abraham can receive salvation.

Children of Abraham are not physical children, but those that believe in the Covenant of Circumcision.

7Being descendants of Abraham doesn't make them truly Abraham's children. For the Scriptures say, "Isaac is the son through whom your descendants will be counted," though Abraham had other children, too. 8This means that Abraham's physical descendants are not necessarily children of God. Only the children of the promise are considered to be Abraham's children.

Romans 9:7-8

God established the Covenant of Circumcision and Abraham believed what God can do. As a result, God performed the circumcision, that is, He provided unwavering faith in Abraham (c.f. Romans 4:17-22). The result of this faith was the physical birth of Isaac. In a similar way, those that believe in this Covenant are like those being born as children of Abraham.

It is the same when we are born again with the life that comes from God. It first requires the same Covenant God made with Abraham. It is because we believe in the promise of Circumcision that God fulfills the unwavering faith in us. Through this steadfast faith, we are born again with the life that comes from God. This is why the Bible says this:

> *And you, dear brothers and sisters, are children of the promise, just like Isaac.*
> *Galatians 4:28*

This means that just as Isaac was born because Abraham believed in God's Covenant of Circumcision, we too can be born again as children of God by believing in the Covenant of Circumcision.

We must believe in the Covenant of Circumcision that God established with the father-of-faith Abraham.

4-7. Covenant Fulfilled in Abraham: Circumcision

God promised the Original Covenant (the Kingdom Gospel) and fulfilled it by sending Christ to be borne by a woman.

He called Abraham from Ur of the Chaldeans, a person who believed in this Covenant, and said to him that all nations will be blessed through him. Abraham believed this promise and obeyed.

God promised Abraham a son (c.f. Galatians 3:16) and Abraham believed this promise. God considered Abraham's belief as righteousness.

However, Abraham's faith was not strong.

To say one's faith is not strong means that he still had *thoughts, emotions, and experiences of the flesh* that he could not fully get rid of.

Abraham was captive by his own ways of thinking and emotions.

He was so weak in faith, that is, so *captured by the ways of his flesh*, that perhaps just by hunger, he may give his wife away.

God promised to give him a son (c.f. Genesis 15:1-6), but Abraham could not wait for God to fulfill the promise. He goes on to bear a child with Hagar by the *fleshly-thinking suggestion* by Sarai. This shows that Abraham could not separate himself from his earthly thinking.

> *The son of the slave wife was born in a human attempt to bring about the fulfillment of God's promise. But the son of the freeborn wife was born as God's own fulfillment of his promise.*
>
> *Galatians 4:23*

Ishmael, the son of the slave wife, was not the son God had promised. Abraham, in his weak faith, tried to fulfill God's promise on his own strength and understanding.

God could not and was unwilling to send His Son through the bloodline of Abraham with this kind of weak faith.

It is no different for us today.

No matter how much we try on our own to believe in the Gospel; or no matter how much we try on our own to believe in Christ, it will be imperfect faith. With imperfect and wavering faith, we cannot be born again with the life that comes from God, see God, nor can we hear Him (c.f. John 6:40, 10:27).

This is why God provided a new Covenant, the Covenant of Circumcision.

It was because of Abraham's lack of faith God was silent with him for 13 years. Then He appeared to Abraham and declared that He is an almighty God, One that can enable Abraham to live a "blameless" life. This promise is the same for us; that is what enables us to be born again with the life that comes from God, live in Christ, place Christ as our head, receive the heart of Christ, and live in the Name of Jesus (c.f. Colossians 1:24-29).

When Abram was ninety-nine years old the LORD appeared to Abram and said to him, "I am God Almighty; walk before me, and be blameless
Genesis 17:1 (ESV)

In this way, God declared that He would enable Abraham to live a blameless life. To fulfill this, God established the Covenant of Circumcision. It is at this time that Abram received a new name and began to be called Abraham.

2I will make a Covenant with you, by which I will guarantee to give you countless descendants." 4"This is my Covenant with you: I will make you the father of a multitude of nations! 5What's more, I am changing your name. It will no longer be Abram. Instead, <u>you will be called Abraham</u>, for you will be the father of many nations.
Genesis 17:2,4-5

The Covenant God established with Abraham is an eternal (everlasting) Covenant, and anyone else that believes in this promise too can become children of God.

7"I will confirm my Covenant with you and your descendants after you, from generation to generation. <u>This is the everlasting Covenant</u>: I will always be your God and the God of your descendants after you. 9Then God said to Abraham, "Your responsibility is to obey the terms of the Covenant. You and all your descendants have this continual responsibility. 10<u>This is the Covenant that you and your descendants must keep: Each male among you must be circumcised.</u>
Genesis 17:7, 9-10

Verse 9 and 10 above shares the details of this Covenant.

The Covenant states that anyone that believes in this promise will circumcise (cut off the flesh of one's foreskin) themselves as a sign of their faith.

> *11You must cut off the flesh of your foreskin as a sign of the Covenant between me and you. 12From generation to generation, every male child must be circumcised on the eighth day after his birth. This applies not only to members of your family but also to the servants born in your household and the foreign-born servants whom you have purchased. 13All must be circumcised. Your bodies will bear the mark of my everlasting Covenant. 14Any male who fails to be circumcised will be cut off from the Covenant family for breaking the Covenant."*
>
> *Genesis 17:11-14*

This physical circumcision was a sign that the person believed in God's Covenant of Circumcision. On verse 14, it says that anyone that failed to be circumcised would have no further relationship with God. This Covenant simply stated that those that do not believe would not have salvation.

Before God provided this Covenant with Abraham, what kind of faith do you think Abraham had?

> *15Then God said to Abraham, "Regarding Sarai, your wife - her name will no longer be Sarai. From now on her name will be Sarah. 16And I will bless her and give you a son from her! Yes, I will bless her richly, and she will become the mother of many nations. Kings of nations will be among her descendants." 17Then Abraham bowed down to the ground, but he laughed to himself in disbelief. "How could I become a father at the age of 100?" he thought. "And how can Sarah have a baby when she is ninety years old?" 18So Abraham said to God, "May Ishmael live under your special blessing!"*
>
> *Genesis 17:15-18*

Abraham was completely a person of the flesh, a person that had no faith.

In earthly, or possibly scientific or medical, thinking, one cannot have a child when the man is over 100 years old, especially if his partner is past the age of menopause. That is why Abraham figured God had made a mistake—that God had meant for Ishmael to receive the blessings (v. 18).

In this way, Abraham was captive to his own knowledge and experiences and was not able to see God's ways.

The story certainly does not end there. God corrects Abraham:

> *19But God replied, "No - Sarah, your wife, will give birth to a son for you. You will name him Isaac, and I will confirm my Covenant with him and his descendants as an everlasting Covenant. 21But my Covenant will be confirmed with Isaac, who will be born to you and Sarah about this time next year."*
>
> *Genesis 17:19, 21*

Verse 19 reiterates that this Covenant is everlasting and given to anyone that believes, so that the people that believe may become children of God.

Abraham heard this and was finally able to accept the message. It was only then that Abraham began to believe without wavering.

Abraham then circumcised himself with faith that God would do what He had promised:

Abraham was ninety-nine years old when he was circumcised,
Genesis 17:24

Now God began to fulfill the Covenant in Abraham. These are the stories you can read in Genesis 18-20, including the events of Sodom and Gomorrah and king Abimelech.

Abraham experiences firsthand the things that God is doing and comes to recognize that He is truly God almighty and grows in faith. That is how God fulfilled His part of the Covenant in Abraham.

God's part of the Covenant of Circumcision is to remove the thinking that is limited to the flesh so that the person may be able to see God fully then believe without wavering.

God uses regular life events to fulfill His part of the Covenant in Abraham. As Abraham sees God in action, he begins toward a perfect faith in God.

16So the promise is received by faith. It is given as a free gift. And we are all certain to
receive it, whether or not we live according to the law of Moses, if we have faith like
Abraham's. For Abraham is the father of all who believe. 17That is what the Scriptures
mean when God told him, "I have made you the father of many nations." This happened
because Abraham believed in the God who brings the dead back to life and who creates
new things out of nothing. 18Even when there was no reason for hope, Abraham kept
hoping—believing that he would become the father of many nations. For God had said to
him, "That's how many descendants you will have!" 19And Abraham's faith did not
weaken, even though, at about 100 years of age, he figured his body was as good as
dead—and so was Sarah's womb. 20Abraham never wavered in believing God's
promise. In fact, his faith grew stronger, and in this he brought glory to God. 21He was
fully convinced that God is able to do whatever he promises. 22And because of
Abraham's faith, God counted him as righteous.
Romans 4:16-22

Once Abraham did his part, which was to believe and take action to remove his foreskin (circumcision) as a sign of his faith, God began to fulfill His part of the Covenant. He began to circumcise Abraham's heart so that Abraham would have perfect faith.

Just like that, we too should follow the "father of all who believe" and take the step of faith so that we may become Abraham's children:

7Being descendants of Abraham doesn't make them truly Abraham's children. For the Scriptures say, "Isaac is the son through whom your descendants will be counted," though Abraham had other children, too. 8This means that Abraham's physical descendants are not necessarily children of God. Only the children of the promise are considered to be Abraham's children.

Romans 9:7-8

You do not have salvation if you are not a child of Abraham, that is, you do not believe in the Covenant of Circumcision. This means you cannot be born again and become a child of God without your faith in God's Covenant.

The reason is simple. If God does not fulfill the Covenant in you, you cannot have perfect faith that is required to become a child of God.

Then does that mean we need to be circumcised?

No.

Jesus our Redeemer has received the physical circumcision on our behalf. As a result, the Holy Spirit was sent through Jesus and the Holy Spirit now circumcises the hearts of all who believe in the Covenant of Circumcision.

No, a true Jew is one whose heart is right with God. And true circumcision is not merely obeying the letter of the law; rather, it is a change of heart produced by God's Spirit. And a person with a changed heart seeks praise from God, not from people.

Romans 2:29

When you came to Christ, you were "circumcised," but not by a physical procedure. Christ performed a spiritual circumcision—the cutting away of your sinful nature.

Colossians 2:11

God sent the Holy Spirit through Christ to all who believes in the Covenant of Circumcision. Let us now look at details of how He fulfills the perfect faith in us so that we may be born again with His life.

The journey of God's fulfillment of the Covenant of Circumcision involves "tests" to identify the level of one's faith. Jesus appears to the person once his faith reaches the level of perfection.

We can see this in Genesis 22:

Some time later, God tested Abraham's faith. "Abraham!" God called. "Yes," he replied. "Here I am."

Genesis 22:1

The word used in verse above is "test."

What do you think God tested?

He tests the faith of Abraham that has been circumcised in heart.

"Take your son, your only son - yes, Isaac, whom you love so much - and go to the land of Moriah. Go and sacrifice him as a burnt offering on one of the mountains, which I will show you."

Genesis 22:2

God tells Abraham to sacrifice his son Isaac. Sacrifice means to separate out the bones from the flesh and divide it into specific sections:

10"If the animal you present as a burnt offering is from the flock, it may be either a sheep or a goat, but it must be a male with no defects. 11Slaughter the animal on the north side of the altar in the LORD's presence, and Aaron's sons, the priests, will splatter its blood against all sides of the altar. 12Then cut the animal in pieces, and the priests will arrange the pieces of the offering, including the head and fat, on the wood burning on the altar. 13But the internal organs and the legs must first be washed with water. Then the priest will burn the entire sacrifice on the altar as a burnt offering. It is a special gift, a pleasing aroma to the LORD.

Leviticus 1:10-13

God was telling Abraham to separate out His Son Isaac's body into different parts as an offering!

How could Abraham follow such a request?

However, we see Abraham fully obeying the Lord's command (c.f. Genesis 22:1-10). How was Abraham able to follow this request?

17It was by faith that Abraham offered Isaac as a sacrifice when God was testing him. Abraham, who had received God's promises, was ready to sacrifice his only son, Isaac, 18even though God had told him, "Isaac is the son through whom your descendants will be counted." 19Abraham reasoned that if Isaac died, God was able to bring him back to life again. And in a sense, Abraham did receive his son back from the dead.

Hebrews 11:17-19

It was simply because Abraham believed in God. He believed that God always fulfills any promise He makes.

God promised this:

4Then the LORD said to him, "No, your servant will not be your heir, for you will have a son of your own who will be your heir." 5Then the LORD took Abram outside and said to him, "Look up into the sky and count the stars if you can. That's how many descendants you will have!"

Genesis 15:4-5

God had already promised that Abraham would bear many children through Isaac.

Abraham believed in God and His promises. Since God had already promised nations through his child Isaac (c.f. Genesis 15:4-5, Hebrews 11:18), Abraham figured God will fulfill His promise in a way that Abraham perhaps does not yet understand, such as maybe even resurrecting Isaac from the dead.

God sees this faith of Abraham and sends and angel to say the following:

"Don't lay a hand on the boy!" the angel said. "Do not hurt him in any way, for now I know that you truly fear God. You have not withheld from me even your son, your only son."

Genesis 22:12

People who live with the same firm faith are called people that "fear God."

God sees this faith and makes this promise:

15Then the angel of the LORD called again to Abraham from heaven. 16"This is what the LORD says: Because you have obeyed me and have not withheld even your son, your only son, I swear by my own name that 17I will certainly bless you. I will multiply your descendants beyond number, like the stars in the sky and the sand on the seashore. Your descendants will conquer the cities of their enemies. 18And through your descendants all the nations of the earth will be blessed - all because you have obeyed me."

Genesis 22:15-18

Verse 16 says, "because … you have not withheld even your son, your only son." This is acknowledgement of Abraham's great, or grown, faith.

It was because of this faith that Jesus was sent to us through Abraham's lineage; God would not have used Abraham unless he reached this level of faith. Through Abraham's faith given through the Covenant of Circumcision, Jesus was sent to destroy the work of Satan (c.f. 1 John 3:8) fulfilling the Original Covenant.

The faith of Abraham is the perfect faith given to those whose hearts are circumcised. God gave this faith to Abraham and his descendants to fulfill the Original Covenant.

To say that we live with the faith of Abraham means that we believe in the Covenant of Circumcision that was given to the "father of faith" Abraham. Just as God made Abraham's faith perfect through the circumcision of his heart, we believe that He will do the same for us. He will also consider us as the *children of the promise* just like Isaac. When we live with that faith, Jesus will be evident in the way we live of our heritage as children of God.

Sarah, the wife of Abraham, was no different from Abraham in her ways of thinking in the flesh:

9"Where is Sarah, your wife?" the visitors asked. "She's inside the tent," Abraham replied. 10Then one of them said, "I will return to you about this time next year, and your wife, Sarah, will have a son!" Sarah was listening to this conversation from the tent. 11Abraham and Sarah were both very old by this time, and Sarah was long past the age of having children. 12So she laughed silently to herself and said, "How could a worn-out woman like me enjoy such pleasure, especially when my master - my husband - is also so old?"

Genesis 18:9-12

Verses above shows Sarah laughing in unbelief of what God is able to do. She was captive by her thoughts of the flesh, that is, her limitation of her logical understanding and experiences. Then God responds:

13Then the LORD said to Abraham, "Why did Sarah laugh? Why did she say, 'Can an old woman like me have a baby?' 14Is anything too hard for the LORD? I will return about this time next year, and Sarah will have a son." 15Sarah was afraid, so she denied it, saying, "I didn't laugh." But the LORD said, "No, you did laugh."

Genesis 18:13-15

God made the promise, and through events at Sodom and Gomorrah and with King Abimelech, God circumcises the heart of Sarah. In another words, Sarah began to believe that there is nothing impossible with God, that He is an almighty God.

17Then Abraham prayed to God, and God healed Abimelech, his wife, and his female servants, so they could have children. 18For the LORD had caused all the women to be infertile because of what happened with Abraham's wife, Sarah.

Genesis 20:17-18

Through this event, Sarah began to perfect her faith in the almighty God.

11It was by faith that even Sarah was able to have a child, though she was barren and was too old. She believed that God would keep his promise. 12And so a whole nation came from this one man who was as good as dead - a nation with so many people that, like the stars in the sky and the sand on the seashore, there is no way to count them.

Hebrews 11:11-12

We can see that even Sarah was freed from her captivity of thinking with the flesh. Isaac was born through her perfected faith.

To conclude, without believing in the Covenant of Circumcision that God gave to Abraham, one will have no relationship with God.

This Covenant of Circumcision was given to the *Father of Faith* and it is an everlasting promise. **We too must believe in this Covenant.**

4-8. God of Abraham, Isaac, and Jacob

The Bible iterates that the Lord is the God of Abraham, Isaac, and Jacob.

15God also said to Moses, "Say this to the people of Israel: Yahweh, the God of your ancestors - the God of Abraham, the God of Isaac, and the God of Jacob - has sent me to you. This is my eternal name, my name to remember for all generations. 16"Now go and call together all the elders of Israel. Tell them, 'The LORD, the God of your ancestors - the God of Abraham, Isaac, and Jacob - has appeared to me. He told me, "I have been watching closely, and I see how the Egyptians are treating you.

Exodus 3:15-16

"Perform this sign," the LORD told him. "Then they will believe that the LORD, the God of their ancestors - the God of Abraham, the God of Isaac, and the God of Jacob - really has appeared to you."

Exodus 4:5

Even Jesus referred to God in the same way:

`I am the God of Abraham, the God of Isaac, and the God of Jacob.' So he is the God of the living, not the dead."

Matthew 22:32

Why do you think God continually repeats that He is the God of Abraham, Isaac, and Jacob?

The reason is that after He gave the everlasting Covenant of Circumcision to Abraham (c.f. Genesis 17:19), He continued this Covenant through Isaac then to Jacob to form the nation of Israel.

God gave the Covenant to Abraham that people will be blessed through Isaac. This promise was fulfilled through Isaac's son, Jacob. Since this same Covenant has been passed through three generations before it was fulfilled, all three of these characters are named together.

God sent His only son Jesus to fulfill the Covenant He made with Abraham, Isaac, and Jacob. Beyond this Covenant (Gospel), there is none other.

So if one does not understand this Covenant, then s/he cannot know God, Jesus, or the Holy Spirit.

And this is the way to have eternal life—to know you, the only true God, and Jesus Christ, the one you sent to earth.

John 17:3

Eternal life here has these three meanings:

1. Living forever
2. Life of God in us (c.f. 1 John 5:11-12)
3. Immanuel, because it means to live in Christ.

To reiterate our points so far, we need to know Jesus, whom God sent to us, in order to live in Him and receive the new life that comes from God.

What exactly do we need to know about Him?

We need to believe that **Jesus fulfills the Covenant of Circumcision in us so that we may have eternal life**. God initiated the Covenant of Circumcision and sent Jesus to fulfill this Covenant (c.f. Hebrews 9:15). Jesus fulfilled this Covenant by dying on the cross for us, and this was God's will.

If you do not know and believe in this fact, even though you have been a good "Christian," you have no relationship with God.

This is why Jesus said this:

On judgment day many will say to me, `Lord! Lord! We prophesied in your name and cast out demons in your name and performed many miracles in your name.'
Matthew 7:22

"Many" in this verse worked hard to live good "Christian" lives. Perhaps these are people in church leadership, including pastors, who have been successful in their ministry.

However, Jesus warns these same people:

But I will reply, '<u>I never knew you</u>. Get away from me, you who break God's laws.'
Matthew 7:23

Why did Jesus say this to them?

The reason is that they did not live according to the will of God the Father.

"Not everyone who calls out to me, `Lord! Lord!" will enter the Kingdom of Heaven. <u>Only those who actually do the will of my Father in heaven will enter.</u>
Matthew 7:21

To what could the "will of the Father" be referring?

In order to fulfill the will of the Father, Jesus came to earth to endure much humiliation and contempt and He ultimately died on the cross.

9Then he said, "<u>Look, I have come to do your will." He cancels the first Covenant in order to put the second into effect.</u> 10For <u>God's will</u> was for us to be made holy by the sacrifice of the body of Jesus Christ, once for all time.

Hebrews 10:9-10

The reason why Jesus died on the cross was to establish the Second Covenant replacing the First Covenant that God had established with Israel through Moses.

28They replied, "<u>We want to perform God's works, too. What should we do?</u>" 29Jesus told them, "<u>This is the only work God wants from you: Believe in the one he has sent</u>."
38<u>For I have come down from heaven to do the will of God who sent me, not to do my own will.</u> 39<u>And this is the will of God</u>, that I should not lose even one of all those he has given me, but that I should raise them up at the last day. 40<u>For it is my Father's will that all who see his Son and believe in him should have eternal life.</u> I will raise them up at the last day."

John 6:28-29, 38-40

Verse 40 refers to the "last day." This refers to the time between his ascension (c.f. 1 Peter 1:20) to this return (c.f. 1 Peter 1:5). This is today, our present times.

To live in the will of God the Father in heaven means to cancel the First Covenant and replace it with the second. The second calls us to *see Jesus and believe in Him so that we may have eternal life* (c.f. John 6:40). This is what it means to live in the Father.

Jesus' resurrection was part of fulfilling the Covenant made with Abraham, Isaac, and Jacob:

32"<u>And now we are here to bring you this Good News. The promise was made to our ancestors,</u> 33<u>and God has now fulfilled it for us, their descendants, by raising Jesus</u>. This is what the second psalm says about Jesus: `You are my Son Today I have become your Father.'

Acts 13:32-33

So then, Jesus' dying on the cross and even his resurrection was to fulfill the Second Covenant God made with Abraham, Isaac, and Jacob.

We then need to understand this clearly: if we do not see and believe in Jesus, through whom God fulfills the Second Covenant, then there is no salvation and eternal life for us.

11So Christ has now become the High Priest over all the good things that have come. He has entered that greater, more perfect Tabernacle in heaven, which was not made by human hands and is not part of this created world. 12With his own blood - not the blood of goats and calves - he entered the Most Holy Place once for all time and secured our redemption forever. 13Under the old system, the blood of goats and bulls and the ashes of a young cow could cleanse people's bodies from ceremonial impurity. 14Just think how much more the blood of Christ will purify our consciences from sinful deeds so that we can worship the living God. For by the power of the eternal Spirit, Christ offered himself to God as a perfect sacrifice for our sins. 15That is why he is the one who mediates a new covenant between God and people, so that all who are called can receive the eternal inheritance God has promised them. For Christ died to set them free from the penalty of the sins they had committed under that first Covenant.

Hebrews 9:11-15

The "new covenant" mentioned in verse 15 refers to the Covenant given when Israel was on their exodus from Egypt (c.f. Deuteronomy 29:1-30:20) on Mount Moab (Sinai). Jesus fulfilled this same Covenant when He ascended to enter into the eternal sanctuary.

The law **(the Old Covenant)** *appointed high priests who were limited by human weakness. But after the law was given, God appointed his Son with an oath* **(the New Covenant)***, and his Son has been made the perfect High Priest forever.*

Remarks added in parenthesis, Hebrews 7:28

7If the first Covenant had been faultless, there would have been no need for a ***second Covenant*** *to replace it. 8But when God found fault with the people, he said: "The day is coming, says the LORD, when I will make a* ***new Covenant*** *with the people of Israel and Judah.*

Hebrews 8:7-8

Therefore, the Second Covenant and the New Covenant are the same and Jesus came to earth as the mediator for it.

We are people who firmly believe that Jesus will fulfill the Second Covenant, the Covenant of Circumcision, in us.

30Then he brought them out and asked, "Sirs, what must I do to be saved?" 31They replied, "Believe in the Lord Jesus and you will be saved, along with everyone in your household." 32And they shared the word of the Lord with him and with all who lived in his household.

Acts 16:30-32

Verse 31 says to "believe in the Lord Jesus." What do you think it is saying to *believe* about Jesus?

It is saying to believe that Jesus will fulfill in you the Covenant that God has promised. When you believe, Jesus will come to your home and fulfill the Covenant in you and your family.

4-9. The First Covenant The Old Promise that is No Longer Valid

What was the First (Old) Covenant that Jesus came to replace by dying on the cross?

This is described in Scriptures by illustrating a parallel between the two sons of Abraham:

21Tell me, you who want to live under the law, do you know what the law actually says?
22The Scriptures say that Abraham had two sons, one from his slave wife and one from
his freeborn wife. 23The son of the slave wife was born in a human attempt to bring
about the fulfillment of God's promise. But the son of the freeborn wife was born as
God's own fulfillment of his promise. 24 ***These two women serve as an***
illustration of God's two Covenants. *The first woman, Hagar, represents*
Mount Sinai where people received the law that enslaved them. 25And now Jerusalem is
just like Mount Sinai in Arabia, because she and her children live in slavery to the law.
26But the other woman, Sarah, represents the heavenly Jerusalem. She is the free woman,
and she is our mother. 27As Isaiah said, "Rejoice, O childless woman, you who have
never given birth! Break into a joyful shout, you who have never been in labor! For the
desolate woman now has more children than the woman who lives with her husband!"
28And you, dear brothers and sisters, are children of the promise, just like Isaac. 29But
you are now being persecuted by those who want you to keep the law, just as Ishmael, the
child born by human effort, persecuted Isaac, the child born by the power of the Spirit.
30But what do the Scriptures say about that? "Get rid of the slave and her son, for the
son of the slave woman will not share the inheritance with the free woman's son." 31So,
dear brothers and sisters, we are not children of the slave woman; we are children of the
free woman.

Galatians 4:21-31

Verse 24 points to the two Covenants. One was born of the flesh and another was born of the Spirit based on the belief in the promise (c.f. Galatians 3:29).

In that way, the Covenant God made with Israel can be seen as two kinds. The reason is that people have two kinds of life: one of the flesh and another of the life that comes from God.

The Covenant that is connected to the life of the flesh is called the First, or Old, Covenant (c.f. Hebrews 7:16). The one that is connected to the life that comes from God is called the Second, or New, Covenant (c.f. Deuteronomy 30:6).

Let us focus on the First Covenant first.

After about two months after beginning the exodus out of Egypt, Moses and the people of Israel arrive at Horeb/Sinai.

At the mountain of Horeb/Sinai, God calls Moses and gives this Covenant, which we call the First (Old) Covenant:

*Moses called all the people of Israel together and said, "Listen carefully, Israel. Hear the decrees and regulations I am giving you today, so you may learn them and obey them! 2"The LORD our God made a Covenant with us at Mount Sinai. (*Sinai is translated as Horeb in other translations) 3The LORD did not make this Covenant with our ancestors, but with all of us who are alive today.*

** Notes added in parenthesis, Deuteronomy 5:1-3*

As it says in verse 3, this is not the same Covenant made with Father Abraham and his children.

Then what was the Covenant God made with Abraham, Isaac, and Jacob?

The Covenant made with Abraham, Isaac, and Jacob was a promise from God that He will send the Messiah through Abraham's seed to fulfill the Original Covenant.

However, the *First Covenant* is not the Covenant of Circumcision. The First Covenant is one established through Moses and people that were with him on mountain of Sinai/Horeb (see verse 2).

4At the mountain the LORD spoke to you face to face from the heart of the fire. 5I stood as an intermediary between you and the LORD, for you were afraid of the fire and did not want to approach the mountain. He spoke to me, and I passed his words on to you. This is what he said. 6"I am the LORD your God, who rescued you from the land of Egypt, the place of your slavery.

Deuteronomy 5:4-6

People were afraid of the fire and did not go up the mountain. Moses went on behalf of the people as an intermediary between Israel and the Lord. He received details of this First Covenant from God and communicated it to the people of Israel. This command is called the Ten Commandments, and it is written from verses 7 through 21. God etched these commandments on a stone.

The LORD spoke these words to all of you assembled there at the foot of the mountain. He spoke with a loud voice from the heart of the fire, surrounded by clouds and deep darkness. This was all he said at that time, and he wrote his words on two stone tablets and gave them to me.

Deuteronomy 5:22

Moses continues to speak:

> *23"But when you heard the voice from the heart of the darkness, while the mountain was*
> *blazing with fire, all your tribal leaders and elders came to me. 24They said, 'Look, the*
> *LORD our God has shown us his glory and greatness, and we have heard his voice from*
> *the heart of the fire. Today we have seen that God can speak to us humans, and yet we*
> *live! 25But now, why should we risk death again? If the LORD our God speaks to us*
> *again, we will certainly die and be consumed by this awesome fire. 26Can any living thing*
> *hear the voice of the living God from the heart of the fire as we did and yet survive? 27Go*
> *yourself and listen to what the LORD our God says. Then come and tell us everything he*
> *tells you, and we will listen and obey.'*
>
> *Deuteronomy 5:23-27*

The elder and heads of Israel came to speak with Moses. They feared that if they heard the voice of God themselves, they might die. For that reason, they ask Moses to be the intermediary and that they would listen to the commands of God that Moses brings back.

Even God agrees with their views (see verses 28-29) and tells them to return to their tents. Then He speaks to Moses telling him to teach the people of Israel His commands so they may follow it when they reach the Promised Land Canaan.

> *30Go and tell them, "Return to your tents." 31But you stand here with me so I can give*
> *you all my commands, decrees, and regulations. You must teach them to the people so they*
> *can obey them in the land I am giving them as their possession."'*
>
> *Deuteronomy 5:30-31*

God promises that if the people are obedient to the commands, He will bless them (see verses 32-33) and will consider them righteous (c.f. Deuteronomy 6:25).

This Law was given through Moses and we call it the Law of Moses (c.f. Luke 2:22, Acts 13:39, 1 Corinthians 9:9). Also, since it was written in stone, it is also called the "written code" or the "letter of the law."

> *But now we have been released from the law, for we died to it and are no longer captive to its power. Now we can serve God, not in the old way of obeying the letter of the law, but in the new way of living in the Spirit.*
>
> *Romans 7:6*

This Law, or the "Letter of the Law" is something whose acts are physically visible or that can be physically heard. They are to be kept with physical actions, which can be done strictly logically with human (physical) thoughts. This is why this law is also called "law of a fleshly commandment" (c.f. Hebrews 7:16, NKJV).

To recap, both the first man Adam and first woman Eve fell into Satan's temptations. Adam obeyed Eve, where Eve was a captive to Satan. As a result, all of Adam's descendants would be slaves to their flesh and live with thoughts and minds of the flesh (c.f. Romans 6:16).

They would be captives of Satan and live on their own accords. They would have the thoughts and mind of flesh and believe that they can live without God.

To such people associated with the things of the flesh, God gave the First Covenant, the Ten Commandments, as the written code through Moses. The people of the flesh would then be able to hear, see, and evaluate their obedience in their minds of flesh. In short, God was letting them see for themselves how impossible it is to be perfectly obedient to God's laws without God's intervention. The law was given to show what sin looks like in a clear way:

Why, then, was the law given? It was given alongside the promise to show people their sins. But the law was designed to last only until the coming of the child who was promised. God gave his law through angels to Moses, who was the mediator between God and the people.

Galatians 3:19

The First Covenant, or the Law of Moses, was given through a man and were to be taught by men. In order to teach and disseminate the law, men were also appointed as high priests:

Every high priest is a man chosen to represent other people in their dealings with God. He presents their gifts to God and offers sacrifices for their sins.

Hebrews 5:1

The high priest had two major roles:

1. Serve God (c.f. Exodus 28:1)
2. Teach the Word of the Lord (c.f. Deuteronomy 31:9-13, Nehemiah 8:1-12)

Reiterating a very important point:

To live under the Law of Moses, or the "written code," means to see, hear and learn from another person.

In order to be acceptable to God under the Law of Moses, one must continue learning from other people and conquering one's ways of the flesh by self-discipline. They must continually strive to live in obedience to the law.

We must recognize the reason why God established this First Covenant.

All people born of Adam's seed is bound to be slaves of their flesh because of Satan's rule over them. They have the mind and thoughts of the flesh.

6So letting your sinful nature control your mind leads to death. But letting the Spirit control your mind leads to life and peace. 7For the sinful nature is always hostile to God. It never did obey God's laws, and it never will. 8That's why those who are still under the control of their sinful nature can never please God. 13For if you live by its dictates, you will die. But if through the power of the Spirit you put to death the deeds of your sinful nature, you will live.

Romans 8:6-8, 13

As the verses above show, people with the mind and thoughts of the flesh are under the control of their sinful natures, or in complete control of Satan.

That is the reason Jesus came to earth; however, it may not be as many believers understand it. *Jesus did not come to change the hearts of flesh-thinking people.*

Even God cannot change the mind and thinking of flesh. If God were able to do that, there would not have been a need to send Jesus to suffer and die on the cross.

The reason why God sent Jesus was to allow Jesus to die on the cross, then overcome the power of death, then send the Holy Spirit so that we can be born again with the life that comes from God. It was not to change our existing hearts, which was beyond repair, but to bring about new hearts, the heart of God.

Jesus did not come to change our hearts, but He came to give us new lives through His death, resurrection, and by returning to us as the Holy Spirit so that we may believe and receive circumcision of our hearts.

All religions in this world has to do with listening and being taught by other people. This only reinforces the thoughts and hearts of the flesh and relies on people's self-discipline or own efforts to be acceptable to God.

Satan uses this to trick people that do not know that it is impossible to please God on our own strength and abilities. If one were truly able to accomplish state of holiness acceptable to the Lord by one's own good works, then even Satan would be able to become God by living a perfect life. This is simply not possible.

So then, we can easily quell any new religions that may appear in our days, as any other that believes in salvation other than through the Name of Jesus is a false religion that is being deceived by Satan. All of these so-called religions has the root of the Law of Moses, which are strict rules to follow taught by other humans (c.f. Romans 2:14-15, 1 Corinthians 15:55-56).

The following terms mean the same:

- To live according to the Law of Moses, or the letter of the law
- To live according to the flesh
- To live according to the thoughts and minds of the flesh
- To live hearing and learning about God's Word from other people

There was a time when one of the churches in city of Kwang Yuk were in a state of discord. The congregation separated into two factions. As they continued to argue, one of them grabbed the senior pastor by the neck and pulled him down from the pulpit.

How could such situations happen? The pastor probably shared God's Word in the best way to his congregation declaring to "love one another," "forgive one another," "be thankful," "be united," and other good teachings.

Even when the best is intended, how could such a terrible event occur at his church?

The problem is that both the pastor and all congregation members only listened to the Word of God through a person only. This is why all people in that church felt they belong in the seat of Moses to make judgments toward one another in the way they understood the Scriptures.

We know that God's commandments are holy, righteous and good (c.f. Romans 7:12).

However, when this perfect Word is heard through the life (mind and heart) of the flesh, Satan plants the thoughts of the flesh and causes people to sin. Even though the Word is indeed holy, righteous, and good, it can be distorted by Satan to cause us to sin.

To give an example, consider a pastor sharing during his sermon to "forgive, love, and serve your enemies." This is certainly a righteous, holy, and good Word of God. However, when a person hears this message only through another person, s/he can only understand this with one's thoughts and mind of the flesh. As a slave to sinful nature, the person cannot but place Satan as their head. So then, even with the Words that are meant to bring about life, man can only desire to be God just like Satan did. Therefore, the man will seek to take the seat that only belongs to God and makes judgment on the other person.

"Why doesn't my husband love me?", "Why doesn't Deacon John forgive deacon Bob?" "Why does my pastor say something, but doesn't live out what he says?" These are examples of people judging one another and therefore sinning.

This is why Apostle Paul says this:

7Well then, am I suggesting that the law of God is sinful? Of course not! In fact, it was the law that showed me my sin. I would never have known that coveting is wrong if the law had not said, "You must not covet." 8But sin used this command to arouse all kinds of covetous desires within me! If there were no law, sin would not have that power. 9At one time I lived without understanding the law. But when I learned the command not to covet, for instance, the power of sin came to life, 10and I died. So I discovered that the law's commands, which were supposed to bring life, brought spiritual death instead. 11Sin took advantage of those commands and deceived me; it used the commands to kill me.

Romans 7:7-11

As the verses above say, even though the law is righteous, holy, and good, Satan deceives us to sin by arousing covetous desires within us.

This is why there is punishment:

For the law always brings punishment on those who try to obey it. (The only way to avoid breaking the law is to have no law to break!)

Romans 4:15

Professionals say "stress" is the most prevalent cause of diseases experienced by many adults. Satan's deception that one must receive and learn the law from other people is the greatest cause of this sickness and curse.

55O death, where is your victory? O death, where is your sting?" 56For sin is the sting that results in death, and the law gives sin its power.

1Corinthians 15:55-56

When a person is a captive of sin, he becomes like Satan. Continuation leads to sickness and curse.

The authority of Satan is the law.

The way Satan kills humans is by deception, especially using the Law, which is the Word of God. He makes people to believe that this Law is something that is to be *heard from other people,* ones that have the heart and mind of the world.

This is why people refer to the "Word of God," but misuses it with the mind that Satan gives to be greedy, blame, and judge others.

We may see good qualities such as diligence and seeking to be holy (c.f. Romans 10:2) in such people. We may even see this person serving and contributing to others.

This person may share a story about Jesus' love and may even volunteer to help the poor, sick and the underprivileged.

However, if they do not know the Second Covenant that God established, they are no different from any worldly businesspersons.

Apostle Paul refers to himself and says that he "obeyed the law without fault" (c.f. Philippians 3:6). He was saying that in comparison with others, he had no faults.

Jindo dogs are said to be very obedient. However, they are obedient when compared to other dogs, but they cannot be compared in the same way with other humans.

Apostle Paul was simply making the point that he lived as a role model that has very little blemish in the law in comparison with other people.

Even around us, we can easily spot people that do not know the Second Covenant and are living religiously on their own accord. Even the best and near-perfect people will have minds that are very filthy when we see them in comparison with the life of God.

The Pharisees, Sadducees, and highest priests during time of Jesus worked hard to obey the law. They even talked about God with their lips:

> *But Jesus remained silent. Then the high priest said to him, "I demand in the name of the living God—tell us if you are the Messiah, the Son of God."*
>
> *Matthew 26:63*

They even received respect from the people (c.f. Acts 5:34).

However, Jesus looks to them and calls them snakes and children of them (Satan):

> *Snakes! Sons of vipers! How will you escape the judgment of hell?*
>
> *Matthew 23:33*

Why did Jesus criticize the people that diligently worked hard to obey the commandments of God?

It is simply because they only listened to the Word *from other people*. They eventually use the same Word, which is righteous, holy, and good, to accuse Jesus as a sinner and executes Him.

That is why Jesus said this:

> *44For no one can come to me unless the Father who sent me draws them to me, and at the last day I will raise them up. 45As it is written in the Scriptures, 'They will all be taught by God.' Everyone who listens to the Father and learns from him comes to me.*
>
> *John 6:44-45*

It is no different even today. We must first hear the voice of and be taught by the Holy Spirit.

For it is not you who will be speaking - it will be the Spirit of your Father speaking through you.

Matthew 10:20

But when you are arrested and stand trial, don't worry in advance about what to say. Just say what God tells you at that time, for it is not you who will be speaking, but the Holy Spirit.

Mark 13:11

for the Holy Spirit will teach you at that time what needs to be said."

Luke 12:12

When the Holy Spirit talks, let us listen and obey.

But when the Father sends the Advocate as my representative—that is, the Holy Spirit—he will teach you everything and will remind you of everything I have told you.

John 14:26

When the Spirit of truth comes, he will guide you into all truth. He will not speak on his own but will tell you what he has heard. He will tell you about the future.

John 16:13

Obviously, we must be wary of Christians that say they are teaching with the words of the Holy Spirit when they are of the flesh and hear only other people. They may even proclaim to others to hear the voice of the Holy Spirit, but do not even know His voice themselves. In their hearts, they believe there is nothing beyond the written law.

But people who aren't spiritual can't receive these truths from God's Spirit. It all sounds foolish to them and they can't understand it, for only those who are spiritual can understand what the Spirit means.

1Corinthians 2:14

That is why we must understand this very clearly:

13When we tell you these things, we do not use words that come from human wisdom.
Instead, we speak words given to us by the Spirit, using the Spirit's words to explain
spiritual truths. 14But people who aren't spiritual can't receive these truths from God's
Spirit. It all sounds foolish to them and they can't understand it, for only those who are

spiritual can understand what the Spirit means. 15Those who are spiritual can evaluate all things, but they themselves cannot be evaluated by others. 16For, "Who can know the LORD's thoughts? Who knows enough to teach him?" But we understand these things, for we have the mind of Christ.

1Corinthians 2:13-16

We must receive the teachings of the Holy Spirit so that we may have the mind of Christ. Remember the inverse: if we do not receive the teachings of the Holy Spirit, we cannot have the mind of Christ.

We are not people who hear the Word of God through people and try to obey them; rather, we are people who receive teachings from the Holy Spirit. We are people who live with the mind of Christ that is given to us from Him as we live in Him.

The mind of Christ is the life of Christ, Name of Jesus, our salvation, and ultimately, our faith.

We must be careful to not be in association with the devil.

It may be easy to mistaken someone as a prophet of God when many people may gather because someone says s/he comes in the Name of Jesus. This person may even show signs and wonders.

However, false prophets are able to show signs and wonders like those of true prophets. Some may not even know that they are false prophets themselves. I know because *I too was one of them.*

One key fruit to distinguish between a true or false prophet is by examining whether their character, their inner person, is continually changing.

Beware of false prophets who come disguised as harmless sheep but are really vicious wolves.

Matthew 7:15

25"What sorrow awaits you teachers of religious law and you Pharisees. Hypocrites! For you are so careful to clean the outside of the cup and the dish, but inside you are filthy—full of greed and self-indulgence! 26You blind Pharisee! First wash the inside of the cup and the dish, and then the outside will become clean, too.

Matthew 23:25-26

22On judgment day many will say to me, `Lord! Lord! We prophesied in your name and cast out demons in your name and performed many miracles in your name.' 23But I will reply, `I never knew you. Get away from me, you who break God's laws.'

Matthew 7:22-23

People who break God's laws are those that live by the *Law of Moses* that do not enter the narrow gate as a result. This means they also do not lead others to this narrow gate (c.f. Matthew 7:13-15).

The narrow gate is referring to heaven (the Kingdom of Heaven), or Jesus Himself (c.f. John 10:7, 9).

Jesus said this:

> *13"What sorrow awaits you teachers of religious law and you Pharisees. Hypocrites! For you shut the door of the Kingdom of Heaven in people's faces. You won't go in yourselves, and you don't let others enter either. 14 15"What sorrow awaits you teachers of religious law and you Pharisees. Hypocrites! For you cross land and sea to make one convert, and then you turn that person into twice the child of hell you yourselves are!*
>
> *Matthew 23:13-15*

> *For false messiahs and false prophets will rise up and perform great signs and wonders so as to deceive, if possible, even God's chosen ones.*
>
> *Matthew 24:24*

In Scriptures, there are only two kinds of laws. The reason is simply that there are two kinds of spirits: one of man (or of flesh), and one of God.

The law given to the life of the flesh is called the *Law of Moses* (c.f. Hebrews 7:16). The law given to living according to the life of God is called *the Law of Christ* or *the Law of the Spirit of Life* (c.f. 1 Corinthians 9:21, Romans 8:2).

The Law of the Spirit of Life refers to living in Christ through the Holy Spirit with the life that comes from God.

To review, it is by the Second Covenant, which God has sworn to fulfill, that the Holy Spirit was sent. The Holy Spirit enables us to see the glory of God (c.f. 2 Corinthians 3:18) and listen to the voice of the Holy Spirit so that we may live with the mind of Christ (c.f. Luke 8:15). That is how God fulfilled the Second Covenant.

Living only by faith and reliance only on the grace of God is how we can live according to the *Law of the Spirit of Life.*

Referring back to Matthew 7:23, people who break God's laws range from both extremes:

1. People who listen to the Law of Moses and strives on his/her accord to keep them
2. People who, in the Name of Jesus, perform many miracles that may attract many people.

There are three common points for people who break God's laws:

1. Such people say that the Gospel just requires simple belief in Jesus, and this faith leads people to heaven.

   That is not the full truth.

   We must first welcome and accept Jesus who first came to find us and live as Jesus did (the Kingdom of Heaven) so that we can enter into heaven.

2. They do not understand the secrets of heaven.

   Jesus clearly said that without knowing the secrets of the Kingdom of God (heaven), there is no forgiveness (c.f. Mark 4:10-12) and salvation (c.f. Luke 8:10-12).

3. They do not know the Second (New) Covenant

   As we have seen before, those that do not know the Second (New) Covenant do not know the Son of God, nor can they know the Secret of Heaven.

Let us recap:

First Covenant was established by God with the people of Israel by giving the commands to a middle-person, Moses. First Covenant was to be communicated and taught by *other people*. The purpose of this Covenant is to show that with one's own (flesh) thoughts and mind, the law cannot be perfectly kept.

For no one can ever be made right with God by doing what the law commands. The law simply shows us how sinful we are.

Romans 3:20

Yet we know that a person is made right with God by faith in Jesus Christ, not by obeying the law. And we have believed in Christ Jesus, so that we might be made right with God because of our faith in Christ, not because we have obeyed the law. For no one will ever be made right with God by obeying the law.

Galatians 2:16

People who try to be considered "righteous" by obeying the law are people that are cursed:

But those who depend on the law to make them right with God are under his curse, for the Scriptures say, "Cursed is everyone who does not observe and obey all the commands that are written in God's Book of the Law."

Galatians 3:10

They are also people that have fallen away from the grace of God:

For if you are trying to make yourselves right with God by keeping the law, you have been cut off from Christ! You have fallen away from God's grace.

Galatians 5:4

The false teachers share what sounds like the Gospel. They say to believe in Jesus for salvation, be grateful for His grace, be filled with His power, be blessed, obey the written Word of God, and repent of your sins. These false teachers may even perform miracles and act as if they are true prophets of God.

That is why we must recognize this clearly:

He did this by ending the system of law with its commandments and regulations. He made peace between Jews and Gentiles by creating in himself one new people from the two groups.

Ephesians 2:15

Where it says "ending the system of law," it doesn't refer to the good law itself (c.f. Romans 7:12), but the First Covenant where people were required to communicate and teach the law.

He canceled the record of the charges against us and took it away by nailing it to the cross.

Colossians 2:14

And now he has made all of this plain to us by the appearing of Christ Jesus, our Savior. He broke the power of death and illuminated the way to life and immortality through the Good News.

2Timothy 1:10

Jesus took away the First Covenant, the Law of Moses, which has been the source of our death.

To say again:

Until John the Baptist, the law of Moses and the messages of the prophets were your guides. But now the Good News of the Kingdom of God is preached, and everyone is eager to get in.

Luke 16:16

The time of listening to the Law (of Moses) from prophets and other people have ended with John the Baptist.

Now, we can live with the mind of Christ that He provides us by placing Him as the Head and by being in Him.

Beloved, do not be brainwashed by teachings of *other people*, especially when they try to teach you what seems to be the Word of God.

In North Korea, people are brainwashed and commit their lives to serving Jung Eun Kim.

When they learn that this belief to which they were brainwashed is false, all their faith will quickly disappear.

Such faith that can easily disappear is not what we call "perfect" faith.

Therefore, perfect faith cannot come of something that any person has made.

14But how can they call on him to save them unless they believe in him? And how can they believe in him if they have never heard about him? And how can they hear about him unless someone tells them? 15And how will anyone go and tell them without being sent? That is why the Scriptures say, "How beautiful are the feet of messengers who bring good news!" 16But not everyone welcomes the Good News, for Isaiah the prophet said, "LORD, who has believed our message?" 17So faith comes from hearing, that is, hearing the Good News about Christ.

Romans 10:14-17

As verse 16 says, faith does not come from *hearing from a person*. This is why we need to hear from Christ as verse 17 reveals.

Until we hear the Word of Jesus who lives inside us (c.f. Romans 10:6-8), we cannot have faith.

When people cannot hear the Word from Christ directly and continues to hear from other people, they may be able to say with their lips about their allegiance to God, but their hearts would not be in alignment.

And so the Lord says, "These people say they are mine. They honor me with their lips, but their hearts are far from me. And their worship of me is nothing but man-made rules learned by rote.

Isaiah 29:13

The Master said: "These people make a big show of saying the right thing, but their hearts aren't in it. Because they act like they're worshiping me but don't mean it,

Isaiah 29:13 (MSG)

As the verse above says, with the teachings of man, we cannot believe in God with our hearts, and this means we cannot obey God's Word with all of our hearts.

20You have died with Christ, and he has set you free from the spiritual powers of this world. So why do you keep on following the rules of the world, such as, 21"Don't handle! Don't taste! Don't touch!"? 22Such rules are mere human teachings about things that deteriorate as we use them. 23These rules may seem wise because they require strong devotion, pious self-denial, and severe bodily discipline. But they provide no help in conquering a person's evil desires.

Colossians 2:20-23

The Law of Moses has already ended:

For Christ has already accomplished the purpose for which the law was given. As a result, all who believe in him are made right with God.

Romans 10:4

Then he said, "Look, I have come to do your will." He cancels the first Covenant in order to put the second into effect.

Hebrews 10:9

Then the questions that arise may be:

- Do we still need to listen to sermons of the pastor?
- Do we still need to study the Word of God?

Yes, we do.

We still need to listen to sermons and study the Word of God, even though from another person.

However, the purpose for listening and learning from another person is so that we may be led by Christ to continue to live in Him.

Let me put it another way. The law was our guardian until Christ came; it protected us until we could be made right with God through faith.

Galatians 3:24

The reason for our listening to other people about the Word of God is so that we can live with the mind of Christ that He gives by being led by Christ the Rock and drinking the living water that comes from Him.

In another words, we hear and learn from other people so that we may know more about Jesus (God) who fulfills the Second (New) Covenant.

So,

25And now that the way of faith has come, we no longer need the law as our guardian.
26For you are all children of God through faith in Christ Jesus. 27And all who have been united with Christ in baptism have put on Christ, like putting on new clothes.

Galatians 3:25-27

Now we must live lives showing Christ by putting Him on like clothes, which can occur when we listen to His Word and believe in Him.

27My sheep listen to my voice; I know them, and they follow me. 28I give them eternal life, and they will never perish. No one can snatch them away from me, 29for my Father has given them to me, and he is more powerful than anyone else. No one can snatch them from the Father's hand. 30The Father and I are one."

John 10:27-30

We must hear His voice and move according to His guidance.

To summarize:

To hear and learn the Word of God through people alone is to follow the First Covenant, the Law of Moses. This Law is canceled, and anyone that still clings to this Law is cursed (c.f. Galatians 3:10), fallen from grace of Christ (c.f. Galatians 5:4), and are people who break God's laws (c.f. Matthew 7:23).

Such people too speak of the "Good News" and the "Holy Spirit," but they do not know the Second (New) Covenant and the Secret of Heaven.

A person can never fully love God with all of his/her heart, mind and strength and will only be self-focused on discipline by only hearing and learning the Word of God from other people.

Perhaps outwardly or with their lips, they may seem to be people that love God, but they are filled with greed on the inside and seek to fulfill their own pursuits by saying it is in the "Name of Jesus" and acting as if they are living out their spiritual lives correctly. They deceive others by their outward acts, but they too may be deceived by Satan and not know that.

Let me repeat this important point:

9Then he said, "Look, I have come to do your will." He cancels the first Covenant in order to put the second into effect. 10For God's will was for us to be made holy by the sacrifice of the body of Jesus Christ, once for all time.

Hebrews 10:9-10

The reason why Jesus died on the cross was to eliminate the First Covenant.

The Second (New) Covenant is the promise God has sworn to us that He will enable us to live by teaching and speaking to us directly. We will be living in Christ and with the life that comes from God because the Holy Spirit has been sent to us to live in us.

4-10. The Law of Sin and Death

But when people keep on sinning, it shows that they belong to the devil, who has been sinning since the beginning. But the Son of God came to destroy the works of the devil.
1John 3:8

Because God's children are human beings - made of flesh and blood - the Son also became flesh and blood. For only as a human being could he die, and only by dying could he break the power of the devil, who had the power of death.
Hebrews 2:14

The Law of Sin and Death is the method by which Satan causes people to commit sin and lead them toward death with him.

Satan certainly uses the obvious methods: craving for physical pleasure, lust of the eyes, and pride in achievements and possessions (c.f. 1John 2:15-16) to lead people toward death; however, I want us to focus on the less obvious that is leading masses to death. Satan, the father of lies, uses false prophets to lead "Christians" to death. Let us examine this further.

Jesus said this:

Beware of false prophets who come disguised as harmless sheep but are really vicious wolves.
Matthew 7:15

The verse above says false prophets come disguised as sheep as if they were representing God.

Some of these "sheep" say they are prophets in the Name of Jesus and hold titles such as *pastors*, *elders*, etc. They may "cast out" demons and perform other "miracles" claiming to be a follower of Jesus. However:

On judgment day many will say to me, `Lord! Lord! We prophesied in your name and cast out demons in your name and performed many miracles in your name.'
Matthew 7:22

The people mentioned in verse 22 believed they were Christians. They worked diligently and apparently performed many major feats. However, Jesus says to them:

But I will reply, `I never knew you. Get away from me, you who break God's laws.'
Matthew 7:23

Jesus calls them people that have broken the laws of God. He has also referred to them as false prophets (verse 15). These people are bound to hell (c.f. Revelations 20:10).

Similar story appears in Luke 13:22-27.

When Jesus was traveling through Jerusalem, someone asked Jesus, "only a few people will be saved, right?"

22Jesus went through the towns and villages, teaching as he went, always pressing on toward Jerusalem. 23Someone asked him, "Lord, will only a few be saved?" He replied,

Luke 13:22-23

Jesus responds like this:

24"Work hard to enter the narrow door to God's Kingdom, for many will try to enter but will fail. 25When the master of the house has locked the door, it will be too late. You will stand outside knocking and pleading, `Lord, open the door for us!' But he will reply, `I don't know you or where you come from.' 26Then you will say, `But we ate and drank with you, and you taught in our streets.'

Luke 13:24-26

The people in these verses too were people that believed they were following Christ. They believed they had been taught by Christ and doing works for Him. Unfortunately, they were wrong.

Even today, many people have fallen for Satan's trickery. Some have lived as false prophets leading others toward the same path. In the end, they will all go to death with Satan.

Jesus says this to them:

And he will reply, `I tell you, I don't know you or where you come from. Get away from me, all you who do evil.'

Luke 13:27

The two stories we have examined above shares two common points about the false prophets Satan uses to lead people to death:

First,

<u>You can enter God's Kingdom only through the narrow gate</u>. The highway to hell is broad, and its gate is wide for the many who choose that way.

Matthew 7:13

<u>Work hard to enter the narrow door to God's Kingdom</u>, for many will try to enter but will fail.

Luke 13:24

False prophets, those that have been deceived by Satan, do not enter into the narrow door AND prevents others from entering into it (c.f. Matthew 23:13-15).

As mentioned previously, the "narrow door" refers to Jesus Himself.

7so he explained it to them: "I tell you the truth, <u>I am the gate for the sheep</u>. 9<u>Yes, I am the gate</u>. Those who come in through me will be saved. They will come and go freely and will find good pastures.

John 10:7, 9

Jesus Himself is the gate for the sheep.

That is why we must enter into Him, who is the gate. That is the way to our salvation, and there is no other way.

We must accept Jesus, our Heaven, and live in Him.

The common point of these false prophets is that they do not know the Law of the Spirit that enables us to live in Christ.

Even though they may say many seeming truths, because they do not know the New Covenant and the Secret of Heaven, they cannot know the *Law of the Spirit of Life* that truly gives life.

Second,

But I will reply, `<u>I never knew you</u>. Get away from me, you who break God's laws.'

Matthew 7:23

And he will reply, `I tell you, <u>I don't know you or where you come from</u>. Get away from me, all you who do evil.'

Luke 13:27

Jesus says He does not know them.

Why did Jesus say He does not know them?

The reason is that they are not His sheep. This is because they were not ones that listened to His voice and followed Him.

My sheep listen to my voice; I know them, and they follow me.
John 10:27

Jesus' sheep hear and follow His Word. Jesus says *He knows* those that hear Him and follow Him.

The way to hear His voice is through the *Law of the Spirit of Life* that is now available to us because of what Christ has done.

Back to the original point, in the two passages we saw above, the false prophets, or people in pastorate positions in churches, did not know the *Law of the Spirit of Life* and as a result, they lived their lives with false faith, or as shown in verse below, "breaking God's laws."

22On judgment day many will say to me, `Lord! Lord! We prophesied in your name and cast out demons in your name and performed many miracles in your name.' 23But I will reply, `I never knew you. Get away from me, you who break God's laws.'
Matthew 7:22-23

They broke God's laws.

The "law" that Satan is using to cause people to sin here is *the Law of Moses.*

The Law of Moses is one related with the flesh where people can only hear and learn from other people, not directly from God. This is the Law that Jesus abolished (c.f. Ephesians 2:15, Colossians 2:14, 2 Timothy 1:10, Hebrews 10:9).

Even though Jesus sacrificed much to get rid of the Law that cannot be kept, Satan continues to use it.

That is why Jesus says it is not lawful for people to continue to live by the Law of Moses.

Even today, Satan makes this outdated law to stand out as something of great importance and awaits to devour his next prey (c.f. 1 Peter 5:8).

The sting of death is sin, and the power of sin is the law.
1Corinthians 15:56 NIV

Sin is the cause of sickness, curses, poverty, and many other negative effects. This sin comes from Satan.

It is because Satan has power over the law.

Satan uses Law of Moses and raises up false prophets to deceive many others. The deceived live by that faith, but unfortunately for them, they end up in death along with the false prophets and Satan.

This method of how Satan uses the Law of Moses to bring others with him toward death is called the "Law of Sin and Death."

From here on, let us look at how Satan causes people to sin so that they may be led toward death with him.

Satan's sin began with greed to obtain what he desired. He uses that same desire to cause people to fall:

> *You are of your father the devil, and your will is to do your father's desires. He was a murderer from the beginning, and has nothing to do with the truth, because there is no truth in him. When he lies, he speaks out of his own character, for he is a liar and the father of lies.*
>
> *John 8:44 (ESV)*

All sinful desires comes from Satan and they lead to death:

> *14Temptation comes from our own desires, which entice us and drag us away. 15These desires give birth to sinful actions. And when sin is allowed to grow, it gives birth to death.*
>
> *James 1:14-15*

Let us examine how Satan gives these desires to people.

He gives the desires to our physical bodies:

> *2in which you once walked, following the course of this world, following the prince of the power of the air, the spirit that is now at work in the sons of disobedience— 3among whom we all once lived in the* ***passions of our flesh****, carrying out the* ***desires of the body and the mind****, and were by nature children of wrath, like the rest of mankind.*
>
> *Ephesians 2:2-3 (ESV)*

Verse 3 distinguishes two parts of the flesh: one is the physical body made from dust, and another is the thoughts and minds of the flesh.

Of these two parts, on where do you think Satan focuses to lead us to focus on our desires?

He focuses on our minds:

6So letting your sinful nature control your mind leads to death. But letting the Spirit control your mind leads to life and peace. 7For the sinful nature is always hostile to God. It never did obey God's laws, and it never will.

Romans 8:6-7

In that way, Satan focuses his attack on our minds so that we may act in hostility toward God and His ways.

What do you think is embedded in our minds of the flesh?

Anyone born of the seed of Adam, who ate the fruit from the tree of the knowledge of good and evil, has law in their minds (c.f. Romans 7:12), and that is what we call the conscience.

14Even Gentiles, who do not have God's written law, show that they know his law when they instinctively obey it, even without having heard it. 15They demonstrate that God's law is written in their hearts, for their own conscience and thoughts either accuse them or tell them they are doing right.

Romans 2:14-15

Remember, the law is holy, righteous and good (c.f. Romans 7:12).

So then, all people on earth, children of Adam, have conscience, or the law, in them. As a result, they feel they may be able to live lives that are holy, righteous, and good.

Based on logic of their minds, it may seem that if children are educated well, they may be able to remain holy, righteous, and good.

That is what Satan does to deceive us. He causes us to believe that we can keep God's commandments on our own lives of flesh. *Remember, the conscience is the law that is rooted in the flesh. We cannot keep the perfect law of God on our own accord!*

For such people that rely on their conscience, the law that is in them, God used Moses to establish the First Covenant.

God promises to bless them if they keep the physical commandments (c.f. Deuteronomy 5:1-6:25, 28:1-14).

The purpose of the Law was to show that people could not keep the law with the limitations of their physical flesh (c.f. Romans 3:20, Galatians 3:19).

However, those that have received the Law of Moses *strives* to keep the commands with the minds of their flesh.

This is how Satan places desires into our thoughts of the flesh so that there is a conflict between our thoughts and mind. Eventually, the mind loses to the thoughts and we are led toward sin, which leads to death (c.f. Romans 7:14-24).

14So the trouble is not with the law, for it is spiritual and good. The trouble is with me, for I am all too human, a slave to sin. 15I don't really understand myself, for I want to do what is right, but I don't do it. Instead, I do what I hate. 16But if I know that what I am doing is wrong, this shows that I agree that the law is good. 17So I am not the one doing wrong; it is sin living in me that does it. 18And I know that nothing good lives in me, that is, in my sinful nature. I want to do what is right, but I can't. 19I want to do what is good, but I don't. I don't want to do what is wrong, but I do it anyway. 20But if I do what I don't want to do, I am not really the one doing wrong; it is sin living in me that does it. 21I have discovered this principle of life—that when I want to do what is right, I inevitably do what is wrong. 22I love God's law with all my heart. 23But there is another power within me that is at war with my mind. This power makes me a slave to the sin that is still within me. 24Oh, what a miserable person I am! Who will free me from this life that is dominated by sin and death?

Romans 7:14-24

We can see from the verses above that Satan causes our minds of the flesh (our inner person) and the thoughts of the flesh (the law or conscience) to be in conflict in order to cause us to be slaves to sin.

When faced with such conflicts, we may pray: "Father in Heaven, help us to overcome sin and be obedient to your Word. Give us strength and ability to do so." Then after placing these before God, we may again strive to meet the commandments again on our own strength.

This way, there is a continual battle within us. We may fall at times, and then fight again. *The Law of Sin and Death* is in work when we continually fall and are led toward the downward spiral of death (c.f. Romans 6:23).

Remember, the reason why God gave the Law of Moses was so that we can know that we cannot overcome the thoughts of the flesh (the thoughts that Satan gives) with our limited mind of the flesh (c.f. Romans 7:12). Once we recognize our limitations, we would turn to God and follow Jesus' leadership.

For no one can ever be made right with God by doing what the law commands. The law simply shows us how sinful we are.

Romans 3:20

Oh, what a miserable person I am! Who will free me from this life that is dominated by sin and death?

Romans 7:24

Let me put it another way. The law was our guardian until Christ came; it protected us until we could be made right with God through faith.

Galatians 3:24

Jesus has abolished the Law because as humans, we cannot keep the Law with our limited minds of the flesh.

He did this by ending the system of law with its commandments and regulations. He made peace between Jews and Gentiles by creating in himself one new people from the two groups.

Ephesians 2:15

Where it says "ending the system of law," it doesn't refer to the good law itself (c.f. Romans 7:12), but the First Covenant where people were required to communicate and teach the law (c.f. Hebrews 10:9-10).

For Christ has already accomplished the purpose for which the law was given. As a result, all who believe in him are made right with God.

Romans 10:4

If we have been, we must get rid out of our desire to follow the Law of Moses and rather, come to faith in Christ and live in Him.

God had sworn to fulfill the Second (New) Covenant through Jesus Christ and He has done it, and it is now available to us! This can only come by faith. Through the Holy Spirit, we can live in Christ, place Him as the head of our lives, and live with the mind that He gives us.

When we live with the mind of Christ, the requirements of the law are automatically fulfilled.

This kind of lifestyle is to live according to *the Law of the Spirit of Life.*

Even then, Satan, the father of lies, continues to raise up false prophets to use the Law of Moses, which Jesus has already abolished, to lead people to their deaths along with him.

They teach people that once they believe in Jesus and receive salvation, they must now obey the written law so that they may continue to be blessed.

The people that are deceived with that message then looks to Scriptures with the eyes of the flesh, listen to the Word with ears of the flesh, then grow in the mind of the flesh, and strive with their flesh to keep the commandments.

In that way, their minds will be in battle with the thoughts that Satan gives. They fall prey to Satan and may continue to fail, going down a spiral of destruction.

This is how people of the First Covenant lives. They commit sin because of Satan's trickery and will eventually die with him.

One other interesting pattern of people that follow the First Covenant is that they pray, "I am a sinner" whenever they come before God to pray. One way of interpreting this prayer is that "I am not a person that belongs to the Lord, because I belong to Satan."

Apostle Paul's life was like that before he met Christ:

> *19I want to do what is good, but I don't. I don't want to do what is wrong, but I do it anyway. 20But if I do what I don't want to do, I am not really the one doing wrong; it is sin living in me that does it. 21I have discovered this principle of life—that when I want to do what is right, I inevitably do what is wrong. 22I love God's law with all my heart. 23But there is another power within me that is at war with my mind. This power makes me a slave to the sin that is still within me.*
>
> *Romans 7:19-23*

Apostle Paul was confessing that with his mind of flesh, he wants to keep the commands, but whenever he tries another "power" (the thoughts given by Satan) appears. He struggles to fight it, but he cannot overcome it and ends up sinning and heading toward the spiral of death.

Let me share an example:

Consider you are a wife of a man that has cheated on you. You cannot forgive him for his acts. However, one day, your pastor shares a message to forgive as Jesus forgave you. Since your pastor has said this, you make a commitment to forgive and love your husband.

Now, Satan begins his acts of deception.

You get recurring thoughts of your husband cheating on you with someone else and other things he may have done wrong as well. In your mind, you are fighting to still forgive and love your husband because you have heard this is the Word of God and you have already committed to do this. However, because of your recurring thoughts, there is constant conflict between your mind to forgive and the thoughts of your husband hurting you. Eventually, the thoughts overcome your mind and leads you toward the impacts of *the Law of Sin and Death.*

The result is that you condemn your husband and get a divorce. Of course, through the process you experience the results of death too, that is, anger, stress, depression, sickness, corruption, and even suicide.

This is how Satan uses *the Law of Sin and Death* to lead us to death with him.

That is why Apostle Paul confesses this:

22I love God's law with all my heart. 23But there is another power within me that is at war with my mind. This power makes me a slave to the sin that is still within me. 24Oh, what a miserable person I am! Who will free me from this life that is dominated by sin and death?

Romans 7:22-24

Satan continues to operate the same way today.

He continues to raise up false prophets, namely pastors, to deceive many to follow the First Covenant.

They say, "obey the Word of God. Follow the written commands of God. If you sin, you will not be blessed, so stop sinning." By doing so, they get believers to focus their strength on the mind of the flesh (conscience). They do this persuasively, some including emotional stories or works of miracles.

As a result, the believers listen to the Word of God through another person and strives on their own strength to keep the commands given by man. They continue to deal with conflict of their minds with the thoughts that Satan gives.

Unfortunately, in the end, they cannot keep the Law nor overcome the thoughts that Satan gives. They come back to the sanctuary and confess that they do not belong to the Lord, but to Satan.

This is how many so-called Christians live today because they have fallen prey to Satan's deception. Many false prophets, pastors, are doing this and may not even be aware of it.

We must know with certainty!

We are not people who hear, learn, and obey the Word of God as taught by other people only. That is what Satan tells people to deceive them and lead them toward eternal death.

The written code (the Law) kills:

He has enabled us to be ministers of his new Covenant. This is a Covenant not of written laws, but of the Spirit. <u>The old written Covenant ends in death</u>; but under the new Covenant, the Spirit gives life.

2Corinthians 3:6

We are not people that live only by the written Word (The Law of Moses). We are people who live with the mind of Christ that He gives through the Holy Spirit. We live in the Living Word, our Christ, and place Him as our head! This is what it means to live according to Christ's *Law of Spirit of Life.*

When we live this way:

So now there is no condemnation for those who belong to Christ Jesus. 2And because you belong to him, the power of the life-giving Spirit has freed you from the power of sin that leads to death. 3The law of Moses was unable to save us because of the weakness of our sinful nature. So God did what the law could not do. He sent his own Son in a body like the bodies we sinners have. And in that body God declared an end to sin's control over us by giving his Son as a sacrifice for our sins. 4He did this so that the just requirement of the law would be fully satisfied for us, who no longer follow our sinful nature but instead follow the Spirit.

Romans 8:1-4

God has sworn to enable us to live in freedom. That was the promise He made with Abraham through the Covenant of Circumcision. This is what is now known as the Second (New) Covenant, which was fulfilled through Jacob, who became known as Israel.

4-11. The Second Covenant

As Israel was completing the 40 years of exodus in the wilderness, circa 1406 BC, they just needed to cross the Jordan River to get to the Promised Land of Canaan. God met Moses at Moab to establish the Second Covenant.

The reason God stopped them there was to illustrate that the Second Covenant must be established in order to cross the Jordan River.

Ark of God was needed to cross the Jordan River (c.f. Joshua 3). In order to carry the Ark of God, Jesus, we must become a sanctuary for Him. We cannot become a sanctuary for Jesus unless we are born again with the life that comes from God. We cannot be born again without God's establishment of the Second Covenant. We will revisit this in detail at a later section.

The Second Covenant is God's re-establishing the Covenant of Circumcision He originally established with the Father-of-Faith Abraham.

To be clear, let me reiterate that there was only one Covenant.

Then what is the so-called "First Covenant" that God established with Moses on Mount Horeb (Sinai)?

God established one Covenant that can bring life. This one Covenant is the Original Covenant established with Adam, which was re-established with Abraham as the Covenant of Circumcision, and was re-established as the Second Covenant at Moab with Moses.

The First Covenant that God established with Moses was only established to show that people cannot keep the commandments on their own, and it is now abolished and no longer in use.

Therefore, those that do not know the Second Covenant does not know God, Jesus, the Holy Spirit, or even the Scriptures.

Satan prowls like a lion so that we cannot see or understand this Covenant. That is the reason why there are many people in our days that read the Bible often but do not see or understand the Second Covenant while they may know the First.

To such people, Jesus says he does not know them.

Matthew 5-7 shows Jesus teaching his disciples from on top of a mountain.

This is called the Sermon on the Mount. Jesus's conclusion of his message was this:

Not everyone who calls out to me, `Lord! Lord!' will enter the Kingdom of Heaven. Only those who actually do the will of my Father in heaven will enter.

Matthew 7:21

What is the will of the Father?

9Then he said, "Look, I have come to do your will." He cancels the first Covenant in order to put the second into effect. 10For God's will was for us to be made holy by the sacrifice of the body of Jesus Christ, once for all time.

Hebrews 10:9-10

God's will was to fulfill what God had sworn, which was to fulfill the Second Covenant. In order to fulfill this, Jesus had to come as a human to die on the cross and rise again from the dead (c.f. Acts 13:32-33).

As we have seen before:

28They replied, "We want to perform God's works, too. What should we do?" 29Jesus told them, "This is the only work God wants from you: Believe in the one he has sent." 38For I have come down from heaven to do the will of God who sent me, not to do my own will. 39And this is the will of God, that I should not lose even one of all those he has given me, but that I should raise them up at the last day. 40For it is my Father's will that all who see his Son and believe in him should have eternal life. I will raise them up at the last day."

John 6:28-29, 38-40

The last day mentioned here refers to the time between his ascension (c.f. 1 Peter 1:20) to this return (c.f. 1 Peter 1:5). This is today, our present times.

The will of the Father God is for His Son Jesus to fulfill the Second Covenant that He had sworn to provide, and for people to see the fulfillment of that Covenant and live by faith.

Let us look at how Jesus devoted His entire life on earth to fulfill the Second Covenant:

> *1These are the terms of the Covenant the LORD commanded Moses to make with the Israelites while they were in the land of Moab, in addition to the Covenant he had made with them at Mount Sinai. 2Moses summoned all the Israelites and said to them, "You have seen with your own eyes everything the LORD did in the land of Egypt to Pharaoh and to all his servants and to his whole country - 3all the great tests of strength, the miraculous signs, and the amazing wonders. 4But to this day the LORD has not given you minds that understand, nor eyes that see, nor ears that hear!*
>
> *Deuteronomy 29:1-4*

Israel has been in the wilderness for 40 years and only about 5 miles separates them from the Jordan River. It is here in Moab that God establishes the Second Covenant.

Verse 4 reveals to us that the First Covenant that was established in Horeb (Sinai) did not give the ability for people's hearts to understand the Word of God, see the glory of God, or hear the voice of the Lord.

The deficiencies of the First Covenant is mentioned here to foretell what is to come in the Second Covenant. Through the Second Covenant, *people would be able to have the hearts to understand the Word of God, see the glory of God, and hear the voice of the Lord.*

> *Therefore, obey the terms of this Covenant so that you will prosper in everything you do.*
>
> *Deuteronomy 29:9*

Receiving this Covenant is the way we can reign in the blessings of God.

> *10All of you - tribal leaders, elders, officers, all the men of Israel - are standing today in the presence of the LORD your God. 11Your little ones and your wives are with you, as well as the foreigners living among you who chop your wood and carry your water. 12You are standing here today to enter into the Covenant of the LORD your God. The LORD is making this Covenant, including the curses. 13By entering into the Covenant today, he will establish you as his people and confirm that he is your God, just as he promised you and as he swore to your ancestors Abraham, Isaac, and Jacob.*
>
> *Deuteronomy 29:10-13*

Verse 12 confirms that God has initiated and is committed to fulfilling this Covenant.

The Second Covenant is an extension of the promise God made to Abraham, Isaac, and Jacob. It gives guidance to how we can take part in the nation of God and God would be our God.

22"Then the generations to come, both your own descendants and the foreigners who come from distant lands, will see the devastation of the land and the diseases the LORD inflicts on it. 23They will exclaim, 'The whole land is devastated by sulfur and salt. It is a wasteland with nothing planted and nothing growing, not even a blade of grass. It is like the cities of Sodom and Gomorrah, Admah and Zeboiim, which the LORD destroyed in his intense anger.' 24"And all the surrounding nations will ask, 'Why has the LORD done this to this land? Why was he so angry?' 25"And the answer will be, 'This happened because the people of the land abandoned the Covenant that the LORD, the God of their ancestors, made with them when he brought them out of the land of Egypt. 26Instead, they turned away to serve and worship gods they had not known before, gods that were not from the LORD.

Deuteronomy 29:22-26

God has explained to Israel the curses that comes with the Covenant. These curses would come because they have abandoned this, the Second, Covenant (v. 25).

If one does not know the Second Covenant and does not faithfully follow it, then they cannot see God and are following another Christ.

Yes. Anyone that does not know the Second Covenant has no relations with God and s/he is following another Christ.

In another words, they believe in another "gospel," which is no gospel at all.

What are the details of the Second Covenant?

The LORD your God will change your heart and the hearts of all your descendants, so that you will love him with all your heart and soul and so you may live!

Deuteronomy 30:6

We can be born again with the life that comes from God because He will circumcise our and our children's hearts so that we may love God with all our hearts and souls.

The Life that God promised is in the Second Covenant, and there is no other Covenant that gives us life.

So if we fail to recognize and believe in the Second Covenant, we cannot love God with all our hearts and soul (remember, 1 Corinthians 16:22 says "If anyone does not love the Lord, that person is cursed. Our Lord, come!"), nor can they be born again with the life that comes from God.

By believing in the Second Covenant, we are born again with the life that comes from God. As a result, we become children of God, Heaven (Kingdom of

God), and sanctuary for the living God. We now live in Christ. When we live this way, God will bring to ruin all of Satan's schemes against us.

7The LORD your God will inflict all these curses on your enemies and on those who hate and persecute you. 11"This command I am giving you today is not too difficult for you to understand, and it is not beyond your reach. 12It is not kept in heaven, so distant that you must ask, 'Who will go up to heaven and bring it down so we can hear it and obey?' 13It is not kept beyond the sea, so far away that you must ask, 'Who will cross the sea to bring it to us so we can hear it and obey?' 14No, the message is very close at hand; it is on your lips and in your heart so that you can obey it.

Deuteronomy 30:7, 11-14

Romans 10 also shares the same message:

6But faith's way of getting right with God says, "Don't say in your heart, `Who will go up to heaven' . 7And don't say, `Who will go down to the place of the dead' (to bring Christ back to life again.)" 8In fact, it says, "The message is very close at hand; it is on your lips and in your heart." And that message is the very message about faith that we preach. 9If you confess with your mouth that Jesus is Lord and believe in your heart that God raised him from the dead, you will be saved. 10For it is by believing in your heart that you are made right with God, and it is by confessing with your mouth that you are saved.

Romans 10:6-10

Verse 9 and 10 tells us from when we can begin to hear His voice and be His sheep (c.f. John 10:27). It is when the Second Covenant is fulfilled in us.

This is where salvation begins.

That is why God said this:

15"Now listen! Today I am giving you a choice between life and death, between prosperity and disaster. 16For I command you this day to love the LORD your God and to keep his commands, decrees, and regulations by walking in his ways. If you do this, you will live and multiply, and the LORD your God will bless you and the land you are about to enter and occupy.

Deuteronomy 30:15-16

God says that we will be able to love God and follow His commands, decrees, and regulations with the heart He gives once He circumcises our and our children's hearts as He had sworn to do for us.

17"But if your heart turns away and you refuse to listen, and if you are drawn away to serve and worship other gods, 18then I warn you now that you will certainly be destroyed. You will not live a long, good life in the land you are crossing the Jordan to occupy. 19"Today I have given you the choice between life and death, between blessings and curses. Now I call on heaven and earth to witness the choice you make. Oh, that you would choose life, so that you and your descendants might live! 20You can make this choice by loving the LORD your God, obeying him, and committing yourself firmly to him. This is the key to your life. And if you love and obey the LORD, you will live long in the land the LORD swore to give your ancestors Abraham, Isaac, and Jacob."

Deuteronomy 30:17-20

In verse 17, if any other gods are worshipped, it means the person does not know or have faith in the Second Covenant.

Here, the Lord (v. 20) is speaking about Jesus of the New Testament (c.f. John 8:56, Genesis 18:10; Isaiah 40:10-11; Ezekiel 34:15, John 10:27)

Once again, let us recommit and check our understanding:

The Covenant God has established is:

1. The Original Covenant established with Adam and Eve
2. The Covenant of Circumcision established with Abraham
3. Everlasting, as he revealed to Isaac
4. Second (New) Covenant established with Jacob (Israel)

All four listed above are part of the same Covenant. They are promises sworn by God and there is no other Covenant that God has made. Faith in this Covenant gives us life.

The reason why God sent His Son Jesus Christ was to fulfill this Covenant (c.f. Hebrews 10:9-10).

Let us now examine further, how the Son of God, Jesus Christ, came to earth to fulfill this Covenant.

Chapter 5 – Fulfillment of God's Covenant through the Ministry of Jesus

5-1. The Fulfillment of God's Covenant

God promised to send the Christ through the seed of Abraham and David in order to fulfill the Covenant that He had sworn to accomplish.

The reason and purpose God sent His Son, the Christ, as a descendant of David is so that He may fulfill the Covenant God had sworn to accomplish.

> *14 "The day will come, says the Lord, when I will do for Israel and Judah all the good things I have promised them. 15 "In those days and at that time I will raise up a righteous descendant from King David's line. He will do what is just and right throughout the land.*
>
> *Jeremiah 33:14-15*

Verse 15 above refers to Christ ("a righteous descendant") that would be sent through King David's lineage.

Verse 14 shares the reason and purpose, which is to fulfill the "good things I have promised them."

Here, the "good things" promised to Israel and Judah is the New Covenant.

"The day is coming," says the Lord, "when I will make a new Covenant with the people of Israel and Judah.

Jeremiah 31:31

Jesus Christ came to earth in the lineage of David in order to fulfill the New Covenant.

> *This is a record of the ancestors of Jesus the Messiah, a descendant of David and of Abraham.*
>
> *Matthew 1:1*

> *That is why he is the one who mediates a new Covenant between God and people, so that all who are called can receive the eternal inheritance God has promised them. For Christ died to set them free from the penalty of the sins they had committed under that first Covenant.*
>
> *Hebrews 9:15*

9Then he said, "Look, I have come to do your will." He cancels the first Covenant in order to put the second into effect. 10For God's will was for us to be made holy by the sacrifice of the body of Jesus Christ, once for all time.

Hebrews 10:9-10

As the verses above share, Jesus came as a descendant of Abraham and David in order to fulfill the Second (New) Covenant that He has sworn to accomplish.

People of Israel that lived during Jesus' lifetime on earth knew that God would send His Son as the Christ (or the Messiah) from lineage of David.

27After Jesus left the girl's home, two blind men followed along behind him, shouting, "Son of David, have mercy on us!" 28They went right into the house where he was staying, and Jesus asked them, "Do you believe I can make you see?" "Yes, Lord," they told him, "we do." 29Then he touched their eyes and said, "Because of your faith, it will happen." 30Then their eyes were opened, and they could see! Jesus sternly warned them, "Don't tell anyone about this." 31But instead, they went out and spread his fame all over the region.

Matthew 9:27-31

Verse 27 reveals that they knew the Christ, the Son of God, would come through the lineage of King David.

22Then a demon-possessed man, who was blind and couldn't speak, was brought to Jesus. He healed the man so that he could both speak and see. 23The crowd was amazed and asked, "Could it be that Jesus is the Son of David, the Messiah?"

Matthew 12:22-23

30Two blind men were sitting beside the road. When they heard that Jesus was coming that way, they began shouting, "Lord, Son of David, have mercy on us!" 31"Be quiet!" the crowd yelled at them. But they only shouted louder, "Lord, Son of David, have mercy on us!" 32When Jesus heard them, he stopped and called, "What do you want me to do for you?" 33"Lord," they said, "we want to see!" 34Jesus felt sorry for them and touched their eyes. Instantly they could see! Then they followed him.

Matthew 20:30-34

Jesus was in the center of the procession, and the people all around him were shouting, "Praise God for the Son of David! Blessings on the one who comes in the name of the LORD! Praise God in highest heaven!"

Matthew 21:9

41Then, surrounded by the Pharisees, Jesus asked them a question. 42"What do you think about the Messiah? Whose son is he?" They replied, "He is the son of David."

Matthew 22:41-42

As the verses above show, the people of that time knew the Christ would come through the lineage of David. Jesus said the following to them:

*21Then Jesus left Galilee and went north to the region of Tyre and Sidon. 22A Gentile woman who lived there came to him, pleading, "Have mercy on me, O Lord, Son of David! For my daughter is possessed by a demon that torments her severely." 23But Jesus gave her no reply, not even a word. Then his disciples urged him to send her away. "Tell her to go away," they said. "She is bothering us with all her begging." 24Then Jesus said to the woman, "I was sent **only** to help God's lost sheep - the people of Israel."*

Matthew 15:21-24

Verse 24 says Jesus came "only" to help the people of Israel. What does this mean?

He was saying that He has only come to accomplish the Second (New) Covenant that God had promised to the people of Israel.

How will Jesus accomplish this Second (New) Covenant?

Let us examine that further in the following sections.

5-2. John the Baptist

God sent a prophet before sending Jesus, the Christ, to fulfill the Second (New) Covenant that God had sworn to accomplish.

3Listen! It's the voice of someone shouting, "Clear the way through the wilderness for the Lord! Make a straight highway through the wasteland for our God! 4Fill in the valleys, and level the mountains and hills. Straighten the curves, and smooth out the rough places. 5Then the glory of the Lord will be revealed, and all people will see it together. The Lord has spoken!"

Isaiah 40:3-5

The "someone shouting" refers to John the Baptist:

2just as the prophet Isaiah had written: "Look, I am sending my messenger ahead of you, and he will prepare your way. 3He is a voice shouting in the wilderness, `Prepare the way for the LORD's coming! Clear the road for him!'" 4This messenger was John the Baptist. He was in the wilderness and preached that people should be baptized to show that they had repented of their sins and turned to God to be forgiven. 5All of Judea, including all the people of Jerusalem, went out to see and hear John. And when they confessed their sins, he baptized them in the Jordan River.

Mark 1:2-5

This was even mentioned by Malachi, the last prophet in the Old Testament:

"Look! I am sending my messenger, and he will prepare the way before me. Then the Lord you are seeking will suddenly come to his Temple. The messenger of the Covenant, whom you look for so eagerly, is surely coming," says the Lord of Heaven's Armies.

Malachi 3:1

In verse 1, the first "messenger" is John the Baptist, and the second is Jesus Christ.

Before sending the Christ, God promised to send a messenger before Him.

10John is the man to whom the Scriptures refer when they say, `Look, I am sending my messenger ahead of you, and he will prepare your way before you.' 11"I tell you the truth, of all who have ever lived, none is greater than John the Baptist. Yet even the least person in the Kingdom of Heaven is greater than he is!

Matthew 11:10-11

Look, I am sending you the prophet Elijah before the great and dreadful day of the Lord arrives.

Malachi 4:5

God said He will send the prophet Elijah, and this "Elijah" is referring to John the Baptist.

10Then his disciples asked him, "Why do the teachers of religious law insist that Elijah must return before the Messiah comes?" 11Jesus replied, "Elijah is indeed coming first to get everything ready. 12But I tell you, Elijah has already come, but he wasn't recognized, and they chose to abuse him. And in the same way they will also make the Son of Man suffer." 13Then the disciples realized he was talking about John the Baptist.

Matthew 17:10-13

In that way, God sent "Elijah," or John the Baptist, before sending the Christ to fulfill the Second (New) Covenant.

John the Baptist was not just born by accident, and it is clear that God had sent him for a purpose:

God sent a man, John the Baptist,

John 1:6

It says that of all that have ever lived, John the Baptist was the greatest (c.f. Matthew 11:11). The reason for these words is that John the Baptist would be the last and final prophet (c.f. Matthew 11:11-13).

This can be seen when Jesus receives baptism from John at the River of Jordan.

13Then Jesus went from Galilee to the Jordan River to be baptized by John. 14But John tried to talk him out of it. "I am the one who needs to be baptized by you," he said, "so why are you coming to me?" 15But Jesus said, "It should be done, for we must carry out all that God requires." So John agreed to baptize him. 16After his baptism, as Jesus came up out of the water, the heavens were opened and he saw the Spirit of God descending like a dove and settling on him. 17And a voice from heaven said, "This is my dearly loved Son, who brings me great joy."

Matthew 3:13-17

Verse 15 says, "It should be done, for we must carry out all that God requires." This can be read, "You must baptize me in order to fulfill the Second Covenant that God has sworn to accomplish."

When John, the "greatest" of all people, laid his hand the on the head of Jesus (c.f. Leviticus 1:3-4, 4:27-31), sins of all people were transferred to Jesus.

Transferring sins of all humankind to Jesus was not through just any person; God did it through John the Baptist, the messenger He had prepared in advance (c.f. Malachi 3:1).

We can clearly see this today and we must believe that Jesus took all of our sins:

The next day John saw Jesus coming toward him and said, "Look! The Lamb of God who takes away the sin of the world!

John 1:29

The "next day" is the day after Jesus was baptized.

In addition to our sins, other problems of sin such as sickness, disobedience, rebellion, curse, and any other negative effects were transferred to Jesus.

4Yet it was our weaknesses he carried; it was our sorrows that weighed him down. And we thought his troubles were a punishment from God, a punishment for his own sins! 5But he was pierced for our rebellion, crushed for our sins. He was beaten so we could be whole. He was whipped so we could be healed. 6All of us, like sheep, have strayed away. We have left God's paths to follow our own. <u>Yet the Lord laid on him the sins of us all.</u>

Isaiah 53:4-6

As a result, there is no one that would go to hell because of one's sinfulness. Instead, the only reason people would go to hell is that they do not believe in Jesus that has taken care of all of their sins.

The baptism of Jesus has deeper meaning of God's grace, but it will not be discussed in this book.

5-3. Disciples of Jesus

1Jesus knew the Pharisees had heard that he was baptizing and making more disciples than John 2(though Jesus himself didn't baptize them - his disciples did.)

John 4:1-2

Jesus made disciples by having his disciples to baptize others in the Name of Jesus.

Now, there are three kinds of baptisms:

1. Baptism of John the Baptist in the River of Jordan

As the last prophet (c.f. Matthew 11:13), John the Baptist performed the *baptism of repentance* that would free people from the sins that came from disobedience to the Law of Moses.

This messenger was John the Baptist. He was in the wilderness and preached that people should be baptized to show that they had repented of their sins and turned to God to be forgiven.

Mark 1:4

Then John went from place to place on both sides of the Jordan River, preaching that people should be baptized to show that they had repented of their sins and turned to God to be forgiven.

Luke 3:3

The passages above show that baptism of John was not the method of receiving forgiveness in itself; rather, they would recognize and confess their sinfulness as they receive the baptism, then they would "turn to God," or look to the One that comes afterwards to receive forgiveness from Him.

That is why John says this:

I baptize with water those who repent of their sins and turn to God. But someone is coming soon who is greater than I am - so much greater that I'm not worthy even to be his slave and carry his sandals. He will baptize you with the Holy Spirit and with fire.

Matthew 3:11

4This messenger was John the Baptist. He was in the wilderness and preached that people should be baptized to show that they had repented of their sins and turned to God to be forgiven. 5All of Judea, including all the people of Jerusalem, went out to see and hear John. And when they confessed their sins, he baptized them in the Jordan River. 6His clothes were woven from coarse camel hair, and he wore a leather belt around his waist. For food he ate locusts and wild honey. 7John announced: "Someone is coming soon who is greater than I am - so much greater that I'm not even worthy to stoop down like a slave and untie the straps of his sandals.

Mark 1:4-7

Therefore, the baptism of John was to enable people to confess their sinfulness and turn from their ways so that they may look to the coming Jesus for forgiveness of their sins.

John says the following the day after he baptized Jesus:

The next day John saw Jesus coming toward him and said, "Look! The Lamb of God who takes away the sin of the world!"

John 1:29

John was the greatest person that has ever lived (c.f. Matthew 11:11) and the messenger God has sent (c.f. Malachi 3:1). His role was to baptize Jesus the Lamb of God so that all sins of the world would be transferred to Him.

2. Baptism of Jesus given through His disciples, through which one may be forgiven of sins and become a disciple of Jesus.

3. Baptism of the Holy Spirit – salvation of spirit/soul

All sins of the world has been transferred to Jesus by John's baptism.

Those that believe in that fact are able to receive baptism in Jesus' Name to be forgiven from their sins and be His disciple.

38Peter replied, "Each of you must repent of your sins and turn to God, and be baptized in the name of Jesus Christ for the forgiveness of your sins. Then you will receive the gift of the Holy Spirit. 41Those who believed what Peter said were baptized and added to the church that day—about 3,000 in all. 42All the believers devoted themselves to the apostles' teaching, and to fellowship, and to sharing in meals (including the Lord's Supper), and to prayer.

Acts 2:38,41-42

In parallel to John 4, there are two distinct steps to be a follower of Jesus. First is to repent of one's sins then second is to receive the baptism of Jesus so that one may be forgiven and become a disciple of Jesus. The disciples that were with Jesus spent the next three years to learn from Jesus and received the Holy Spirit, the gift/grace of God, so that they would be reborn as a child of God.

One thing we need to understand with certainty is that we are not saved from our spirit/souls when we become a disciple of Jesus. In another words, we are not eternally saved just because we are forgiven from our sins by the baptism of Jesus' Name and call ourselves disciples of Jesus. Forgiveness of sins only gives salvation to our flesh, which is not eternal.

To explain this concept from the Old Testament, when the people of Israel began the exodus, they were able to cross the Red Sea by foot. This was a salvation for their physical bodies to escape Egypt; this was not a salvation of their spirits/souls.

So I want to remind you, though you already know these things, that Jesus first rescued the nation of Israel from Egypt, but later he destroyed those who did not remain faithful.

Jude 1:5

The verse above simply refers to physical rescue from Egypt.

Their entry, forty years later, into land of Canaan would be the correct parallel for the salvation of their spirits/souls. This is because prior to their entry, God established the Second Covenant with them in the land of Moab. People of Israel would believe in His promises and carry the Ark of God to cross the Jordan River.

Even if Adam and Eve did not commit sin, it would not have meant they would enter into eternal heaven. In order to do so, they must have eaten from the Tree of Life and been born again with the life that comes from God.

In the same way, just because one repents and receives baptism through the Name of Jesus does not mean this person has received salvation of their spirit/souls.

Instead, repentance and baptism is the beginning of a journey of being a disciple of Jesus. S/he would still need to learn from the Holy Spirit and truly recognize the Gospel so that s/he would be born again with the life that comes from God—only that would be the salvation of their spirit/souls. This is the way to eternal heaven.

Jesus replied, "I assure you, no one can enter the Kingdom of God without being born of water and the Spirit.

John 3:5

That is why not all of Jesus' disciples stayed with Him until the end. Judas Iscariot was one of them.

At this point, many of his disciples turned away and deserted him.

John 6:66

The reason why the so-called "disciples" of Jesus desert their faith is that they have not received the Holy Spirit.

The eternal heaven that we will enter is a spiritual realm.

The reward for trusting him will be the salvation of your souls.

1Peter 1:9

In order for one's spirit/soul to be saved, one must receive the baptism by the Holy Spirit. Only then, the person may be born again with the life that comes from God.

There is no life or salvation in baptism of man.

15And then he told them, "Go into all the world and preach the Good News to everyone. 16Anyone who believes and is baptized will be saved. But anyone who refuses to believe will be condemned.

Mark 16:15-16

Verses above refer to baptism of the Holy Spirit that comes from faith after hearing the Good News.

For even if you had ten thousand others to teach you about Christ, you have only one spiritual father. For I became your father in Christ Jesus when I preached the Good News to you.

1Corinthians 4:15

5which come from your confident hope of what God has reserved for you in heaven. You have had this expectation ever since you first heard the truth of the Good News. 6This same Good News that came to you is going out all over the world. It is bearing fruit everywhere by changing lives, just as it changed your lives from the day you first heard and understood the truth about God's wonderful grace.

Colossians 1:5-6

As the Scripture shares above, one first becomes a disciple of Jesus and begins to learn from the Holy Spirit about who God is. Along the way, one would begin to understand the Gospel, recognize that God is almighty, and understand the fullness of the love of God. It is when this person learns from the Holy Spirit and is built up to have unwavering faith that this person would be born again in the life that comes from God.

This is the third kind of baptism, the baptism of the Spirit.

We will revisit this topic in greater depth at a later section.

5-4. Circumcision of Christ, Part I Ministry of Jesus

Covenant of Circumcision is a promise that God has sworn to accomplish. The promise is that He will enable us to know Him as the almighty God that has sent the Christ to save us.

Before the Father-of-Faith Abraham received circumcision, he did not fully know or believe in God (c.f. Genesis 17:15-18).

Regardless, God promised the Covenant of Circumcision with Abraham, and Abraham believed in God and cut his foreskin to demonstrate that he believes that God will do as He promised (c.f. Genesis 17:9-14, 24).

God saw Abraham's faith and fulfilled His end of the Covenant by circumcising Abraham's heart. As a result, Abraham was able to fully know God and have an unwavering faith in God (c.f. Romans 4:17-22). God gave Abraham a son as He promised and that is how Isaac was born (c.f. Galatians 4:28).

God swore to accomplish the Second Covenant with Israel. Israel refers to all people that believe in the promises of God.

7Being descendants of Abraham doesn't make them truly Abraham's children. For the Scriptures say, "Isaac is the son through whom your descendants will be counted," though Abraham had other children, too. 8This means that Abraham's physical descendants are not necessarily children of God. Only the children of the promise are considered to be Abraham's children.

Romans 9:7-8

As the verses above state, the people of Israel are not the physical nation of Israel, but all of us who believe in the Second (New) Covenant that God swore to fulfill.

Second Covenant says that God will circumcise our and our children's hearts so that we would love God with all our hearts and souls. We reach this state when we are born again with His life and become His children (c.f. Deuteronomy 30:6). In another words, His circumcision of our hearts causes us to be born again as His children.

The circumcision of Christ is performed on our hearts by the Holy Spirit.

No, a true Jew is one whose heart is right with God. And true circumcision is not merely obeying the letter of the law; rather, <u>it is a change of heart produced by God's Spirit</u>. And a person with a changed heart seeks praise from God, not from people.

Romans 2:29

10So you also are complete through your union with Christ, who is the head over every ruler and authority. 11When you came to Christ, you were "circumcised," but not by a physical procedure. Christ performed a spiritual circumcision—the cutting away of your sinful nature.

Colossians 2:10-11

Through the circumcision by the Holy Spirit, the believer will be able to live life having unwavering faith. S/he would love God with all her/his heart and mind without the thoughts and minds of the flesh.

Then, what do you think is the process by which the Holy Spirit causes us to be born again by circumcising our hearts in Christ so that we would know the True God and Jesus Christ and love Him with all our hearts and mind?

The Second Covenant is fulfilled in this order (c.f. Deuteronomy 30:6-14):

- Holy Spirit, through Christ, circumcises our and our children's hearts, which
- Enables us to truly know the Almighty God and His Son Jesus, which in turn
- Enables us to love God with all our hearts and mind so that
- We would be born again with the life that comes from God
- Enabling us to accept Jesus Christ
- We would be able to hear the voice of God as He speaks from within us

These are the terms of the Covenant the LORD commanded Moses to make with the Israelites while they were in the land of Moab, in addition to the Covenant he had made with them at Mount Sinai.

Deuteronomy 29:1

6"The LORD your God will change your heart and the hearts of all your descendants, so that you will love him with all your heart and soul and so you may live! 11"This command I am giving you today is not too difficult for you to understand, and it is not beyond your reach. 12It is not kept in heaven, so distant that you must ask, 'Who will go up to heaven and bring it down so we can hear it and obey?' 13It is not kept beyond the sea, so far away that you must ask, 'Who will cross the sea to bring it to us so we can hear it and obey?' 14No, the message is very close at hand; it is on your lips and in your heart so that you can obey it.

Deuteronomy 30:6, 11-14

This message is also revealed in Romans:

6But faith's way of getting right with God says, "Don't say in your heart, `Who will go up to heaven' . 7And don't say, `Who will go down to the place of the dead' (to bring Christ back to life again.)" 8In fact, it says, "The message is very close at hand; it is on your lips and in your heart." And that message is the very message about faith that we preach.

Romans 10:6-8

To summarize the verses above:

- God sends the Holy Spirit (c.f. Romans 2:29) through Christ (c.f. Colossians 2:11)
- Then circumcises our hearts so that
- We may love God with all our hearts and soul, which then
- Enables us to receive the life that comes from God so that
- We may accept Jesus Christ. This will enable us to
- Hear the voice of Jesus and live according to His guidance

Jesus came for that purpose, and declared this Gospel (Joyful News).

Let us now look at how the Holy Spirit circumcises our hearts through Christ so that we may know the Father and the Son fully and love Him with all our hearts and souls.

5-5. Circumcision of Christ, Part II Heaven that has come to us

As we have seen in previous chapters, Jesus declared the Gospel as the "heaven that has come to us."

From then on Jesus began to preach, "Repent of your sins and turn to God, for the Kingdom of Heaven is near."

Matthew 4:17

The verse above clarifies that heaven is not a destination where we ought to go, but rather, it is one that is near us.

In New King James Version, it says, "for the kingdom of heaven is at hand," or at a distance close enough to be touched at a hand-distance.

Jesus Himself is the heaven that has come to us:

But if I am casting out demons by the Spirit of God, then the Kingdom of God has arrived among you.

Matthew 12:28

Here, the Holy Spirit was in Jesus, and Jesus has come to earth as the Kingdom of God.

Jesus came to earth as heaven, the Kingdom of God, to declare Himself as the Kingdom Gospel.

However, there is a major limitation with the physical body of Jesus. We cannot invite Jesus to live inside us while He is human on earth. We would not be a sanctuary for God nor can we live in Him as long as He is living in the flesh.

This is why after He completes the requirements of the Second (New) Covenant (c.f. John 19:30), that is, dying on the cross (c.f. Hebrews 10:9-10), coming back to life in three days (c.f. Acts 13:32-33), and then ascending to heaven in 40 days, He returns to us as Spirit, namely the Holy Spirit.

And I tell you the truth, some standing here right now will not die before they see the Son of Man coming in his Kingdom.

Matthew 16:28

Jesus was saying to his listeners that some in the audience would see the "Son of Man coming in his Kingdom." He was referring to his return in the Holy Spirit.

Luke shares the same message:

I tell you the truth, some standing here right now will not die before they see the Kingdom of God.

Luke 9:27

Note that in the same message, Matthew says "Son of Man coming in his Kingdom" while Luke says "the Kingdom of God." This means that Jesus will come with the authority of the Kingdom in the Holy Spirit and that He Himself is the Kingdom of God, or heaven.

In short, Jesus now dwells in our hearts within the Holy Spirit as the Kingdom of God. We must accept Jesus who is heaven (the Kingdom of God) that has come to us within the Holy Spirit.

9The one who is the true light, who gives light to everyone, was coming into the world.
10He came into the very world he created, but the world didn't recognize him. 11He
came to his own people, and even they rejected him. 12But to all who believed him and
accepted him, he gave the right to become children of God. 13They are reborn—not with
a physical birth resulting from human passion or plan, but a birth that comes from God.

John 1:9-13

How can we believe and accept Him?

When we are "reborn" with the life that comes from God, the Holy Spirit, who is one with Jesus, can live in us.

We will examine this in greater depth, but to share briefly, when we are born with the life that comes from God, we become transformed into the likeness of Christ. This transformation is not outwardly such that religious persons may feign on the outside, but a true conversion of the heart.

Oh, my dear children! I feel as if I'm going through labor pains for you again, and they will continue until Christ is fully developed in your lives.

Galatians 4:19

Spiritual birth occurs when Christ's likeness is developed in us. Christ's likeness is what the sanctuary of God looks like. Jesus was the sanctuary for the living God (c.f. John 2:19-21).

To say we accepted Jesus means that the life of God that has been planted in us as a seed has grown to the image of Christ and that we have become a sanctuary for God.

Christ's image or the house of Christ (c.f. 1 Corinthians 3:9, Hebrews 3:6) must be made in us so that we may be born spiritually. This birth is required for Jesus to come to live in us.

Then, what would it look like if we have the image of Christ (sanctuary of God) made in us?

The LORD your God will change your heart and the hearts of all your descendants, so that you will love him with all your heart and soul and so you may live!

Deuteronomy 30:6

A person who has the image of Christ (sanctuary of God) made in him/her will love God with all one's heart and soul.

When the sanctuary of God was built during the Old Testament, glory of the Lord filled it:

33Then he hung the curtains forming the courtyard around the Tabernacle and the altar. And he set up the curtain at the entrance of the courtyard. So at last Moses finished the work. 34Then the cloud covered the Tabernacle, and the glory of the LORD filled the Tabernacle. 35Moses could no longer enter the Tabernacle because the cloud had settled down over it, and the glory of the LORD filled the Tabernacle.

Exodus 40:33-35

The verses above say that once the work of building the sanctuary was complete, God's glory filled it.

When God's glory fills something, it means God's love was overflowing. This is because glory of God refers to both that He is light (c.f. 1 John 1:5) and love (c.f. 1 John 4:8).

This means that when the glory of God fills us, we are able to love God with all our hearts and soul. We are then able to love our neighbors with the same kind of overflowing love.

This is a picture of what we would look like when we are a completed sanctuary for the living God.

Even when King Solomon built the temple:

So King Solomon finished all his work on the Temple of the LORD. Then he brought all the gifts his father, David, had dedicated - the silver, the gold, and the various articles - and he stored them in the treasuries of the LORD's Temple.

1Kings 7:51

6Then the priests carried the Ark of the LORD's Covenant into the inner
sanctuary of the Temple - the Most Holy Place - and placed it beneath the wings of
the cherubim. 7The cherubim spread their wings over the Ark, forming a canopy
over the Ark and its carrying poles. 8These poles were so long that their ends could
be seen from the Temple's main room - the Holy Place - but not from the outside.
They are still there to this day. 9Nothing was in the Ark except the two stone tablets
that Moses had placed in it at Mount Sinai, where the LORD made a Covenant with
the people of Israel when they left the land of Egypt. 10When the priests came out
of the Holy Place, a thick cloud filled the Temple of the LORD. 11The priests could
not continue their service because of the cloud, for the glorious presence of the
LORD filled the Temple.

1Kings 8:6-11

As the passage above shows, the installation of the Ark of God was the final step in completing the temple of God. Inside this ark was only the two stone tablets, which included the commandment to love God and others, known as the Ten Commandments (c.f. Exodus 31:18).

So then, we, who are the sanctuary of God, are filled with the ability to love God and others with all our hearts and soul when we are completed. This is what it means to be filled with His glory.

Jesus speaks about this kind of results in our lives:

31Here is another illustration Jesus used: "The Kingdom of Heaven is like a mustard
seed planted in a field. 32It is the smallest of all seeds, but it becomes the largest of
garden plants; it grows into a tree, and birds come and make nests in its branches."

Matthew 13:31-32

Here, we can consider the birds as enemies, the ones that come and eat the seed. However, when the glory of God overflows, we become large enough to wrap our enemies with the love of God and allow him/her to nest in our branches. This is a picture of a person that has been perfected into an image of Christ (or has completed the building of sanctuary for the Living God) looks like.

Note: Loving God with all our hearts, soul, mind, and strength and loving others as we love ourselves are the same.

The reason is that as we love God with all our hearts and soul to be born again with the life that comes from God (c.f. Deuteronomy 30:6), God becomes our head and we become His body. With the heart He gives us, we would be able to love our neighbors wholly as we love God.

Reference:

- Matthew 22:37-40 (Note on verse 39, it says "second is equally important)
- Matthew 5:43-48
- 1 John 4:19-21

Mark shares the same message:

26Jesus also said, "The Kingdom of God is like a farmer who scatters seed on the ground. 27Night and day, while he's asleep or awake, the seed sprouts and grows, but he does not understand how it happens. 28The earth produces the crops on its own. First a leaf blade pushes through, then the heads of wheat are formed, and finally the grain ripens. 29And as soon as the grain is ready, the farmer comes and harvests it with a sickle, for the harvest time has come." 30Jesus said, "How can I describe the Kingdom of God? What story should I use to illustrate it? 31It is like a mustard seed planted in the ground. It is the smallest of all seeds, 32but it becomes the largest of all garden plants; it grows long branches, and birds can make nests in its shade."

Mark 4:26-32

The grains mentioned in verses 26-29 refer to children of God that have been born again with the image of Christ (or image of heaven). This image is described further in verses 30-32.

In this way, we, as the sanctuary of God, are filled with His glory, which is light (c.f. 1 John 1:5) and love (c.f. 1 John 4:8). We are filled with His glory when we are born again as children of God. This time of rebirth is also when we accept Jesus as our Lord. From that point forward, we live with the new life of Christ (c.f. 1 John 5:11-12). We will be able to hear His voice as He speaks from within us and we will be able to follow Him wholeheartedly (c.f. Deuteronomy 30:6, 11-14 and Romans 10:6-10).

"The LORD your God will change your heart and the hearts of all your descendants, so that you will love him with all your heart and soul and so you may live!

Deuteronomy 30:6

Read this verse with the following considerations:

"So that you will love him with all your heart and soul" means that "you will be changed into His image" or "you will be built into a sanctuary of God."

"So you may live" means "you will receive new life" or "you will be born again with the life that comes from God and be considered a child of God"

In short, it means we will welcome Jesus into our hearts, which means we will be a sanctuary for Him. We will listen to His voice and live according to His guidance (c.f. Deuteronomy 30:11-14).

> *6But the righteousness based on faith says, "Do not say in your heart, 'Who will ascend into heaven?'" (that is, to bring Christ down) 7or "'Who will descend into the abyss?'" (that is, to bring Christ up from the dead). 8But what does it say? "The word is near you, in your mouth and in your heart" (that is, the word of faith that we proclaim);*
>
> *Romans 10:6-8 (ESV)*
> *also see Deuteronomy 30:11-14*

These verses point to the Second (New) Covenant that God has sworn to accomplish. He will enable us to live as holy sanctuaries where God will dwell; He will be heaven (the Kingdom of God) in our hearts. The Son of God, Jesus Christ, came to earth to fulfill this Covenant.

5-6. Fulfillment of the Circumcision of Christ

Let us examine how the Holy Spirit, through Jesus Christ the Son of God, fulfills the Second Covenant that God has sworn to accomplish. We will examine how He circumcises our hearts so that we may love God with all our hearts and soul to enable us accept Jesus and be reborn as heaven (the Kingdom of God) (c.f. Deuteronomy 30:6, 11-14).

We can see this through the life of Peter, a disciple of Jesus.

Before Peter was a disciple of Jesus, he saw Jesus being baptized by John the Baptist (c.f. John 1:29-42).

After Jesus took Peter as His disciple, Peter followed Him and saw all that Jesus did.

The Holy Spirit uses these kinds of experiences to fulfill the Second (New) Covenant in Peter. Peter did not fully have faith in Jesus when he became a disciple; only over time he began to realize that Jesus is the Christ and got to know him (love him) fully. Look at the procession of Jesus' life:

Matthew 3 – Jesus received baptism from John at the Jordan River. John proclaimed that Jesus is the Lamb of God that takes the sin of the world.

Matthew 4 – Jesus overcame Satan's temptations; proclamation of the Gospel; Calling of Peter

Matthew 5-7 – Sermon on the Mount; Jesus' teachings on living the life of heaven, prayer, and will of God (note 7:21 is parallel to Hebrews 10:9-10).

Matthew 8 – Authority of God; Jesus is Christ, who is the Almighty God

Matthew 9 – Old and New Covenant (v. 14-17). Jesus who came from the lineage of King David.

Matthew 10 – Calling of the twelve disciples; the activities of the Holy Spirit

Matthew 11 – John the Baptist is the Elijah; conclusion of the Law; and Repentance

Matthew 12 – the Name of Jesus, Christ is King, God upon us, and the will of God

Matthew 13 – Old and New Covenant

Matthew 14 – Jesus is Christ who is the almighty God (c.f. 1 John 5:20)

Matthew 15 – Christ has come to fulfill the Second (New) Covenant that God had sworn to accomplish with the people of Israel; All creation submits to Christ

After all these experiences, Jesus asks his disciples in chapter 16:

13When Jesus came to the region of Caesarea Philippi, he asked his disciples, "Who do people say that the Son of Man is?" 14"Well," they replied, "some say John the Baptist, some say Elijah, and others say Jeremiah or one of the other prophets." 15Then he asked them, "But who do you say I am?" 16Simon Peter answered, "You are the Messiah, the Son of the living God."

Matthew 16:13-16

Christ means the anointed one (c.f. Psalms 2:2, which parallels Acts 4:26), the King (c.f. 1 Kings 19:15-16), Prophet (c.f. 1 Kings 19:16), and High Priest (c.f. Exodus 40:13).

This means that when one says, "Jesus is Christ," s/he is also saying, "Jesus is an almighty King, prophet, and high priest."

Peter followed Jesus wherever He went and learned through the Holy Spirit (c.f. 1 Corinthians 12:3) that Jesus is the almighty King of kings.

The reason Jesus is called the "Son" because He came to fulfill the Second (New) Covenant.

32"<u>And now we are here to bring you this Good News. The promise was made to our ancestors,</u> 33and God has now fulfilled it for us, their descendants, by raising Jesus. <u>This is what the second psalm says about Jesus: `You are my Son Today I have become your Father.</u>'

Acts 13:32-33

The law (First Covenant) appointed high priests who were limited by human weakness. <u>But after the law was given, God appointed his Son with an oath (Second, New Covenant), and his Son has been made the perfect High Priest forever.</u>

Hebrews 7:28

The verses above explain that the word "Son" is used to fulfill the promise God had made with Abraham, Isaac, and Jacob (c.f. Galatians 3:16).

When Peter confessed that Jesus is Lord, he was actually confessing the following: "Jesus, You have come to fulfill Second (New) Covenant."

Jesus replied, "You are blessed, Simon son of John, because my Father in heaven has revealed this to you. You did not learn this from any human being.

Matthew 16:17

Yes. The Holy Spirit led Peter to come to know that Jesus is the almighty King through his life as he experienced the works and teachings of Jesus.

The Holy Spirit led Peter to see that Jesus is the Christ, the Son that has come to fulfill the Second Covenant, which God had promised the Father of Faith Abraham, Isaac, and Jacob.

Jesus used the life of Jesus here on earth to circumcise the heart of Peter so that he may come to know that Jesus is the Christ.

When you came to Christ, you were "circumcised," but not by a physical procedure. Christ performed a spiritual circumcision—the cutting away of your sinful nature.
Colossians 2:11

Once Peter achieved this faith, Jesus tells him that upon him, He will build a church that would be His body. He is speaking of the Church that has been circumcised through the fulfillment of the Second (New) Covenant.

The following point is very important.

The reason is that only the Holy Spirit can enable us to love God with all our hearts and souls so that we may be born again with the life that comes from God (c.f. Deuteronomy 30:6).

Matthew 16:21 begins with words, "From then on." This signifies that the disciples now recognized that Jesus is the almighty King of kings, the Christ. They now believed that Jesus is the Son of God that came to fulfill the Second Covenant.

From then on Jesus began to tell his disciples plainly that it was necessary for him to go to Jerusalem, and that he would suffer many terrible things at the hands of the elders, the leading priests, and the teachers of religious law. He would be killed, but on the third day he would be raised from the dead.
Matthew 16:21

From this time forward, Jesus begins to explain to his disciples about His coming death and resurrection because they have now come to believe that Jesus is the Son of God that came to fulfill the Second (New) Covenant.

He explains these to them because His death and resurrection is required to fulfill the Second (New) Covenant.

9Then he said, "Look, I have come to do your will." He cancels the first Covenant in order to put the second into effect. 10For God's will was for us to be made holy by the sacrifice of the body of Jesus Christ, once for all time.
Hebrews 10:9-10

The verses below explain that the resurrection of Jesus also plays a role in fulfillment of the Second Covenant.

32"And now we are here to bring you this Good News. The promise was made to our ancestors, 33and God has now fulfilled it for us, their descendants, by raising Jesus. This is what the second psalm says about Jesus: `You are my Son Today I have become your Father.'

Acts 13:32-33

In summary, Jesus died and resurrected from the grave so that His disciples may fully believe and declare, "Jesus is Lord" and that "Jesus, you are Christ, the Son of God that came to fulfill the Second Covenant."

Another very important fact is that no matter how many people may tell and teach us about Jesus that died on the cross to forgive us from our sins, we would not be able to know God's (Christ's) love for us fully.

We know from prior sections that if we do not fully know God's (Christ's) love for us, then we cannot love Him back with all our hearts and souls; and if we cannot love Him that way, we cannot be born again with the life that comes from God (c.f. Deuteronomy 30:6).

So then, how can we know God's love so that we may love Him back with all our hearts and souls?

We need the Holy Spirit! Only the Holy Spirit is able to show and teach our hearts that Jesus died for our sins so that He may fulfill the Second Covenant in us. Holy Spirit alone is able to help us truly experience and know God's love that will enable us to recognize that Jesus died to give us new life.

For it is my Father's will that all who see his Son and believe in him should have eternal life. I will raise them up at the last day ("last day" refers to present day, c.f. 1 Peter 1:20).

John 6:40

Oh, foolish Galatians! Who has cast an evil spell on you? For the meaning of Jesus Christ's death was made as clear to you as if you had seen a picture of his death on the cross.

Galatians 3:1

We can only see the true meaning of Jesus' death on the cross through the Holy Spirit. Only when the Holy Spirit shows us, are we able to see the overflowing fountain of God's love. When we drink from this fountain, we will experience His love fully so that we may love Him back with all our hearts and souls.

To summarize, we can only see Jesus who died on the cross to fulfill the Second Covenant in us only through the Holy Spirit.

Then to does God enable us to receive the Holy Spirit?

Oh, foolish Galatians! Who has cast an evil spell on you? For the meaning of Jesus Christ's death was made as clear to you as if you had seen a picture of his death on the cross. 2Let me ask you this one question: Did you receive the Holy Spirit by obeying the law of Moses? Of course not! You received the Spirit because you believed the message you heard about Christ.

Galatians 3:1-2

In the verses above, what must you hear in order to believe and receive the Holy Spirit?

What's more, the Scriptures looked forward to this time when God would declare the Gentiles to be righteous because of their faith. God proclaimed this good news to Abraham long ago when he said, "All nations will be blessed through you."

Galatians 3:8

The Holy Spirit is given to those who believe in the Covenant of Circumcision that God had promised Abraham, which is now called the Second (New) Covenant. Only such people can see Jesus who died on the cross to fulfill this Covenant in them.

We can certainly try to learn and hear stories about Jesus' death on the cross from many people. However, no amount of teachings of other people will enable us to experience the true and full love of God.

We need to see Jesus who died on the cross for us through the Holy Spirit.

However, not everyone will be able to do this.

It is only allowed for those that believe in the Covenant of Circumcision that was promised through Abraham, Isaac, and Jacob, which is now known as the Second (New) Covenant.

In another words, only those that are able to say "Jesus, you are the Son of God, the Christ that has come to fulfill the Second Covenant" can see Jesus who died on the cross through the Holy Spirit.

The reason is that Jesus died on the cross to fulfill the New Covenant.

We can see why Zechariah says Jesus can only be seen by family of David and people of Jerusalem:

Then I will pour out a spirit of grace and prayer on the family of David and on the people of Jerusalem. They will look on me whom they have pierced and mourn for him as for an only son. They will grieve bitterly for him as for a firstborn son who has died.
Zechariah 12:10

In the verse above, who is the family of David?

14The day will come, says the Lord, when I will do for Israel and Judah all the good things I have promised them. 15"In those days and at that time I will raise up a righteous descendant from King David's line. He will do what is just and right throughout the land.
Jeremiah 33:14-15

The verses above explain that Christ will be sent in order to fulfill a promise for Israel and Judah through the lineage of David. This is pointing to the New Covenant.

"The day is coming," says the Lord, "when I will make a new Covenant with the people of Israel and Judah."

Jeremiah 31:31

When we place those verses together, we can see that those that believe in the Christ that will come through the lineage of David to fulfill this New Covenant can be called the Family of David (*People of Israel and Judah*).

People of Jerusalem can be seen in the following passages:

24These two women serve as an illustration of God's two Covenants. The first woman, Hagar, represents Mount Sinai where people received the law that enslaved them. 26But the other woman, Sarah, represents the heavenly Jerusalem. She is the free woman, and she is our mother. 28And you, dear brothers and sisters, are children of the promise, just like Isaac. 29But you are now being persecuted by those who want you to keep the law, just as Ishmael, the child born by human effort, persecuted Isaac, the child born by the power of the Spirit.
Galatians 4:24, 26, 28-29

When we look at the verses above together, we can see that Jerusalem refers to the Holy Spirit. The Holy Spirit gives birth to those that believe in the Second Covenant and calls them His children. *People of Jerusalem* then means those that believe in the Second Covenant by the activity of the Holy Spirit.

Yes, it is true.

God only gives His Spirit to the *Family of David* and *People of Jerusalem* that believes in the Second (New) Covenant. He enables them to see Jesus who died on the cross, His overflowing love for us that allows us to love Him back with all our heart, soul, and strength. This is how the Second Covenant is fulfilled in us.

10 "Then I will pour out a spirit of grace and prayer on the family of David and on the people of Jerusalem. They will look on me whom they have pierced and mourn for him as for an only son. They will grieve bitterly for him as for a firstborn son who has died. 12 "All Israel will mourn, each clan by itself, and with the husbands separate from their wives. The clan of David will mourn alone, as will the clan of Nathan, 13the clan of Levi, and the clan of Shimei. 14Each of the surviving clans from Judah will mourn separately, and with the husbands separate from their wives."

Zechariah 12:10, 12-14

On that day a fountain will be opened for the dynasty of David and for the people of Jerusalem, a fountain to cleanse them from all their sins and impurity.

Zechariah 13:1

In the last verse, "on that day" refers to the day when we will see Jesus dying on the cross through the enablement of His Spirit.

When we see Jesus who died on the cross, His fountain of living water (the love that overflows from the Living God) begins to flow from within us.

Not everyone can drink from this fountain (overflowing Love).

This fountain is reserved only for the *Family of David* and *People of Jerusalem.* For us to take part in this, we must believe in the Second Covenant that God had sworn to accomplish through His Son Jesus Christ.

We absolutely must drink from this fountain.

3Jesus replied, "Anyone who drinks this water will soon become thirsty again. 14But those who drink the water I give will never be thirsty again. It becomes a fresh, bubbling spring within them, giving them eternal life."

John 4:13-14

37On the last day, the climax of the festival, Jesus stood and shouted to the crowds, "Anyone who is thirsty may come to me! 38Anyone who believes in me may come and drink! For the Scriptures declare, `Rivers of living water will flow from his heart.'" 39(When he said "living water," he was speaking of the Spirit, who would be given to everyone believing in him. But the Spirit had not yet been given, because Jesus had not yet entered into his glory.)

John 7:37-39

The Spirit and the bride say, "Come." Let anyone who hears this say, "Come." Let anyone who is thirsty come. Let anyone who desires drink freely from the water of life.
Revelation 22:17

We must see Jesus who died on the cross so that we may drink from this fountain of Love. Only then, will we see the power of God working in and around us; we shall see demons being cast out.

"On that day a fountain will be opened for the dynasty of David and for the people of Jerusalem, a fountain to cleanse them from all their sins and impurity. 2"And on that day," says the Lord of Heaven's Armies, "I will erase idol worship throughout the land, so that even the names of the idols will be forgotten. I will remove from the land both the false prophets and the spirit of impurity that came with them.
Zechariah 13:1-2

Jesus Himself too said that He will come showing Himself only to those people that would proclaim Him as the Christ, the Son of the Living God, and the One who came to fulfill the Second Covenant.

16And I will ask the Father, and he will give you another Advocate, who will never leave you. 17He is the Holy Spirit, who leads into all truth. The world cannot receive him, because it isn't looking for him and doesn't recognize him. But you know him, because he lives with you now and later will be in you. 18No, I will not abandon you as orphans—I will come to you. 19Soon the world will no longer see me, but you will see me. Since I live, you also will live.
John 14:16-19

Verse 19 shares that some will see Jesus after He resurrects from the dead.

So you have sorrow now, but I will see you again; then you will rejoice, and no one can rob you of that joy.
John 16:22

As the verses above infer, Jesus will come back to be seen by those that believe that He is the Son of God, the mediator of the New Covenant.

Jesus had to die and resurrect from the grave to fulfill the Second Covenant (c.f. Acts 13:32-33).

However, one cannot see the resurrected Jesus that has the power to overcome death nor receive the Name of Jesus by listening and learning from other people.

He Himself must come and teach us Himself.

22So you have sorrow now, but <u>I will see you again</u>; then you will rejoice, and no one can rob you of that joy. 23At that time you won't need to ask me for anything. I tell you the truth, you will ask the Father directly, and he will grant your request <u>because you use my name</u>. 24You haven't done this before. <u>Ask, using my name</u>, and you will receive, and you will have abundant joy.

John 16:22-24

Reading the verses above, to whom do you believe He gives the power and authority that is in His Name?

26<u>Then you will ask in my name.</u> I'm not saying I will ask the Father on your behalf, 27for the Father himself loves you dearly <u>because you love me</u> and believe that I came from God.

John 16:26-27

The power and authority that is in His Name is given to those that love God with all his/her heart because they have seen Jesus who died on the cross through the work of the Holy Spirit. To such people, Jesus comes to them and gives His Name to them as an inheritance.

Jesus died and resurrected from the grave (c.f. Acts 13:32-33) so that He may fulfill the Second (New) Covenant in all people that believe.

In another words, sole purpose of Jesus' coming to earth and all His activities on earth was to fulfill the Second Covenant. During Jesus' life on earth, He circumcised the hearts of His disciples, just as God circumcised heart of Abraham, so that they may come to see the true and almighty God and fully know the Son Jesus.

<u>Through the Holy Spirit, Peter had confessed that Jesus is Christ who is the Son of the living God. After His resurrection, Jesus comes to meet Peter at Tiber River in order to fulfill the Second Covenant in him.</u>

Jesus asks Peter:

15After breakfast Jesus asked Simon Peter, "<u>Simon son of John, do you love me more than these?</u>" "Yes, Lord," Peter replied, "you know I love you." "Then feed my lambs," Jesus told him. 16Jesus repeated the question: "<u>Simon son of John, do you love me?</u>" "Yes, Lord," Peter said, "you know I love you." "Then take care of my sheep," Jesus said. 17A third time he asked him, "<u>Simon son of John, do you love me?</u>" Peter was hurt that Jesus asked the question a third time. He said, "Lord, you know everything. You know that I love you." Jesus said, "Then feed my sheep.

John 21:15-17

Peter says he loves Jesus. Since Peter has this heart, Jesus returns to him through the Holy Spirit at Pentecost so that he may be born again with the life that comes from God (also known as image of Christ and sanctuary for the Living God).

The LORD your God will change your heart and the hearts of all your descendants, so that you will love him with all your heart and soul and so you may live!
Deuteronomy 30:6

When we receive this heart change is when we can say we have accepted Jesus Christ as our Lord and Savior.

11"This command I am giving you today is not too difficult for you to understand, and it is not beyond your reach. 12It is not kept in heaven, so distant that you must ask, 'Who will go up to heaven and bring it down so we can hear it and obey?' 13It is not kept beyond the sea, so far away that you must ask, 'Who will cross the sea to bring it to us so we can hear it and obey?' 14No, the message is very close at hand; it is on your lips and in your heart so that you can obey it.
Deuteronomy 30: 11-14

Letter to Romans says this:

6But the righteousness based on faith says, "Do not say in your heart, 'Who will ascend into heaven?'" (that is, to bring Christ down) 7or "'Who will descend into the abyss?'" (that is, to bring Christ up from the dead). 8But what does it say? "The word is near you, in your mouth and in your heart" (that is, the word of faith that we proclaim); 9because, if you confess with your mouth that Jesus is Lord and believe in your heart that God raised him from the dead, you will be saved. 10For with the heart one believes and is justified, and with the mouth one confesses and is saved.
Romans 10:6-10 (ESV)

That is the beginning of salvation.

In this way, Jesus was the mediator for the Second (New) Covenant through His life on earth.

Chapter 6 – Requirements of the New Covenant

6-1. The New Covenant, Part I Another Name for the Second Covenant

History of Israel:

1. Entry into Land of Canaan
2. Time of the Judges
3. Leadership of Samuel
4. King David
5. King Solomon (building of the temple)
6. Jeroboam – Northern Israel – destroyed by Assyria in 722 B.C.
7. Rehoboam – Southern Judah – invaded three times since 605 B.C.
8. King Nebuchadnezzar of Babylon Invades

God declared the the Second Covenant at around 1406 BC. 810 years later at about 596 B.C., God re-declared the Second Covenant through Jeremiah the prophet.

Second (New) Covenant is fulfilled by the Holy Spirit who works together in Christ.

7If the first Covenant had been faultless, there would have been no need for a second Covenant to replace it. 8But when God found fault with the people, he said: "The day is coming, says the LORD, when I will make a new Covenant with the people of Israel and Judah.

Hebrews 8:7-8

The Second and New Covenant are the same as shown in the verses above.

God uses Jeremiah the prophet to share the New Covenant.

31 "The day is coming," says the Lord, "when I will make a new Covenant with the people of Israel and Judah. 32This Covenant will not be like the one I made with their ancestors when I took them by the hand and brought them out of the land of Egypt. They broke that Covenant, though I loved them as a husband loves his wife," says the Lord. 33 "But this is the new Covenant I will make with the people of Israel on that day," says the Lord. "I will put my instructions deep within them, and I will write them on their hearts. I will be their God, and they will be my people. 34And they will not need to teach their neighbors, nor will they need to teach their relatives, saying, 'You should know the Lord.' For everyone, from the least to the greatest, will know me already," says the Lord. "And I will forgive their wickedness, and I will never again remember their sins."

Jeremiah 31:31-34

Verse 34 says that through the New Covenant that we will be able to know God fully (c.f. John 17:3). It is through this Covenant that our sins will no longer be remembered.

God had promised to fulfill this Covenant by sending the Christ that will come from the lineage of David.

14 "The day will come, says the Lord, when I will do for Israel and Judah all the good things I have promised them. 15 "In those days and at that time I will raise up a righteous descendant from King David's line. He will do what is just and right throughout the land.

Jeremiah 33:14-15

Verse 14 refers to the New Covenant, and God swears to accomplish this Covenant.

"31 "The day is coming," says the Lord, "when I will make a new Covenant with the people of Israel and Judah. 35It is the Lord who provides the sun to light the day and the moon and stars to light the night, and who stirs the sea into roaring waves. His name is the Lord of Heaven's Armies, and this is what he says. 36 "I am as likely to reject my people Israel as I am to abolish the laws of nature!"

Jeremiah 31:31,35-36

The message of the verses above is that as long as the sun exists during the day time, as long as the moon and the stars exist in the evening time, as long as the waves exist in the seas, God will surely fulfill His promises.

God says this:

This is what the Lord says: "Just as the heavens cannot be measured and the foundations of the earth cannot be explored, so I will not consider casting them away for the evil they have done. I, the Lord, have spoken!

Jeremiah 31:37

This verse is a hyperbole stating that the Covenant may be abandoned when the universe may be measured.

Out of curiosity, Internet was used to understand the size of the universe.

The sun is so large that it can contain earth 1.3 million times! Some other stars are much larger than the sun so that it can contain 50 million suns! Some galaxies contain about 20 billion stars that big! Finally, there are 20 billion galaxies that can contain 50 million suns!

This easily shows that humans cannot even fathom the vastness of the universe. God was jesting to say that what He had promised would be accomplished with absolute certainty.

God sent Jesus His Son to fulfill the New Covenant.

28The law appointed high priests who were limited by human weakness. But after the law was given, God appointed his Son with an oath, and his Son has been made the perfect High Priest forever. 8:1Here is the main point: We have a High Priest who sat down in the place of honor beside the throne of the majestic God in heaven. 6But now Jesus, our High Priest, has been given a ministry that is far superior to the old priesthood, for he is the one who mediates for us a far better Covenant with God, based on better promises. 7If the first Covenant had been faultless, there would have been no need for a second Covenant to replace it. 8But when God found fault with the people, he said: "The day is coming, says the LORD, when I will make a new Covenant with the people of Israel and Judah.

Hebrews 7:28, 8:1, 6-8

God established His Son as the high priest so that He may fulfill the New Covenant.

11So Christ has now become the High Priest over all the good things that have come. He has entered that greater, more perfect Tabernacle in heaven, which was not made by human hands and is not part of this created world. 12With his own blood - not the blood of goats and calves - he entered the Most Holy Place once for all time and secured our redemption forever. 13Under the old system, the blood of goats and bulls and the ashes of a young cow could cleanse people's bodies from ceremonial impurity. 14Just think how much more the blood of Christ will purify our consciences from sinful deeds so that we can worship the living God. For by the power of the eternal Spirit, Christ offered himself to God as a perfect sacrifice for our sins. 15That is why he is the one who mediates a new Covenant between God and people, so that all who are called can receive the eternal inheritance God has promised them. For Christ died to set them free from the penalty of the sins they had committed under that first Covenant.

Hebrews 9:11-15

As verses above show, Jesus shed His blood and died on the cross in order to fulfill the New Covenant. However, note that in the following chapter that it refers to this Covenant as the "Second" Covenant:

9Then he said, "Look, I have come to do your will." He cancels the first Covenant in order to put the second into effect. 10For God's will was for us to be made holy by the sacrifice of the body of Jesus Christ, once for all time.

Hebrews 10:9-10

This is confirmation that the Second Covenant is the New Covenant.

To summarize, God sent His Son Jesus Christ so that He may fulfill the requirements to accomplish the Second, or New, Covenant.

6-2. The New Covenant, Part II
Jesus the Rock Provides the Living Water

Before we look deeper into the New Covenant, there are few points you, the reader, must fully understand.

To simplify, these points have been separated into four parts labeled [II] to [V]. A section about the Law of the Spirit of Life will come afterward labeled [VI]. Finally, the four points will be combined with the latter to complete the understanding of how the New Covenant is accomplished.

First point is that Jesus is the foundation rock.

1I don't want you to forget, dear brothers and sisters, about our ancestors in the wilderness long ago. All of them were guided by a cloud that moved ahead of them, and all of them walked through the sea on dry ground. 2In the cloud and in the sea, all of them were baptized as followers of Moses. 3All of them ate the same spiritual food, 4and all of them drank the same spiritual water. For they drank from the spiritual rock that traveled with them, and <u>that rock was Christ</u>.

1Corinthians 10:1-4

We too need to drink the same spiritual water from Christ the rock.

13Jesus replied, "Anyone who drinks this water will soon become thirsty again. 14But those who drink the water I give will never be thirsty again. <u>It becomes a fresh, bubbling spring within them, giving them eternal life</u>."

John 4:13-14

We need to drink this spiritual water so that we may have eternal life. Eternal life means being born again with the life that comes from God, the image of Christ, or the sanctuary where God may dwell.

However, some people may complain that drinking from this Rock does not guarantee Eternal Life since the verse below refers to the Israelites that died even after drinking from the rock:

Yet God was not pleased with most of them, and their bodies were scattered in the wilderness.

1Corinthians 10:5

The reason why the people of Israel were not successful was that they have drunk the physical water, not the spiritual water.

This is why we must drink the spiritual water through the Holy Spirit.

37On the last day, the climax of the festival, Jesus stood and shouted to the crowds, "Anyone who is thirsty may come to me! 38Anyone who believes in me may come and drink! For the Scriptures declare, `Rivers of living water will flow from his heart.'" 39(When he said "living water," he was speaking of the Spirit, who would be given to everyone believing in him. But the Spirit had not yet been given, because Jesus had not yet entered into his glory.)

John 7:37-39

Those that believe in the Covenant will be the "child of the promise" just like Isaac. This Covenant was initially called the *Covenant of Circumcision* then became known as the Second or New Covenant.

The Bible calls people that believe in the *New Covenant* the "new man."

and that you put on the new man which was created according to God, in true righteousness and holiness.

Ephesians 4:24 NKJV

9Do not lie to one another, since you have put off the old man with his deeds, 10and have put on the new man who is renewed in knowledge according to the image of Him who created him,

Colossians 3:9-10 NKJV

John 13:34 gives a "new command" to the *new man*:

So now I am giving you a new commandment: Love each other. Just as I have loved you, you should love each other.

John 13:34

It says to love one another as Jesus loves us.

Jesus lived in God (c.f. John 14:10-11), placed God as the head (c.f. 1 Corinthians 11:3), saw the glory of God (c.f. John 5:19-20) and lived with the heart that God gave with the Name that God provided, Jesus. He loved us with that love that flowed from God.

Jesus is giving us the *new commandment* to love that way:

And this is his commandment: We must believe in the name of his Son, Jesus Christ, and love one another, just as he commanded us.

1John 3:23

God established everything to be new. He declared that He would do *new things* and sent His Son the Christ to make us a *new man* so that we may be able to follow the *new commandment.*

In Isaiah 42:1-4, God declares that He will send the Christ to bring justice. He continues:

5God, the Lord, created the heavens and stretched them out. He created the earth and everything in it. He gives breath to everyone, life to everyone who walks the earth. And it is he who says, 6"I, the Lord, have called you to demonstrate my righteousness. I will take you by the hand and guard you, and I will give you to my people, Israel, as a symbol of my Covenant with them. And you will be a light to guide the nations. 7You will open the eyes of the blind. You will free the captives from prison, releasing those who sit in dark dungeons. 8"I am the Lord; that is my name! I will not give my glory to anyone else, nor share my praise with carved idols. 9Everything I prophesied has come true, and now I will prophesy again. I will tell you the future before it happens."

Isaiah 42:5-9

Behold, the former things have come to pass, and new things I now declare; before they spring forth I tell you of them."

Isaiah 42:9 (ESV)

God will send the Christ to accomplish the *new thing.*

This *new thing* is:

18"But forget all that - it is nothing compared to what I am going to do. 19For I am about to do something new. See, I have already begun! Do you not see it? I will make a pathway through the wilderness. I will create rivers in the dry wasteland. 20The wild animals in the fields will thank me, the jackals and owls, too, for giving them water in the desert. Yes, I will make rivers in the dry wasteland so my chosen people can be refreshed.

Isaiah 43:18-20

The *new thing* that Christ would do is to provide water for God's chosen people.

God's chosen people are:

"But you are my witnesses, O Israel!" says the Lord. "You are my servant. You have been chosen to know me, believe in me, and understand that I alone am God. There is no other God - there never has been, and there never will be.

Isaiah 43:10

God's chosen people are those that know and believe in God.

For anyone that knows and believes in God, He provides the water of life that s/he can drink freely.

The Spirit and the bride say, "Come." Let anyone who hears this say, "Come." Let anyone who is thirsty come. Let anyone who desires drink freely from the water of life.
Revelation 22:17

As the people of Israel were on their exodus, while they were in the wilderness, God provided the water through Jesus the Rock (c.f. 1 Corinthians 10:1-4).

We can learn two lessons from the events where God provided water from the rock:

First lesson can be seen in Exodus 17:1-3, where the people of Israel were thirsty and complained to Moses about it. Then,

4Then Moses cried out to the LORD, "What should I do with these people? They are ready to stone me!" 5The LORD said to Moses, "Walk out in front of the people. Take your staff, the one you used when you struck the water of the Nile, and call some of the elders of Israel to join you. 6I will stand before you on the rock at Mount Sinai. Strike the rock, and water will come gushing out. Then the people will be able to drink." So Moses struck the rock as he was told, and water gushed out as the elders looked on.
Exodus 17:4-6

God told Moses to strike the rock. He was saying to strike Jesus, who is the Rock, which refers to His death on the cross.

In that way, when we look to Jesus who died on the cross, the Living Water comes gushing out (c.f. Zechariah 12:10-13:2).

Moses named the place Massah (which means "test") and Meribah (which means "arguing") because the people of Israel argued with Moses and tested the LORD by saying, "Is the LORD here with us or not?"
Exodus 17:7

How can we know if Jesus lives inside of us?

If this Living Water gushes out of us, then Jesus is there.

If not, Jesus is not there.

Second lesson can be seen near the end of their forty years in the wilderness. It is the event at Kadesh before they entered Canaan (circa 1406 BC).

They complain to Moses in Numbers 20:2-5. Then,

6Moses and Aaron turned away from the people and went to the entrance of the Tabernacle, where they fell face down on the ground. Then the glorious presence of the LORD appeared to them, 7and the LORD said to Moses, 8"You and Aaron must take the staff and assemble the entire community. As the people watch, speak to the rock over there, and it will pour out its water. You will provide enough water from the rock to satisfy the whole community and their livestock." 9So Moses did as he was told. He took the staff from the place where it was kept before the LORD. 10Then he and Aaron summoned the people to come and gather at the rock. "Listen, you rebels!" he shouted. "Must we bring you water from this rock?" 11Then Moses raised his hand and struck the rock twice with the staff, and water gushed out. So the entire community and their livestock drank their fill.

Numbers 20:6-11

Here, Moses and Aaron make a big mistake before God.

God commanded them to *speak* to the rock to bring out the water, but they were inflamed with their human emotions and struck the rock with their staff. It is for this reason neither Moses nor Aaron was able to enter the Promised Land.

12But the LORD said to Moses and Aaron, "Because you did not trust me enough to demonstrate my holiness to the people of Israel, you will not lead them into the land I am giving them!" 13This place was known as the waters of Meribah (which means "arguing") because there the people of Israel argued with the LORD, and there he demonstrated his holiness among them.

Numbers 20:12-13

Our lesson here is that we cannot enter Canaan, or be in Christ, with our human emotions.

12One day the LORD said to Moses, "Climb one of the mountains east of the river, and look out over the land I have given the people of Israel. 13After you have seen it, you will die like your brother, Aaron, 14for you both rebelled against my instructions in the wilderness of Zin. When the people of Israel rebelled, you failed to demonstrate my holiness to them at the waters." (These are the waters of Meribah at Kadesh in the wilderness of Zin.)

Numbers 27:12-14

32At Meribah, too, they angered the Lord, causing Moses serious trouble. 33They made Moses angry, and he spoke foolishly.

Psalms 106:32-33

We can learn from this second event that this water makes us holy (c.f. 1 Peter 3:15-16, the mind of Christ) and that it is provided by the resurrected Jesus.

When we look to the resurrected Jesus that sits on the right hand of God, Jesus the Rock will provide us spiritual water so that we may have a holy heart, which is, the heart of Christ or the Name of Jesus.

We do this by keeping our eyes on Jesus, the champion who initiates and perfects our faith. Because of the joy awaiting him, he endured the cross, disregarding its shame. Now he is seated in the place of honor beside God's throne.

Hebrews 12:2

When we look to Jesus that sits on the right hand of God, He makes us whole by giving us His heart.

The right hand of God means He is One with authority.

The Lord stands at your right hand to protect you. He will strike down many kings when his anger erupts.

Psalms 110:5

But from now on the Son of Man will be seated in the place of power at God's right hand."

Luke 22:69

Now Christ has gone to heaven. He is seated in the place of honor next to God, and all the angels and authorities and powers accept his authority.

1Peter 3:22

When we look to Jesus that sits on the right hand of God through the Holy Spirit, the Living Water, the overflowing love of Christ, gushes out. When we drink of this Water, we obtain the heart of Christ that makes us holy. Once that occurs, we can see God demonstrating miracles through His heart in us.

8On that day life-giving waters will flow out from Jerusalem, half toward the Dead Sea and half toward the Mediterranean, flowing continuously in both summer and winter.
9And the Lord will be king over all the earth. On that day there will be one Lord - his name alone will be worshiped. 11And Jerusalem will be filled, safe at last, never again to be cursed and destroyed.

Zechariah 14:8-9, 11

As mentioned previously, "Jerusalem" in verse 8 is the Holy Spirit (c.f. Galatians 4:26, 29, which is equivalent to John 7:37-39).

We who are living in the wilderness must drink this water.

We can drink this water by looking to Christ the Rock that has hung on the cross and is at the right hand of God.

6-3. The New Covenant, Part III Seeking the Glory of God

As we go through Christian living, we must recognize that God the Father, Son, and the Holy Spirit does all things through what is written in Scriptures (c.f. 1 Corinthians 4:6). That is why we must pray for the Holy Spirit to show and teach us Scriptures. If we do not know the Scriptures, we cannot possibly know Jesus the Son of God (c.f. Matthew 22:29, 2 Timothy 3:15-17).

Even when Jesus overcame temptation of Satan, He referred to the written Word (the Scriptures) of the Father.

4But Jesus told him, "No! The Scriptures say, `People do not live by bread alone, but by every word that comes from the mouth of God.'" 7Jesus responded, "The Scriptures also say, `You must not test the LORD your God.'" 10"Get out of here, Satan," Jesus told him. "For the Scriptures say, `You must worship the LORD your God and serve only him.'"

Matthew 4:4, 7, 10

So Jesus said, "When you have lifted up the Son of Man on the cross, then you will understand that I AM he. I do nothing on my own but say only what the Father taught me.

John 8:28

From the verses above, we can see that Jesus relied on the Word of God as the Father taught Him.

49I don't speak on my own authority. The Father who sent me has commanded me what to say and how to say it. 50And I know his commands lead to eternal life; so I say whatever the Father tells me to say."

John 12:49-50

Even Satan works using the Scriptures.

and said, "If you are the Son of God, jump off! For the Scriptures say, `He will order his angels to protect you. And they will hold you up with their hands so you won't even hurt your foot on a stone.'"

Matthew 4:6

However, Satan only uses Scriptures as the letter of the law to bring about death (c.f. 2 Corinthians 3:6).

We must fully understand Scriptures so that we may know Jesus.

You search the Scriptures because you think they give you eternal life. But the Scriptures point to me!

John 5:39

27Then Jesus took them through the writings of Moses and all the prophets, explaining from all the Scriptures the things concerning himself. 32They said to each other, "Didn't our hearts burn within us as he talked with us on the road and explained the Scriptures to us?" 44Then he said, "When I was with you before, I told you that everything written about me in the law of Moses and the prophets and in the Psalms must be fulfilled." 45Then he opened their minds to understand the Scriptures. 46And he said, "Yes, it was written long ago that the Messiah would suffer and die and rise from the dead on the third day. 47It was also written that this message would be proclaimed in the authority of his name to all the nations, beginning in Jerusalem: 'There is forgiveness of sins for all who repent.' 48You are witnesses of all these things.

Luke 24:27, 32, 44-48

As the verses above reveal, Jesus used Scriptures to teach others about Himself.

Even Jesus' disciples used Scriptures to teach that Jesus is the Christ:

2As was Paul's custom, he went to the synagogue service, and for three Sabbaths in a row he used the Scriptures to reason with the people. 3He explained the prophecies and proved that the Messiah must suffer and rise from the dead. He said, "This Jesus I'm telling you about is the Messiah."

Acts 17:2-3

1This letter is from Paul, a slave of Christ Jesus, chosen by God to be an apostle and sent out to preach his Good News. 2God promised this Good News long ago through his prophets in the holy Scriptures.

Romans 1:1-2

To summarize, the wisdom for us to live in Christ is all stored in the Scriptures.

15You have been taught the holy Scriptures from childhood, and they have given you the wisdom to receive the salvation that comes by trusting in Christ Jesus. 16All Scripture is inspired by God and is useful to teach us what is true and to make us realize what is wrong in our lives. It corrects us when we are wrong and teaches us to do what is right. 17God uses it to prepare and equip his people to do every good work.

2Timothy 3:15-17

However, when we look through Scriptures, we may find that some points that are difficult to understand. One of those points are passages that tell us to look toward the face of Jesus.

Because I am righteous, I will see you. When I awake, I will see you face to face and be satisfied.

Psalms 17:15

In another passage, it says we need to see the glory of God so that we may be transformed into His image.

So all of us who have had that veil removed can see and reflect the glory of the Lord. And the Lord-who is the Spirit-makes us more and more like him as we are changed into his glorious image.

2Corinthians 3:18

We can see other parts of Scriptures that say to look to either the glory of the Lord or the face of the Lord with the same intent (c.f. Exodus 33:18-23).

We can also see in Scriptures that the Name of God and God Himself are referenced as the same.

No one has ever seen God. But the unique One, who is himself God, is near to the Father's heart. He has revealed God to us.

John 1:18

The verse above says that Jesus revealed God to us.

At another verse, it says:

I have made your name known to those whom you gave me from the world. They were yours, and you gave them to me, and they have kept your word.

John 17:6 (NRSV)

It says that Jesus revealed the "Name of the Father" in the passage above.

The Name of God and God Himself can be interchanged with the word "glory" as well.

I have given them the glory you gave me, so they may be one as we are one.

John 17:22

Here, Jesus said the glory makes them one, and on another verse:

Now I am departing from the world; they are staying in this world, but I am coming to you. Holy Father, you have given me your name; now protect them by the power of your name so that they will be united just as we are.

John 17:11

In the verse above, it says the Name of Jesus makes them one.

All throughout Scriptures, we can see equivalent meanings where it refers to showing God Himself, the glory of God, or the Name of God.

Name of the Father is "Jesus" and the Name "Jesus" is the Name of the Life of the Father. This Life is one lived in Christ (c.f. 1 John 5:11-12) and it is shown as the heart of Christ.

To say we live:

- By God
- By the Name of God
- By the Name of Jesus
- By the Glory of God
- By the Life of Jesus
- In Christ (c.f. 1 John 5:11-12)
- With Christ as our Head
- With the heart that Christ provides
- With Christ as our covering (clothes)
- Revealing Jesus

They all mean the same.

We can also say it this way:

- Seeing the face of God
- Seeing the glory of God
- Revealing the glory of God
- Revealing God
- Revealing the Name of God
- Revealing the Life of God
- Seeing the Heart of God

They also mean the same.

We can clearly see from the following passages:

Glory = face (c.f. Exodus 33:18-23)

Glory = Name (c.f. John 17:22, 11)

Name = Life (c.f. 2 Chronicles 6:1-11; The Ark that holds the Covenant (c.f. 2 Samuel 6:2)

Covenant = Heart (c.f. 1 John 5:11-12, Ephesians 1:10).

In this way, we can see the Scriptures using the words "face," "glory," "name," "life," and "heart" with equivalent meaning.

Getting back to the main subject:

God desires to shine the light of His face (heart) upon us:

22And the LORD spoke to Moses, saying: 23"Speak to Aaron and his sons, saying, 'This is the way you shall bless the children of Israel. Say to them: 25The LORD make His face shine upon you, And be gracious to you; 26The LORD lift up His countenance upon you, And give you peace.'"

Numbers 6:22-23, 25-26 NKJV

In the verses above, we can easily justify that His *shining His face upon us* is the same as *His looking toward us*. We can also see that His blessing us with His face is shown to be with His Name in the following verse:

Whenever Aaron and his sons bless the people of Israel in my name, I myself will bless them."

Numbers 6:27

We can see the equivalence between the light of God's face and the Name of God.

This means that when God shines His face (heart) upon us, then we can have His Name (the Heart of Christ).

What does God do when people sin again Him?

17Then my anger will blaze forth against them. I will abandon them, hiding my face from them, and they will be devoured. Terrible trouble will come down on them, and on that day they will say, 'These disasters have come down on us because God is no longer among us!' 18At that time I will hide my face from them on account of all the evil they commit by worshiping other gods.

Deuteronomy 31:17-18

O Lord, why do you reject me? Why do you turn your face from me?

Psalms 88:14

As the verses above say, we cannot see the face of God when we sin.

When God says He will hide His face from us, it means He will not see us.

They are coming in to fight against the Chaldeans and to fill them with the dead bodies of men whom I shall strike down in my anger and my wrath, for I have hidden my face from this city because of all their evil.

Jeremiah 33:5 (ESV)

There are many other verses in Scripture that say God hides His face when we sin against Him: Ezekiel 39:23-24, Psalm 13:1, 30:7, 44:24.

Scriptures say those destined for ruin are those whose face (presence) of God has turned away from them:

8in flaming fire, inflicting vengeance on those who do not know God and on those who do not obey the gospel of our Lord Jesus. 9They will suffer the punishment of eternal destruction, away from the presence of the Lord and from the glory of his might,

2Thessalonians 1:8-9 (ESV)

The reason for our prayers is to see the face of God.

Look to the LORD and his strength; seek his face always.

1Chronicles 16:11 NIV

Do not hide your face from me when I am in distress. Turn your ear to me; when I call, answer me quickly.

Psalms 102:2 NIV

Look to the LORD and his strength; seek his face always.

Psalms 105:4 NIV

Answer me quickly, O LORD; my spirit fails. Do not hide your face from me or I will be like those who go down to the pit.

Psalms 143:7 NIV

5He will receive blessing from the LORD and vindication from God his Savior. 6Such is the generation of those who seek him, who seek your face, O God of Jacob. Selah

Psalms 24:5-6 NIV

Let your face shine on your servant; save me in your unfailing love.

Psalms 31:16 NIV

Do not hide your face from your servant; answer me quickly, for I am in trouble.

Psalms 69:17 NIV

3Turn us again to yourself, O God. Make your face shine down upon us. Only then will we be saved. 7Turn us again to yourself, O God of Heaven's Armies. Make your face shine down upon us. Only then will we be saved. 19Turn us again to yourself, O Lord God of Heaven's Armies. Make your face shine down upon us. Only then will we be saved.

Psalms 80:3, 7, 19

Prayer is seeking God's face so that He may look toward us. That is why God responds to our prayers in this way:

For he has not despised or disdained the suffering of the afflicted one; he has not hidden his face from him but has listened to his cry for help.

Psalms 22:24 NIV

Why are you cast down, O my soul? And why are you disquieted within me? Hope in God, for I shall yet praise Him For the help of His countenance.

Psalms 42:5 NKJV

They did not conquer the land with their swords; it was not their own strong arm that gave them victory. It was your right hand and strong arm and the blinding light from your face that helped them, for you loved them.

Psalms 44:3

Answers to our prayers is to see the face of God. In another words, prayers are answered as God sees us.

The reason is that when He sees us, we obtain the Name of Jesus (the heart of Christ) through the light (glory) from his face (heart).

After His resurrection, Jesus comes back and says We obtain the Name of Jesus when He sees us.

22So you have sorrow now, but I will see you again; then you will rejoice, and no one can rob you of that joy. 23At that time you won't need to ask me for anything. I tell you the truth, you will ask the Father directly, and he will grant your request because you use my name. 24You haven't done this before. Ask, using my name, and you will receive, and you will have abundant joy.

John 16:22-24

This means that children of God that have been born again with the life that comes from God live seeking the face of God (God's glory) and the heart of Jesus.

Reminder: The heart of Jesus is the overflowing love that God provides.

And I will never again turn my face from them, for I will pour out my Spirit upon the people of Israel. I, the Sovereign Lord, have spoken!"

Ezekiel 39:29

Israel, referred in the verse above, refers to those that believe in the Second (New) Covenant. Only to them will God pour out His Spirit so that they may live seeing His face (glory, heart).

6He has enabled us to be ministers of his new Covenant. This is a Covenant not of written laws, but of the Spirit. The old written Covenant ends in death; but under the new Covenant, the Spirit gives life. 18So all of us who have had that veil removed can see and reflect the glory of the Lord. And the Lord-who is the Spirit-makes us more and more like him as we are changed into his glorious image.

2Corinthians 3:6, 18

3If the Good News we preach is hidden behind a veil, it is hidden only from people who are perishing. 4Satan, who is the god of this world, has blinded the minds of those who don't believe. They are unable to see the glorious light of the Good News. They don't understand this message about the glory of Christ, who is the exact likeness of God. 6For God, who said, "Let there be light in the darkness," has made this light shine in our hearts so we could know the glory of God that is seen in the face of Jesus Christ.

2Corinthians 4:3,4, 6

We are blessed when we have firm faith like that of Abraham and seek the glory (face, heart) of God through the Holy Spirit.

Unless we see God's glory (face, heart) through the Holy Spirit, there can be no change in us.

When we look to the heart of Jesus through the Holy Spirit as he hung on the cross, the love of God overflows. When we drink (realize) this overflow of water (love), we will have the heart of Christ (the Name of Jesus).

We can only be changed into the image of Christ when we see God's glory (face, heart) through the Holy Spirit.

Children of God that has been born again with the life that comes from God do not live by obeying the law; rather, they live seeking the glory (heart) of God and drinking the overflowing water (love). As a result, they have the heart of Christ and live in the Name of Jesus.

They are ministers of the New Covenant, people that can see God's glory (face, life, heart, Name).

6-4. The New Covenant, Part IV Looking to Jesus to become a Suitable Sanctuary for God

God's ultimate purpose on earth is to build a sanctuary for Himself.

That is why God took the people of Israel out of Egypt to go through the Wilderness to reach the land of Canaan so that they may build a temple for Him there.

When Israel turned away from God, the temple was destroyed and they were taken as slaves. When they came to their senses, they would return to the temple and rebuild it. That is how the Old Testament history concluded.

As mentioned in earlier sections, God's reason and purpose of building the temple was to place His Name there (c.f. 1 Kings 8:12-21, 2 Chronicles 6:1-11).

The LORD said to him, "I have heard your prayer and your petition. <u>I have set this Temple apart to be holy - this place you have built where my name will be honored forever. I will always watch over it, for it is dear to my heart.</u>

1Kings 9:3

The reason why our living God causes us to be born again to be the sanctuary for Him is so that He may give His Name to us as an inheritance.

That is why we see this in the last book of the Old Testament:

The Lord of Heaven's Armies says to the priests: "A son honors his father, and a servant respects his master. If I am your father and master, <u>where are the honor and respect I deserve</u>? You have shown contempt for my name! 'But you ask, '<u>How have we ever shown contempt for your name?</u>'

Malachi 1:6

We can see in the verse above that God refers Himself as the Name.

But my name is honored by people of other nations from morning till night. <u>All around the world they offer sweet incense and pure offerings in honor of my name.</u> <u>For my name is great among the nations,</u>" says the Lord of Heaven's Armies.

Malachi 1:11

Listen to me and make up your minds to honor my name," says the Lord of Heaven's Armies, "or I will bring a terrible curse against you. I will curse even the blessings you receive. Indeed, I have already cursed them, because you have not taken my warning to heart.

Malachi 2:2

We would be cursed if we do not place the Name of God in our hearts.

16Then those who feared the Lord spoke with each other, and the Lord listened to what they said. In his presence, a scroll of remembrance was written to record the names of those who feared him and always thought about the honor of his name. 17"They will be my people," says the Lord of Heaven's Armies. "On the day when I act in judgment, they will be my own special treasure. I will spare them as a father spares an obedient child. 18Then you will again see the difference between the righteous and the wicked, between those who serve God and those who do not."

Malachi 3:16-18

The "righteous" are people who have the Name of God in their hearts. The verse above says those that do not have the Name of God in their hearts are people that do not serve Him.

2"But for you who fear my name, the Sun of Righteousness will rise with healing in his wings. And you will go free, leaping with joy like calves let out to pasture. 3On the day when I act, you will tread upon the wicked as if they were dust under your feet," says the Lord of Heaven's Armies.

Malachi 4:2-3

This was written as the Old Testament was coming to close. To accomplish this salvation, God would send Elijah first then the Covenant's Mediator, Jesus (c.f. Malachi 3:1).

The reason and purpose that Jesus the Christ, the Son of God came to earth is to fulfill the Second (New) Covenant in us as God had sworn to accomplish. By fulfilling the Covenant, we would be reborn to be a sanctuary that would bear His Name in us. That is why we must be built up to be an acceptable sanctuary for Him.

This can be done by having the image of Christ in us so that we may be born again with the life that comes from God. By our rebirth, we can welcome Jesus, who is heaven, into our hearts.

Oh, my dear children! I feel as if I'm going through labor pains for you again, and they will continue until Christ is fully developed in your lives.

Galatians 4:19

How can we be built up to be a sanctuary for God?

8"Have the people of Israel build me a holy sanctuary so I can live among them. 9You must build this Tabernacle and its furnishings exactly according to the pattern I will show you.

Exodus 25:8-9

Set up this Tabernacle according to the pattern you were shown on the mountain.

Exodus 26:30

As the verses above show, the sanctuary is to be built according to the pattern God shows us.

The altar must be hollow, made from planks. Build it just as you were shown on the mountain.

Exodus 27:8

Our ancestors carried the Tabernacle with them through the wilderness. It was constructed according to the plan God had shown to Moses.

Acts 7:44

They serve in a system of worship that is only a copy, a shadow of the real one in heaven. For when Moses was getting ready to build the Tabernacle, God gave him this warning: "Be sure that you make everything according to the pattern I have shown you here on the mountain."

Hebrews 8:5

The sanctuary is to be built according to the way it was shown, and the sanctuaries being built in us are no different.

We are to be built according to the way He shows it to us.

We must look to Jesus that has come to us as the sanctuary for the Living God to show us; however, we will not be able to see with our physical eyes, and we must seek Him through the Holy Spirit (c.f. John 6:40, John 14:16-20, 16:22-27).

The ministers of the New Covenant are:

He has enabled us to be ministers of his new Covenant. This is a Covenant not of written laws, but of the Spirit. The old written Covenant ends in death; but under the new Covenant, the Spirit gives life.

2Corinthians 3:6

So all of us who have had that veil removed can see and reflect the glory of the Lord. And the Lord-who is the Spirit-makes us more and more like him as we are changed into his glorious image.

2Corinthians 3:18

We who see the glory (face, heart) of the Lord through the Holy Spirit are those that are being built up to His image.

6-5. The New Covenant, Part V He Forms Us to be the Church

From the beginning, God had in mind to accomplish this one thing: to bear children that are brothers and sisters to Jesus. They would be the Church that receives inheritance that is pure and undefiled, beyond the reach of change and decay.

3All praise to God, the Father of our Lord Jesus Christ. It is by his great mercy that we have been born again, because God raised Jesus Christ from the dead. Now we live with great expectation, 4and we have a priceless inheritance - an inheritance that is kept in heaven for you, pure and undefiled, beyond the reach of change and decay.

1Peter 1:3-4

9I was chosen to explain to everyone this mysterious plan that God, the Creator of all things, had kept secret from the beginning. 10God's purpose in all this was to use the church to display his wisdom in its rich variety to all the unseen rulers and authorities in the heavenly places. 11This was his eternal plan, which he carried out through Christ Jesus our Lord. 12Because of Christ and our faith in him, we can now come boldly and confidently into God's presence.

Ephesians 3:9-12

The author of Hebrews writes it this way:

5And furthermore, it is not angels who will control the future world we are talking about. 6For in one place the Scriptures say, "What are mere mortals that you should think about them, or a son of man that you should care for him?

Hebrews 2:5-6

“Mere mortals” refer to humans, while “son of man” refers to Jesus Christ.

You made him a little lower than the angels; you crowned him with glory and honor
Hebrews 2:7 NIV

God made His Son, the Christ, little lower than the angels to crown him with glory and honor. This means that Jesus came to earth in the flesh to die on the cross but to resurrect from the grave. The result is to be crowned with glory and honor by holding all authority over heaven and earth (c.f. Matthew 28:18).

You gave them authority over all things." Now when it says "all things," it means nothing is left out. But we have not yet seen all things put under their authority.

Hebrews 2:8

All things in heaven and on earth were placed under His authority; however, we cannot readily see this today. Why is that?

This is where we can see God's amazing plan of love.

9What we do see is Jesus, who was given a position "a little lower than the angels"; and because he suffered death for us, he is now "crowned with glory and honor." Yes, by God's grace, Jesus tasted death for everyone. 10God, for whom and through whom everything was made, chose to bring many children into glory. And it was only right that he should make Jesus, through his suffering, a perfect leader, fit to bring them into their salvation.

Hebrews 2:9-10

The reason why Jesus suffered even to His death is so that we may be reborn as children of God and enter into His glory.

11So now Jesus and the ones he makes holy have the same Father. That is why Jesus is not ashamed to call them his brothers and sisters. 12For he said to God, "I will <u>proclaim</u> your name to my brothers and sisters. I will praise you among your assembled people."

Hebrews 2:11-12

God will enable us to be born again with the life of Jesus. As a result, we become brothers and sisters of Jesus. Jesus will proclaim His Name to us.

The word "proclaim" or "declare" means to make known:

"And I have <u>declared</u> to them Your name, and will <u>declare</u> it, that the love with which You loved Me may be in them, and I in them."

John 17:26 NKJV

Summarizing, Jesus came to earth in a form little less than the angels and died then resurrected. As a result, He took away the authority of Satan, the king of the earth, and now holds all authority of heaven and earth. All things are under His authority and submit to Him.

Now, how does He cause us to submit to Him?

Through the suffering of Christ, we are reborn as brothers and sisters of Jesus. By teaching us the Name of Jesus, all things submit to Him through us, *our bodies.*

Jesus shares a similar message to His disciples near Caesarea Philippi:

15Then he asked them, "But who do you say I am?" 16Simon Peter answered, "You are the Messiah, <u>the Son of the living God</u>."

Matthew 16:15-16

Peter says Jesus is the Messiah, the Son of God, that came to fulfill the Second (New) Covenant (c.f. Hebrews 7:28, 8:6-13).

> *17Jesus replied, "You are blessed, Simon son of John, because my Father in heaven has revealed this to you. You did not learn this from any human being. 18Now I say to you that you are Peter (which means `rock'), and upon this rock I will build my church, and all the powers of hell will not conquer it.*
>
> *Matthew 16:17-18*

"Upon this rock" refers to Peter's confession in verse 16, where Peter demonstrated faith. When we have this faith, Jesus is declaring that he will raise us up also as the body of Christ, the Church.

Church is made up people that place Christ as their head (c.f. Ephesians 1:22-23).

> *And I will give you the keys of the Kingdom of Heaven. Whatever you forbid on earth will be forbidden in heaven, and whatever you permit on earth will be permitted in heaven."*
>
> *Matthew 16:19*

The keys of the Kingdom of Heaven is the Name of Jesus.

God causes us to be born again with the life that comes from God so that we may together become the church, or the body of Christ. Through the Holy Spirit, we place Christ as our head and live in Christ with the heart of Christ that He gives us. As we live in the Name of Jesus, all things submits before us.

6-6. The New Covenant, Part VI
The Law of the Spirit of Life

In this section, we will review and amalgamate the last four sections regarding the New Covenant.

10God, for whom and through whom everything was made, chose to bring many children into glory. And it was only right that he should make Jesus, through his suffering, a perfect leader, fit to bring them into their salvation. 11So now Jesus and the ones he makes holy have the same Father. That is why Jesus is not ashamed to call them his brothers and sisters.

Hebrews 2:10-11

The verses above say that we are born with the same Life as Jesus, and therefore we are brothers and sisters with Him.

Jesus says:

I tell you the truth, anyone who believes in me will do the same works I have done, and even greater works, because I am going to be with the Father.

John 14:12

Jesus is telling us with emphasis that we can live as Jesus did.

He also adds that to enable us to live that way, He had to go to the Father.

The reason that He goes to the Father is to enter into the tabernacle in heaven to rid of our sins (c.f. Hebrews 9:11-15) and send the Holy Spirit to make us children of God.

But in fact, it is best for you that I go away, because if I don't, the Advocate won't come. If I do go away, then I will send him to you.

John 16:7

He sends the Holy Spirit so that we may be born again and become siblings of Jesus.

For this reason, children of God that have been reborn with the life that comes from God must live like Jesus by living in the Name of Jesus.

12"I tell you the truth, anyone who believes in me will do the same works I have done, and even greater works, because I am going to be with the Father. 13You can ask for anything in my name, and I will do it, so that the Son can bring glory to the Father. 14Yes, ask me for anything in my name, and I will do it!

John 14:12-14

As brothers and sisters of Christ, we must live as He did:

Those who say they live in God should live their lives as Jesus did.

1John 2:6

To help us to live that way, Jesus showed his brothers and sisters an example of how to live.

For God knew his people in advance, and he chose them to become like his Son, so that his Son would be the firstborn among many brothers and sisters.

Romans 8:29

Now we must live as Jesus did and live in His Name.

When we try to become Jesus, we are sinning as Satan did; but it is natural for us to live as Jesus did as brothers and sisters that have the same Life as Him.

How did Jesus live that we may imitate Him?

because through Christ Jesus the law of the Spirit of life set me free from the law of sin and death.

Romans 8:2 NIV

Jesus lived according to the Law of the Spirit of Life that was in Him.

In another words, He lived according to the guidance of the Holy Spirit and the Father that was in Him. Jesus placed the Father as the head (c.f. 1 Corinthians 11:3), listened to the Word of the Father, and lived in the Father's Name, that is, with the heart of the Father (c.f. John 10:25).

Put in another way, Jesus saw the glory (face, heart) of the Father (c.f. John 5:19-20) as the Holy Spirit that was in Him showed Him. He continued to drink the spiritual water (Word, Life, Love) that the Father provided and came to know the heart of the Father. As a result, He lived in the Name of the Father.

That way of living is called *The Law of the Spirit of Life.*

The New Covenant is:

31 "The day is coming," says the Lord, "when I will make a new Covenant with the people of Israel and Judah. 32This Covenant will not be like the one I made with their ancestors when I took them by the hand and brought them out of the land of Egypt. They broke that Covenant, though I loved them as a husband loves his wife," says the Lord.

Jeremiah 31:31-32

The Covenant (v. 32) made when God brought the people of Israel out of Egypt refers to the Law of Moses. It is the law that must be kept as people hear from or are taught by other people. This is the Ten Commandments shown in Deuteronomy 5.

> *"But this is the new Covenant I will make with the people of Israel on that day," says the Lord. "I will put my instructions deep within them, and I will write them on their hearts. I will be their God, and they will be my people.*
>
> *Jeremiah 31:33*

"I" in the passage above refers to Jesus.

> *And we know that the Son of God has come, and he has given us understanding so that we can know the true God. And now we live in fellowship with the true God because we live in fellowship with his Son, Jesus Christ. He is the only true God, and he is eternal life.*
>
> *1John 5:20*

Putting it together, the promise of the New Covenant is that Jesus will put into our hearts the Law of the Spirit of Life that is in Him so that we may live as He did.

The Law of the Spirit of Life is a promise that He will enable us to live with the heart of Christ by causing us to be born again in the life that comes from God, be the sanctuary for the living God, and through the Holy Spirit in us, live in Christ with the Life of God.

We would be the Church, the Body of Christ, which is in Christ and places Christ as our head. It is a promise that we will be able to live with the heart of Christ that He provides us.

The Holy Spirit in us will help us to see the face (glory, heart) of Jesus that hung on the cross. That will enable us to drink the spiritual water (love) of Jesus, which in turn allows us to live with the heart of Christ that He provides us.

Another way of seeing it is that the Holy Spirit in us will help us to see the face (glory, heart) of Jesus who sits on the right hand of God. That will enable us to drink the spiritual water (love) of Jesus, which in turn allows us to live with a holy heart that He provides us.

The promise is that through the Holy Spirit we are able to see the glory (face, heart) of Jesus. That will enable us to drink the spiritual water (love) that Jesus provides. Then, one may live with the heart of Christ, that is, in the Name of Jesus.

There is therefore now no condemnation for those who are in Christ Jesus. 2For the law of the Spirit of life has set you free in Christ Jesus from the law of sin and death. 3For God has done what the law, weakened by the flesh, could not do. By sending his own Son in the likeness of sinful flesh and for sin, he condemned sin in the flesh, 4in order that the righteous requirement of the law might be fulfilled in us, who walk not according to the flesh but according to the Spirit.

Romans 8:1-4 (ESV)

For that reason, in order to overcome Satan's attacks, we need God the Father, Son, and Holy Spirit to fulfill the New Covenant in us so that *the Law of Spirit of Life* may overcome *the Law of Sin and Death* that Satan uses against us. This begins with our faith in the New Covenant that God swore to accomplish. Through the Law of Spirit of Life, we will be able to fulfill the requirements of the law.

The Covenant must be fulfilled in us so that we may live as the Kingdom of God (heaven).

When we believe in the Covenant that God has sworn to accomplish, even with the shaky faith that Abraham began with, God will send His Son, the Christ, to fulfill the New Covenant in us.

6-7. Image of Christ is Necessary for Rebirth

Jesus replied, "I assure you, no one can enter the Kingdom of God <u>without being born of water and the Spirit</u>.

John 3:5

The "water" in the verse above is the baptism of John the Baptist and the baptism that Jesus' disciples gave (c.f. 1 Peter 3:21).

We must believe that through the baptism of John the Baptist all of our sins have been transferred to Jesus (c.f. John 1:29).

By believing this truth, we receive baptism in the Name of Jesus to be forgiven from our sins. It is from this point forward that we are disciples of Jesus that learns directly from the Holy Spirit/Jesus about the one true God and His Son, the Christ, whom God sent. As a result, we are born again with the life that comes from God. This is the way to eternal life.

And this is the way to have eternal life—to know you, the only true God, and Jesus Christ, the one you sent to earth.

John 17:3

To know the one true God requires us to know the Covenant of Circumcision that He promised with Abraham, Isaac, and Jacob.

To know the Christ whom God sent requires us to know that the Christ the Son came to accomplish the Father's promise of the Covenant of Circumcision.

When we believe this, God strengthens our faith so that we may be born again (obtain eternal life) as a "Child of the Promise" just as Isaac was.

However, we must all understand something:

Even though God had made the Covenant of Circumcision with Abraham, Isaac was not born just because Abraham cut off his foreskin in response to the promise. Cutting the foreskin was simply a sign of his belief that God would do what God promised to accomplish (c.f. Genesis 17:11).

Isaac was not immediately born. Rather, Abraham faced life experiences such as the events at Sodom, with King Abimelech in Gerar, and many others through which God performed circumcision in Abraham's heart, that is, Abraham came to know the one true God. Through these events, Abraham's faith grew and when perfected, Isaac was born.

As God continually circumcised Abraham, Abraham's faith continued to grow. When it grew to perfection, Isaac was fully formed and was born.

It is the same when we too are born with the life that comes from God.

We are forgiven (c.f. Acts 2:38) and are called a disciple of Jesus (c.f. Acts 2:41) when we receive baptism in the Name of Jesus. However, we are not born again at this time of baptism.

Even Jesus' disciples spent three years following Jesus to learn from the Holy Spirit so that they may confess what they did as portrayed in Matthew 16:16-17. At the end of the three years, they saw Jesus die on the cross to take care of their sins; they also saw Jesus resurrect from the grave to demonstrate that He has overcome the power of death.

When Jesus came back to meet them at Tibet River, they saw Jesus and realized His great love for them and confessed their love back to Him.

This is how Image of Christ was fulfilled in them, and that is why they received the Holy Spirit at Pentecost. When they received the Holy Spirit, they were born again as the sanctuary for the Living God, and this is when we can say they have accepted Jesus.

We can see similar events in Antioch:

25Then Barnabas went on to Tarsus to look for Saul. 26When he found him, he brought him back to Antioch. Both of them stayed there with the church for a full year, teaching large crowds of people. (It was at Antioch that the believers were first called Christians.)

Acts 11:25-26

People that live according to the Holy Spirit are considered "believers" (c.f. Romans 8:9, 14).

Disciples were trained for one year at Antioch.

In Ephesus, disciples were trained for two years (c.f. Acts 19:8-10).

This is the truth:

Our receiving baptism in the Name of Jesus does not give us eternal life. That baptism only resolves the problem with our sin in the physical realm. Though this baptism gives the person the title of Christian, or a disciple of Jesus, they have not yet received salvation (life, rebirth) of their spirit/souls.

After receiving baptism of Jesus, the person must learn from the Holy Spirit and Jesus through their life experiences so that the Image of Christ may be formed in them. Once they reach that level, they will be reborn as a sanctuary suitable to accept Jesus into their heart.

The reason why "disciples" do not stay with and depart from Jesus eternally is that they turn away before they have been fully transformed to the Image of Christ.

At this point many of his disciples turned away and deserted him.

John 6:66

That is why Apostle Paul says this:

Oh, my dear children! I feel as if I'm going through labor pains for you again, and they will continue until Christ is fully developed in your lives.

Galatians 4:19

Apostle Paul is certainly scolding the church at Galatia for not being able to distinguish faith of their members, but what is important to us is the second part of the verse. He is saying that the Image of Christ must formed in them so that they may be born again.

Some people ask this:

Did not the criminal that was hung next to Jesus receive salvation?

Yes, the criminal received salvation.

However, the criminal has seen Jesus through the Holy Spirit, recognized Jesus as the Christ, and heard the saving voice of Jesus, while the other criminal did not see or hear Jesus.

We too can receive salvation right now if we can see Jesus through the Holy Spirit and hear His voice.

If we want to see Jesus through the Holy Spirit and hear His voice, we must first begin by becoming a disciple of Jesus and commit to learn from the Holy Spirit/Jesus.

The event of Centurion Cornelius also shows this as shown in Acts 10:1-48.

Cornelius was a God-fearing person.

1In Caesarea there lived a Roman army officer named Cornelius, who was a captain of the Italian Regiment. 2He was a devout, God-fearing man, as was everyone in his household. He gave generously to the poor and prayed regularly to God.

Acts 10:1-2

What does it mean to be a God-fearing man?

When God tested Abraham (c.f. Genesis 22:1-12), God told Abraham to give his son Isaac as a burnt offering. Abraham figured that even if his only son was sacrificed, God would still use Isaac to bear many children because God had promised it (c.f. Genesis 15:4-5). One conjecture he may have had was that God would raise Isaac from the dead (c.f. Hebrews 11:17-19).

God saw Abraham's faith and said:

"Don't lay a hand on the boy!" the angel said. "Do not hurt him in any way, for now I know that you truly fear God. You have not withheld from me even your son, your only son."

Genesis 22:12

The Centurion had the same faith like that of Abraham. That is why when he met Peter and received some teachings, he was able to receive the Holy Spirit.

To recap, we need the Image of Christ, who was a perfect sanctuary where God dwelled to be fulfilled in us so that we may be born again to be a sanctuary for the living God and accept Jesus into our hearts.

Our pursuit to grow into the Image of Christ is called the practice of godliness.

Those that do not practice godliness lacks understanding.

3Some people may contradict our teaching, but these are the wholesome teachings of the Lord Jesus Christ. These teachings promote a godly life. 4Anyone who teaches something different is arrogant and lacks understanding. Such a person has an unhealthy desire to quibble over the meaning of words. This stirs up arguments ending in jealousy, division, slander, and evil suspicions.

1Timothy 6:3-4

6-8. Practice of Godliness

1So now there is no condemnation for those who belong to Christ Jesus. 2And because you belong to him, the power of the life-giving Spirit has freed you from the power of sin that leads to death. 3The law of Moses was unable to save us because of the weakness of our sinful nature. So God did what the law could not do. He sent his own Son in a body like the bodies we sinners have. And in that body God declared an end to sin's control over us by giving his Son as a sacrifice for our sins. 4He did this so that the just requirement of the law would be fully satisfied for us, who no longer follow our sinful nature but instead follow the Spirit.

Romans 8:1-4

16So I say, let the Holy Spirit guide your lives. Then you won't be doing what your sinful nature craves. 17The sinful nature wants to do evil, which is just the opposite of what the Spirit wants. And the Spirit gives us desires that are the opposite of what the sinful nature desires. These two forces are constantly fighting each other, so you are not free to carry out your good intentions. 18But when you are directed by the Spirit, you are not under obligation to the law of Moses. 25Since we are living by the Spirit, let us follow the Spirit's leading in every part of our lives.

Galatians 5:16-18, 25

Practice of godliness is the practice of following and executing the teachings of the Holy Spirit, which is the practice of living by the Law of the Spirit of Life that is in Christ Jesus.

In another words, practice of godliness is live according to the Second Covenant or as a worker of the New Covenant.

Another way of describing practice of godliness is the practice of living according to the ways of the Living God.

If you explain these things to the brothers and sisters, Timothy, you will be a worthy servant of Christ Jesus, one who is nourished by the message of faith and the good teaching you have followed.

1Timothy 4:6

"Worthy servant" means worker of the Living God (c.f. Luke 18:18-19)

"Message of faith" means Word of Jesus that speaks from within us (c.f. Romans 10:6-8), or the voice of God (c.f. John 10:27).

"Good teaching":

I will bless the LORD who guides me; even at night my heart instructs me.

Psalms 16:7

Since only God is truly good (c.f. Luke 18:18-29), "Good teaching" means, to learn from God Himself.

To recap, we become true workers for God when we practice godliness. We will be able to hear the voice of God and learn from Him.

7Do not waste time arguing over godless ideas and old wives' tales. Instead, train yourself to be godly. 8"Physical training is good, but training for godliness is much better, promising benefits in this life and in the life to come." 9This is a trustworthy saying, and everyone should accept it. 10This is why we work hard and continue to struggle, for our hope is in the living God, who is the Savior of all people and particularly of all believers. 11Teach these things and insist that everyone learn them. 12Don't let anyone think less of you because you are young. Be an example to all believers in what you say, in the way you live, in your love, your faith, and your purity. 13Until I get there, focus on reading the Scriptures to the church, encouraging the believers, and teaching them. 14Do not neglect the spiritual gift you received through the prophecy spoken over you when the elders of the church laid their hands on you. 15Give your complete attention to these matters. Throw yourself into your tasks so that everyone will see your progress. 16Keep a close watch on how you live and on your teaching. Stay true to what is right for the sake of your own salvation and the salvation of those who hear you.

1Timothy 4:7-16

Yes, it is true.

Practice of godliness is to live according to the ways of the Living God.

Through our practice of godliness, the Image of Christ can be made complete in us so that we may be born again to become the sanctuary for the Living God. We will then be able to accept Jesus in our hearts.

It is also through the practice of godliness that our faith may grow just as Abraham's faith grew through God's working on (circumcision of) his heart.

How then shall we practice godliness?

Fight the good fight for the true faith. Hold tightly to the eternal life to which God has called you, which you have confessed so well before many witnesses.

1Timothy 6:12

Practice of godliness is a fight for the truth faith. As we know, Satan prowls around like a roaring lion (c.f. 1 Peter 5:8) to interfere with our practice of godliness.

The reason is that without practice of godliness, all of God's plans for us go to ruin.

First, Drink the water that gives eternal life

Practice of godliness is to drink the water that gives eternal life.

In Scriptures:

13Jesus replied, "Anyone who drinks this water will soon become thirsty again. 14But those who drink the water I give will never be thirsty again. It becomes a fresh, bubbling spring within them, giving them eternal life."

John 4:13-14

37On the last day, the climax of the festival, Jesus stood and shouted to the crowds, "Anyone who is thirsty may come to me! 38Anyone who believes in me may come and drink! For the Scriptures declare, `Rivers of living water will flow from his heart.'" 39(When he said "living water," he was speaking of the Spirit, who would be given to everyone believing in him. But the Spirit had not yet been given, because Jesus had not yet entered into his glory.)

John 7:37-39

Practice of godliness to drink through the Holy Spirit the spiritual water that Christ the Rock gives us.

This water is only for the chosen people (c.f. Isaiah 43:19-20), those that know and believe in God (c.f. Isaiah 43:10), and those that know and believe in the Second Covenant that God promised.

First, we must practice looking to Jesus who died on the cross through the Holy Spirit.

To see Jesus is to see His face, glory, and heart. It is to see and recognize how much He loved us and thought of us when He hung on the cross.

Oh, foolish Galatians! Who has cast an evil spell on you? For the meaning of Jesus Christ's death was made as clear to you as if you had seen a picture of his death on the cross.

Galatians 3:1

10"Then I will pour out a spirit of grace and prayer on the family of David and on the people of Jerusalem. They will look on me whom they have pierced and mourn for him as for an only son. They will grieve bitterly for him as for a firstborn son who has died.
11The sorrow and mourning in Jerusalem on that day will be like the great mourning for Hadad-rimmon in the valley of Megiddo. 12"All Israel will mourn, each clan by itself, and with the husbands separate from their wives. The clan of David will mourn alone, as will the clan of Nathan, 13the clan of Levi, and the clan of Shimei. 14Each of the surviving clans from Judah will mourn separately, and with the husbands separate from their wives. 13:1"On that day a fountain will be opened for the dynasty of David and for the people of Jerusalem, a fountain to cleanse them from all their sins and impurity.
2"And on that day," says the Lord of Heaven's Armies, "I will erase idol worship throughout the land, so that even the names of the idols will be forgotten. I will remove from the land both the false prophets and the spirit of impurity that came with them.

Zechariah 12:10-14, 13:1-2

When we look to the cross, to Jesus the Rock who died for us, through the Holy Spirit, the spiritual water (love) flows out from Him. We begin to recognize His great love for us.

And Jesus Christ was revealed as God's Son by his baptism in water and by shedding his blood on the cross - not by water only, but by water and blood. And the Spirit, who is truth, confirms it with his testimony.

1John 5:6

As the Holy Spirit teaches us and shows us Jesus who died on the cross:

5And this hope will not lead to disappointment. For we know how dearly God loves us, because he has given us the Holy Spirit to fill our hearts with his love. 6When we were utterly helpless, Christ came at just the right time and died for us sinners. 7Now, most people would not be willing to die for an upright person, though someone might perhaps be willing to die for a person who is especially good. 8But God showed his great love for us by sending Christ to die for us while we were still sinners.

Romans 5:5-8

We know what real love is because Jesus gave up his life for us. So we also ought to give up our lives for our brothers and sisters.

1John 3:16

9God showed how much he loved us by sending his one and only Son into the world so that we might have eternal life through him. 10This is real love - not that we loved God, but that he loved us and sent his Son as a sacrifice to take away our sins.

1John 4:9-10

As the Scripture says in verses above, the Holy Spirit can show us Jesus who died for us on the cross; this is not through our physical eyes. When we see Him that way, spiritual water, His love, flows out and saturates our hearts. Our hearts would overflow with His love and we would have the heart of God that enables us to love God and others wholeheartedly.

Let us learn from the Holy Spirit and live in faith in Jesus. When we do, this spiritual water (love) will flow out of us (c.f. Exodus 17:1-7).

5The purpose of my instruction is that all believers would be filled with love that comes from a pure heart, a clear conscience, and genuine faith. 6But some people have missed this whole point. They have turned away from these things and spend their time in meaningless discussions.

1Timothy 1:5-6

Second, when we look through the Spirit to Jesus who sits on the right hand of God, the spiritual water (love) will flow

We do this by keeping our eyes on Jesus, the champion who initiates and perfects our faith. Because of the joy awaiting him, he endured the cross, disregarding its shame. Now he is seated in the place of honor beside God's throne.

Hebrews 12:2

8On that day life-giving waters will flow out from Jerusalem, half toward the Dead Sea and half toward the Mediterranean, flowing continuously in both summer and winter. 9And the Lord will be king over all the earth. On that day there will be one Lord - his name alone will be worshiped. 11And Jerusalem will be filled, safe at last, never again to be cursed and destroyed.

Zechariah 14:8-9, 11

When we, through the Holy Spirit, look to Jesus the Rock who sits on the right hand of God, the spiritual water will flow and saturate our hearts. The result would be our hearts becoming holy (c.f. Numbers 20:2-13). God the King who has authority over all heaven and earth will give us holy hearts so that He may work through us.

To recap, the practice of godliness is to learn from the Holy Spirit and look to Christ the Rock. When we do, spiritual water (love) flows. We must practice drinking this water, and through this practice, we grow into the Image of Christ.

To drink this water means to drink the Living Water, which means to drink the love of Living Jesus.

Through the Holy Spirit, we must look to the heart of Jesus who came to earth and died on the cross so that we may drink (realize) the love of Living Jesus.

1 Corinthians 2:6-9 speaks of Jesus' death on the cross:

6Yet when I am among mature believers, I do speak with words of wisdom, but not the kind of wisdom that belongs to this world or to the rulers of this world, who are soon forgotten. 7No, the wisdom we speak of is the mystery of God - his plan that was previously hidden, even though he made it for our ultimate glory before the world began. 8But the rulers of this world have not understood it; if they had, they would not have crucified our glorious Lord. 9That is what the Scriptures mean when they say, "No eye has seen, no ear has heard, and no mind has imagined what God has prepared for those who love him."

1Corinthians 2:6-9

As the verses above reveal, Jesus' death on the cross was the hidden secret that God had prepared for those that love Him.

But it was to us that God revealed these things by his Spirit. For his Spirit searches out everything and shows us God's deep secrets.

1Corinthians 2:10

Holy Spirit teaches us about Jesus who died on the cross and enables us to see the glory (face, heart) of Jesus.

11No one can know a person's thoughts except that person's own spirit, and no one can know God's thoughts except God's own Spirit. 12And we have received God's Spirit (not the world's spirit), so we can know the wonderful things God has freely given us.

1Corinthians 2:11-12

We can understand the amazing heart of God only through the Holy Spirit.

When we tell you these things, we do not use words that come from human wisdom. Instead, we speak words given to us by the Spirit, using the Spirit's words to explain spiritual truths.

1Corinthians 2:13

Only the Holy Spirit is able to teach and show us Jesus' death on the cross.

14But people who aren't spiritual can't receive these truths from God's Spirit. It all sounds foolish to them and they can't understand it, for only those who are spiritual can understand what the Spirit means. 15Those who are spiritual can evaluate all things, but they themselves cannot be evaluated by others. 16For, "Who can know the LORD's thoughts? Who knows enough to teach him?" But we understand these things, for we have the mind of Christ.

1Corinthians 2:14-16

Practice of godliness is to see and realize the heart of Living Jesus through the Holy Spirit. Through this practice, we grow into and secure the heart (Image) of Christ.

To reiterate:

Practice of godliness is to provide the heart of Christ that the Holy Spirit gives to our:

- Wives
- Husbands
- Neighbors
- Enemies

You see, his faith and his actions worked together. His actions made his faith complete.
James 2:22

Through this practice, the seed of Life of Jesus that is planted in us may grow into the Image of God as we drink the spiritual water (love). When we attain His image, we are reborn as a sanctuary for God (heaven, Kingdom of God).

Note: To be *born again with the life that comes from God* or to *accept Jesus* means the same.

11And this is what God has testified: He has given us eternal life, and this life is in his Son. 12Whoever has the Son has life; whoever does not have God's Son does not have life.
1John 5:11-12

26Jesus also said, "The Kingdom of God is like a farmer who scatters seed on the ground. 27Night and day, while he's asleep or awake, the seed sprouts and grows, but he does not understand how it happens. 28The earth produces the crops on its own. First a leaf blade pushes through, then the heads of wheat are formed, and finally the grain ripens. 29And as soon as the grain is ready, the farmer comes and harvests it with a sickle, for the harvest time has come."
Mark 4:26-29

In this way, the seeds in us must grow to bear crops (Image of Christ).

Up until what point should we grow to attain the Image of Christ? And what does this crop look like?

30Jesus said, "How can I describe the Kingdom of God? What story should I use to illustrate it? 31It is like a mustard seed planted in the ground. It is the smallest of all seeds, 32but it becomes the largest of all garden plants; it grows long branches, and birds can make nests in its shade."

Mark 4:30-32

As the verses above say, the birds are enemies that try to eat the seeds. However, we must grow until we can embrace our enemies with the vast love (heart) of Christ. When we are fully grown, we can see the Word of God in effect.

12Fight the good fight for the true faith. Hold tightly to the eternal life to which God has called you, which you have confessed so well before many witnesses. 13And I charge you before God, who gives life to all, and before Christ Jesus, who gave a good testimony before Pontius Pilate, 14that you obey this command without wavering. Then no one can find fault with you from now until our Lord Jesus Christ comes again. 15For at just the right time Christ will be revealed from heaven by the blessed and only almighty God, the King of all kings and Lord of all lords.

1Timothy 6:12-15

As verse 14 says, we must continue to grow until Jesus returns. Then at the right time (v. 15), Christ will be revealed as He speaks from within us (c.f. Deuteronomy 30:6, 11-14, Romans 10:6-8).

9But some became stubborn, rejecting his message and publicly speaking against the Way. So Paul left the synagogue and took the believers with him. Then he held daily discussions at the lecture hall of Tyrannus. 10This went on for the next two years, so that people throughout the province of Asia—both Jews and Greeks—heard the word of the Lord.

Acts 19:9-10

I would like to give a sincere apology to my readers.

I have run several seminars for pastors to teach on the Law of the Spirit of Life.

I was disappointed to see many pastors either preaching the "other" gospel or returning to it. I could not understand the cause of those that returned to the death-producing message.

I know the reason now.

If someone was to study the true Gospel of Jesus, the one and only true Gospel, it may take at most 30 days to study it in detail.

However, Jesus taught His disciples for three years.

In another place, we can see disciples being educated for one year (at Antioch) and at another for two years (at Ephesus). The Word of God was not apparent to them until end of that training.

Life takes some time to grow.

Unfortunately, if a person does not grow until s/he reaches the Image of Christ, s/he will be as a baby being aborted within his/her mother's womb.

However, the opposite extreme is also true. Can a child in the mother's womb grow faster by eating more or taking some special pills?

No.

It is the same for our growth.

I had thought that a person that lacks understanding can attend a seminar that focuses on special topics to learn the materials within a few weeks. That was a lack in my understanding.

They may think they understand the message when they are listening to it, but their hearts may be the footpath, rocky soil, or thorns.

It takes time to practice of godliness, which is similar to process of re-chewing the cud (c.f. Leviticus 11:1-8, Deuteronomy 14:3-8). It is through that process that a person comes to realization and attains the Image of Christ.

During this time, they are to practice and train themselves in loving their neighbors with the love that God provides them.

Through the practice of godliness, which is similar to re-chewing of the cud, people must grow until they are reborn as heaven (c.f. 1 Corinthians 4:15). This timeline for growth is different for every believer.

Now I realize why the Bible says those that do not practice godliness lack understanding (c.f. 1 Timothy 6:3-4).

To summarize, the practice of godliness is the practice of giving our neighbors the heart (love) that Christ gives us as we drink the overflowing spiritual water that is given to us when we look to our Christ the Rock through the Holy Spirit.

This is called the "New Covenant."

34So now I am giving you a new commandment: Love each other. Just as I have loved you, you should love each other. 35Your love for one another will prove to the world that you are my disciples."

John 13:34-35

When someone says s/he has faith, but does not love his/her brothers (parents, spouse, neighbors), then s/he is not someone who believes in the New Covenant.

> *So now we can tell who are children of God and who are children of the devil. Anyone who does not live righteously and does not love other believers does not belong to God.*
> *1John 3:10*

> *19We love each other because he loved us first. 20If someone says, "I love God," but hates a Christian brother or sister, that person is a liar; for if we don't love people we can see, how can we love God, whom we cannot see? 21And he has given us this command: Those who love God must also love their Christian brothers and sisters.*
> *1John 4:19-21*

6-9. Precious Faith

This letter is from Simon Peter, a slave and apostle of Jesus Christ. I am writing to you who share the same precious faith we have. This faith was given to you because of the justice and fairness of Jesus Christ, our God and Savior.

2Peter 1:1

Apostle Peter says he has the "precious faith."

What kind of faith do you think Peter had?

We know the person who is "precious" is Jesus Christ (c.f. 1 Peter 2:4, 6).

Jesus, who is precious, shed His precious blood in order to fulfill the New Covenant.

It was the precious blood of Christ, the sinless, spotless Lamb of God.

1Peter 1:19

In the same way, he took the cup of wine after supper, saying, "This cup is the new Covenant between God and his people—an agreement confirmed with my blood. Do this to remember me as often as you drink it."

1Corinthians 11:25

Then, what is this precious faith?

Precious faith is the faith in the New Covenant that God had sworn to accomplish. This is because precious Jesus accomplished this Covenant by shedding His precious blood.

Precious faith is the belief in the Precious Promise. This faith is something that can only come from God.

Jesus asks his disciples near Caesarea, Philippi:

Then he asked them, "But who do you say I am?"

Matthew 16:15

Peter responds:

Simon Peter answered, "You are the Messiah, the Son of the living God."

Matthew 16:16

The "Son of God" is mentioned here because Peter recognized that Jesus is the Christ that came from the lineage of Abraham and David (the Son) that has come to fulfill the Second (New) Covenant.

Jesus replied, "You are blessed, Simon son of John, because my Father in heaven has revealed this to you. You did not learn this from any human being.
Matthew 16:17

This faith can only be attained through teachings of the Holy Spirit whom God has sent to us (c.f. 1 Corinthians 12:3).

That is why in 1 Peter 1:1 it says "you who share the same precious faith we have."

2May God give you more and more grace and peace as you grow in your knowledge of God and Jesus our Lord. 3By his divine power, God has given us everything we need for living a godly life. We have received all of this by coming to know him, the one who called us to himself by means of his marvelous glory and excellence.
2Peter 1:2-3

The verse above says, "God will give" … "as you grow in your knowledge of God and Jesus our Lord." This means that we will receive when we come to know the work that our One True God and Jesus Christ, whom He sent, is doing.

We will receive when we come to know that the Christ, the Son of God, will accomplish the Second Covenant, which began from the Covenant of Circumcision that God had sworn to bring to fruition.

This faith is what we call the *precious faith*, and it is something that only God can give.

As we come to know the work that God is doing and live with this precious faith, God the Father, Son and Holy Spirit will solidify that faith and give us grace, peace, and everything we need for living a godly life.

And because of his glory and excellence, he has given us great and precious promises. These are the promises that enable you to share his divine nature and escape the world's corruption caused by human desires.
2Peter 1:4

"Great and precious promises" is referring to the Covenant of Circumcision, which is now called the Second (New) Covenant.

5In view of all this, make every effort to respond to God's promises. Supplement your faith with a generous provision of moral excellence, and moral excellence with knowledge, 6and knowledge with self-control, and self-control with patient endurance, and patient endurance with godliness, 7and godliness with brotherly affection, and brotherly affection with love for everyone. 10So, dear brothers and sisters, work hard to prove that you really are among those God has called and chosen. Do these things, and you will never fall away. 11Then God will give you a grand entrance into the eternal Kingdom of our Lord and Savior Jesus Christ.

2Peter 1:5-7, 10-11

Apostle Peter confesses with certainty that Jesus will always be with us when we believe in the precious promise, the Second (New) Covenant. Our faith in this promise will cause us to live loving others with the mind of Christ that the Holy Spirit gives us.

Apostle Peter also confesses soon before his death:

12Therefore, I will always remind you about these things - even though you already know them and are standing firm in the truth you have been taught. 13And it is only right that I should keep on reminding you as long as I live. 14For our Lord Jesus Christ has shown me that I must soon leave this earthly life,

2Peter 1:12-14

Apostle Peter knew about his pending death, and this is why he was pressing to share this truth:

15so I will work hard to make sure you always remember these things after I am gone. 16For we were not making up clever stories when we told you about the powerful coming of our Lord Jesus Christ. We saw his majestic splendor with our own eyes 17when he received honor and glory from God the Father. The voice from the majestic glory of God said to him, "This is my dearly loved Son, who brings me great joy." 18We ourselves heard that voice from heaven when we were with him on the holy mountain.

2Peter 1:15-18

The reason that Apostle Peter confesses he was certain he heard the voice of God at the Transfiguration was that He wanted to share the following words before he died. He wanted to share these words to those with the precious faith, those that spread the love of Christ through the Holy Spirit (c.f. 2 Peter 1:4-7). He wanted to share this:

Because of that experience, we have even greater confidence in the message proclaimed by the prophets. You must pay close attention to what they wrote, for their words are like a lamp shining in a dark place - until the Day dawns, and Christ the Morning Star shines in your hearts.

2Peter 1:19

More clear than the voice Apostle Peter heard at the Transfiguration is the voice of God who speaks to us from within us.

We can hear God's voice because of the Precious Faith, which can now be called the Precious Covenant, or the Second (New) Covenant (c.f. Deuteronomy 30:6-14).

6"The LORD your God will change your heart and the hearts of all your descendants, so that you will love him with all your heart and soul and so you may live! 12It is not kept in heaven, so distant that you must ask, 'Who will go up to heaven and bring it down so we can hear it and obey?' 13It is not kept beyond the sea, so far away that you must ask, 'Who will cross the sea to bring it to us so we can hear it and obey?' 14No, the message is very close at hand; it is on your lips and in your heart so that you can obey it.

Deuteronomy 30:6, 12-14

Children of God, those that are born again with the life that comes from God, ought to hear and follow Him as His sheep as He speaks from within them.

My sheep listen to my voice; I know them, and they follow me.

John 10:27

I apologize for not being able to specify exactly how to hear the voice of God. It is my limits of expression that prevent me from delivering them through words.

However, we know with certainty that we must hear the voice of God.

22Moses said, 'The LORD your God will raise up for you a Prophet like me from among your own people. Listen carefully to everything he tells you.' 23Then Moses said, 'Anyone who will not listen to that Prophet will be completely cut off from God's people.'

Acts 3:22-23

The "Prophet" mentioned in the verse above is referring to Jesus Christ (c.f. Romans 10:6-8)

Starting with Samuel, every prophet spoke about what is happening today.

Acts 3:24

And the seeds that fell on the good soil represent honest, good-hearted people who hear God's word, cling to it, and patiently produce a huge harvest.

Luke 8:15

We can hear the voice of God because Christ the Son came to us through the Holy Spirit to fulfill the Covenant of Circumcision, which is now called the Second (New) Covenant, which the Father God had sworn to accomplish.

6-10. The Lord's Supper

The Lord's Supper was a meal that Jesus had with His disciples on the night before Jesus was captured to be hung on the cross (c.f. Matthew 26:17-30, Mark 14:22-42, Luke 22:14-23).

During this event, Jesus shared with His disciples His reason and purpose for coming to earth.

Pointing to one of several references to this event:

23For I pass on to you what I received from the Lord himself. On the night when he was betrayed, the Lord Jesus took some bread 24and gave thanks to God for it. Then he broke it in pieces and said, "This is my body, which is given for you. Do this to remember me."

1Corinthians 11:23-24

This means that whenever we eat, we ought to remember that it was to make our bodies into His sanctuary (collectively the Church) that he died for us.

In the same way, he took the cup of wine after supper, saying, "This cup is the new Covenant between God and his people—an agreement confirmed with my blood. Do this to remember me as often as you drink it."

1Corinthians 11:25

Whenever we drink, we ought to remember that Jesus shed blood on the cross and died in order to fulfill the New Covenant that the Father God swore to accomplish.

For every time you eat this bread and drink this cup, you are announcing the Lord's death until he comes again.

1Corinthians 11:26

This verse reiterates that whenever we eat or drink, we ought to recall that Jesus made our bodies as a sanctuary for Him (collectively, the Church) through His death by fulfilling the New Covenant that Father God swore to accomplish.

Saying this, he washed the feet of His disciples:

6When Jesus came to Simon Peter, Peter said to him, "Lord, are you going to wash my feet?" 7Jesus replied, "You don't understand now what I am doing, but someday you will." 8"No," Peter protested, "you will never ever wash my feet!" Jesus replied, "Unless I wash you, you won't belong to me." 9Simon Peter exclaimed, "Then wash my hands and head as well, Lord, not just my feet!" 10Jesus replied, "A person who has bathed all over does not need to wash, except for the feet, to be entirely clean. And you disciples are clean, but not all of you." 14And since I, your Lord and Teacher, have washed your feet, you ought to wash each other's feet. 15I have given you an example to follow. Do as I have done to you. 16I tell you the truth, slaves are not greater than their master. Nor is the messenger more important than the one who sends the message. 17Now that you know these things, God will bless you for doing them. 20I tell you the truth, anyone who welcomes my messenger is welcoming me, and anyone who welcomes me is welcoming the Father who sent me.

John 13:6-10, 14-17, 20

Jesus says these things to His disciples just before they were sent out to share the Gospel.

Why did He target the feet?

Reminder: Romans 10:6-8 is equivalent to Second Covenant (c.f. Deuteronomy 30:11-14)

13For "Everyone who calls on the name of the LORD will be saved." 14But how can they call on him to save them unless they believe in him? And how can they believe in him if they have never heard about him? And how can they hear about him unless someone tells them? 15And how will anyone go and tell them without being sent? That is why the Scriptures say, "How beautiful are the feet of messengers who bring good news!"

Romans 10:13-15

The feet refers to the feet of the people that share the Second (New) Covenant.

Jesus continues to wash the feet of those that share the Second (New) Covenant even today.

How beautiful upon the mountains are the feet of him who brings good news, who proclaims peace, who brings glad tidings of good things, who proclaims salvation, who says to Zion, "Your God reigns!"

Isaiah 52:7 NKJV

Since Jesus shed His blood in order to fulfil the New Covenant that God had sworn to accomplish:

In the same way, he took the cup of wine after supper, saying, "This cup is the new Covenant between God and his people—an agreement confirmed with my blood. Do this to remember me as often as you drink it."

1Corinthians 11:25

The blood of Jesus refers to the New Covenant in Scriptures.

So guard yourselves and God's people. Feed and shepherd God's flock - his church, purchased with his own blood - over which the Holy Spirit has appointed you as elders.
Acts 20:28

The church Jesus purchased with His own blood refers to His fulfillment of the New Covenant. He shed His blood so that we may become the body of Christ, the church, and place Jesus as our head and be in Him. As a result, we would be able to have the heart He gives and live in His Name (c.f. Deuteronomy 30:6, 11-14).

Just think how much more the blood of Christ will purify our consciences from sinful deeds so that we can worship the living God. For by the power of the eternal Spirit, Christ offered himself to God as a perfect sacrifice for our sins.
Hebrews 9:14

Since Jesus fulfilled the New Covenant by shedding His blood for us, the Holy Spirit gives us the heart of Christ as we are in Christ, and that enables us to serve the Living God.

18For you know that God paid a ransom to save you from the empty life you inherited from your ancestors. And the ransom he paid was not mere gold or silver. 19It was the precious blood of Christ, the sinless, spotless Lamb of God.
1Peter 1:18-19

"The empty life you inherited from your ancestors" refers to seeking to live under the Law of Moses by following the Word of God (written code) on our own accords to consider ourselves righteous; however, as we have seen in prior chapters, no one can be considered righteous, holy, or good by our acts.

We can be righteous, holy, and good only through Jesus who fulfilled the New Covenant by shedding His blood. Now, we can live in Christ, place Him as our head, and live with the heart He gives us.

But if we are living in the light, as God is in the light, then we have fellowship with each other, and the blood of Jesus, his Son, cleanses us from all sin.
1John 1:7

Since Jesus fulfilled the New Covenant by shedding His blood for us, we can live in Christ, place Him as our head, and stay away from sin because He gives us His heart.

> *and from Jesus Christ. He is the faithful witness to these things, the first to rise from the dead, and the ruler of all the kings of the world. All glory to him who loves us and has freed us from our sins by shedding his blood for us.*
>
> *Revelation 1:5*

"Shedding of His blood" holds the same meaning as prior verses, and:

> *and made us to be a kingdom, priests serving his God and Father, to him be glory and dominion forever and ever. Amen.*
>
> *Revelation 1:6 (NRSV)*

Even His making us His Kingdom (heaven) is because Jesus fulfilled the New Covenant by shedding His blood. As a result, we can be born again and become the Kingdom of God.

> *9And they sang a new song with these words: "You are worthy to take the scroll and break its seals and open it. For you were slaughtered, and your blood has ransomed people for God from every tribe and language and people and nation. 10And you have caused them to become a Kingdom of priests for our God. And they will reign on the earth."*
>
> *Revelation 5:9-10*

Above verses also give us the same message.

Summarizing, it is because of the fulfillment of the New Covenant that:

- We can be the Church (c.f. Acts 20:28)
- We can serve God with a clean heart (c.f. Hebrews 9:14)
- We can be free from the empty ways of the past (c.f. 1 Peter 1:18)
- We can be forgiven and cleansed from our sins (c.f. 1 John 1:7)
- We can be completely free from captivity of sin (c.f. Revelations 1:5)
- We can live as the Kingdom of God (Heaven) (c.f Revelations 1:6)
- We can reign on earth as kings (c.f. Revelations 5:9-10)

To conclude:

There is only one Covenant God has made. It was originally called the Original Covenant, then over time, it became more elaborated and received the following names:

- Covenant of Circumcision

- Eternal Covenant
- Second Covenant
- New Covenant

This is the one and only Covenant that God has made, and no other promises of God exists.

To live in the will of the Father in heaven means to live with faith that the Holy Spirit through Christ will fulfill the New Covenant, which God has sworn to accomplish, in us.

21"Not everyone who calls out to me, `Lord! Lord!' will enter the Kingdom of Heaven. Only those who actually do the will of my Father in heaven will enter. 22On judgment day many will say to me, `Lord! Lord! We prophesied in your name and cast out demons in your name and performed many miracles in your name.' 23But I will reply, `I never knew you. Get away from me, you who break God's laws.'

Matthew 7:21-23

The people mentioned in the verses above did not know the Second (New) Covenant that God has sworn to accomplish through the Christ His Son that He sent, which was fulfilled this way:

9Then he said, "Look, I have come to do your will." He cancels the first Covenant in order to put the second into effect. 10For God's will was for us to be made holy by the sacrifice of the body of Jesus Christ, once for all time.

Hebrews 10:9-10

Returning to the main passage:

24"Anyone who listens to my teaching and follows it is wise, like a person who builds a house on solid rock. 25Though the rain comes in torrents and the floodwaters rise and the winds beat against that house, it won't collapse because it is built on bedrock. 26But anyone who hears my teaching and doesn't obey it is foolish, like a person who builds a house on sand. 27When the rains and floods come and the winds beat against that house, it will collapse with a mighty crash."

Matthew 7:24-27

The people mentioned in Matthew 7:21-23 did not drink the spiritual water from Christ the Rock.

Conclusion

Before all eternity, God planned through Christ to bear children that live like Jesus (the eldest son) and to give them the treasured things in heaven as an inheritance (c.f. 1 Peter 1:3-4, Ephesians 3:9-12).

His plan was to enable us to eat from the Tree of Life so that we may live in Christ (c.f. 1 John 5:11-12), place Christ as our head (c.f. 1 Corinthians 11:3), have the heart of Christ that He gives, and Live in the Name of Jesus. God created people in the image of God and led them through the Garden of Eden so that He may fulfill this plan.

However, Adam and Eve turned away from God. As a result, all people born from Adam's seed would possess Satan's nature. Anyone that is of Satan would be eternally damned to go with him to hell, a place of agony specifically made for him (c.f. Matthew 25:41).

However, God is love.

He established a way that sinners can be saved.

This plan is called the "Law of Faith."

27Where is boasting then? It is excluded. By what law? Of works? No, but by the law of faith. 28Therefore we conclude that a man is justified by faith apart from the deeds of the law.

Romans 3:27-28 NKJV

God first made the promise, and He would fulfill this promise to anyone that believed in it – that was God's plan of salvation.

In order to save sinners, the first promise is called the Original Covenant, and that is the Original Gospel (c.f. Genesis 3:15, 21).

This was the promise God had intended to accomplish in the Garden of Eden.

The Gospel was this promise that would enable us to live as heaven (the Kingdom of God).

15And I will cause hostility between you and the woman, and between your offspring and her offspring. He will strike your head, and you will strike his heel." 21And the LORD God made clothing from animal skins for Adam and his wife.

Genesis 3:15, 21

To Abraham, this promise was called the Covenant of Circumcision; to Isaac, this promise was called Eternal Covenant; and to Jacob (Israel), this promise was called the Second Covenant; and it is now known as the New Covenant.

Though they were given different names, this is one same Covenant of God. Since each of them believed in the promises of God, God responded by sending His Son, the Christ (c.f. Galatians 3:16), so that He may fulfill the Original Covenant (promise), that is, to accomplish the promise of the Gospel that He swore to do.

25And now that the way of faith has come, we no longer need the law as our guardian. 26For you are all children of God through faith in Christ Jesus. 27And all who have been united with Christ in baptism have put on Christ, like putting on new clothes.
Galatians 3:25-27

To say this differently:

God established only one Covenant, the Second (New) Covenant, which is the Gospel that Jesus taught. There was no other promise from God other than this. This is why He sent His Son to fulfill this promise.

For that reason, anyone that shares any other message are people that have not been sent from God. They are people who believe in another god, an incorrect faith (c.f. Deuteronomy 29:22-26).

Yes.

We must now live like Jesus and live as heaven looking at the glory (heart) of God through the Holy Spirit. We must live with the heart He gives us, that is, in the Name of Jesus.

Those who say they live in God should live their lives as Jesus did.
1John 2:6

16For I am not ashamed of this Good News about Christ. It is the power of God at work, saving everyone who believes-the Jew first and also the Gentile. 17<u>This Good News tells us how God makes us right in his sight.</u> This is accomplished from start to finish by faith. As the Scriptures say, "It is through faith that a righteous person has life."
Romans 1:16-17

Verse 17 tells us the Good News tells us how we may be right in His sight (also see 1 Corinthians 1:30).

We must know this with certainty:

If we do not know and believe that Jesus came as our mediator to fulfill the Second (New) Covenant, then Jesus will say He does not know us on that day.

The reason is that He fulfills the Covenant to those that believe in the Second (New) Covenant and considers them as children of the promise like Isaac (c.f. Galatians 4:28)

Nonetheless, many people today do not know about this Covenant that God has sworn to accomplish.

I would like to reiterate this before concluding this book:

The reason and purpose for which Jesus died on the cross is:

9Then he said, "Look, I have come to do your will." He cancels the first Covenant in order to put the second into effect. 10For God's will was for us to be made holy by the sacrifice of the body of Jesus Christ, once for all time.

Hebrews 10:9-10

The reason and purpose for why Jesus resurrected from the dead is:

32"And now we are here to bring you this Good News. The promise was made to our ancestors, 33and God has now fulfilled it for us, their descendants, by raising Jesus. This is what the second psalm says about Jesus: `You are my Son Today I have become your Father.'

Acts 13:32-33

The reason and purpose for why Jesus came to earth to die and to live again is to fulfill the Second (New) Covenant.

After the resurrection, Jesus ascended into heaven. This too was to fulfill the Second (New) Covenant:

11So Christ has now become the High Priest over all the good things that have come. He has entered that greater, more perfect Tabernacle in heaven, which was not made by human hands and is not part of this created world. 12With his own blood - not the blood of goats and calves - he entered the Most Holy Place once for all time and secured our redemption forever. 15That is why he is the one who mediates a new Covenant between God and people, so that all who are called can receive the eternal inheritance God has promised them. For Christ died to set them free from the penalty of the sins they had committed under that first Covenant.

Hebrews 9:11-12, 15

Jesus then returned to us as the Holy Spirit. This too was to fulfill the Second (New) Covenant:

The LORD your God will change your heart and the hearts of all your descendants, so that you will love him with all your heart and soul and so you may live!
Deuteronomy 30:6

6But the righteousness of faith speaks in this way, "Do not say in your heart, 'Who will ascend into heaven?'" (that is, to bring Christ down from above) 7or, " 'Who will descend into the abyss?' " (that is, to bring Christ up from the dead). 8But what does it say? "The word is near you, in your mouth and in your heart" (that is, the word of faith which we preach):
Romans 10:6-8 NKJV

Note: the passage in Romans 10:6-8 is equivalent to Deuteronomy 30:11-14, which refers to the Second Covenant.

In that way, as He promised through the Second Covenant, He came to us in the Holy Spirit so that we may be born again with the life that comes from God. As a result, we may live as heaven and hear Him as He speaks to us from within us.

He enables us to be reborn as heaven and calls us His sanctuary. This is to fulfill the Second Covenant.

7The LORD your God will inflict all these curses on your enemies and on those who hate and persecute you. 8Then you will again obey the LORD and keep all his commands that I am giving you today. 9"The LORD your God will then make you successful in everything you do. He will give you many children and numerous livestock, and he will cause your fields to produce abundant harvests, for the LORD will again delight in being good to you as he was to your ancestors. 10The LORD your God will delight in you if you obey his voice and keep the commands and decrees written in this Book of Instruction, and if you turn to the LORD your God with all your heart and soul.
Deuteronomy 30:7-10

In the passage above, obeying the Lord and keeping His commandments can only be kept with the heart of Jesus that only He can give, which is given to us through the Holy Spirit.

In that way, Jesus' life on earth, death, resurrection, ascension, and His return through the Holy Spirit, our rebirth, and His living in us is to fulfill the Second (New) Covenant in us.

For that reason, anyone that does not know this truth is a false prophet, a person that is not of Christ.

I give thanks to God who has guided us to this point.

Even as I reflect on the message of this book, I am reminded of God's unending grace and love toward us.

I cried out to God because God had responded to prayers of a pastor's wife. It was then that God commanded me to elaborate on the Gospel. I simply obeyed and did it.

I recognize there may be many grammatical errors and lacks in expression. I apologize once again for my lacking.

However, there are so much to be shared within the Bible.

I again apologize if I could not explain and elaborate fully.

If time permits for you, we may be able to look to the face of God and share life and joy together when you join us at "Chun Jae Mo." (Chun Jae Mo is the missionary organization that the author has founded where he teaches about the Gospel that Jesus taught, find out more at http://www.chunjaemo.com).

Thank you.

We love you in Christ.

To repeat one more time:

There is no other promise that God the Father, Son, and Holy Spirit made and fulfilled other than the New Covenant.

… and it will be fulfilled in anyone who believes.

April 14, 2017

Pastor Sang Kwang Lee

Appendices

Introduction to the Appendices:

When reading this for the first time, it may seem confusing, especially because different words are interchanged throughout the text. To make it easier for you, the reader, I produced summary sheets that can be used as quick reference to help as a refresher.

First includes summary of main key points (A-1).

Second is a glossary to help with key words used in the text (A-2).

Finally, since the author progressively added words that meant the same in preceding chapters, an exhaustive list, as used in this book was compiled (A-3).

-Dr. Sang Sur

A-1. Quick Look Sheets

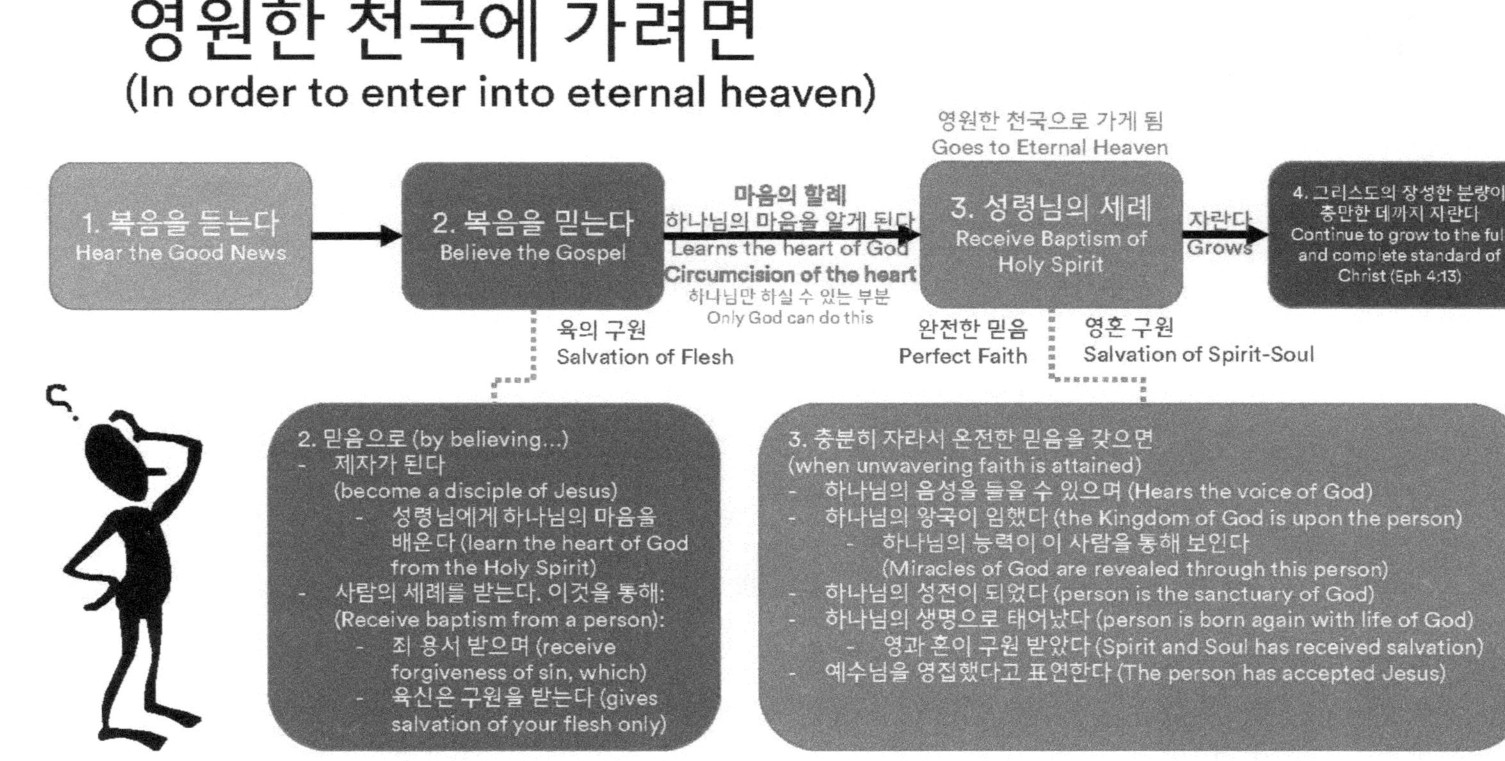
영원한 천국에 가려면
(In order to enter into eternal heaven)
1. 복음을 듣는다
Hear the Good News
2. 복음을 믿는다
Believe the Gospel
마음의 할례
하나님의 마음을 알게 된다
Learns the heart of God
Circumcision of the heart
하나님만 하실 수 있는 부분
Only God can do this
영원한 천국으로 가게 됨
Goes to Eternal Heaven
3. 성령님의 세례
Receive Baptism of Holy Spirit
자란다
Grows
4. 그리스도의 장성한 분량이 충만한 데까지 자란다
Continue to grow to the full and complete standard of Christ (Eph 4:13)
육의 구원
Salvation of Flesh
완전한 믿음
Perfect Faith
영혼 구원
Salvation of Spirit-Soul
2. 믿음으로 (by believing...)
- 제자가 된다
(become a disciple of Jesus)
- 성령님에게 하나님의 마음을 배운다 (learn the heart of God from the Holy Spirit)
- 사람의 세례를 받는다. 이것을 통해:
(Receive baptism from a person):
- 죄 용서 받으며 (receive forgiveness of sin, which)
- 육신은 구원을 받는다 (gives salvation of your flesh only)
3. 충분히 자라서 온전한 믿음을 갖으면
(when unwavering faith is attained)
- 하나님의 음성을 들을 수 있으며 (Hears the voice of God)
- 하나님의 왕국이 임했다 (the Kingdom of God is upon the person)
- 하나님의 능력이 이 사람을 통해 보인다
(Miracles of God are revealed through this person)
- 하나님의 성전이 되었다 (person is the sanctuary of God)
- 하나님의 생명으로 태어났다 (person is born again with life of God)
- 영과 혼이 구원 받았다 (Spirit and Soul has received salvation)
- 예수님을 영접했다고 표현한다 (The person has accepted Jesus)

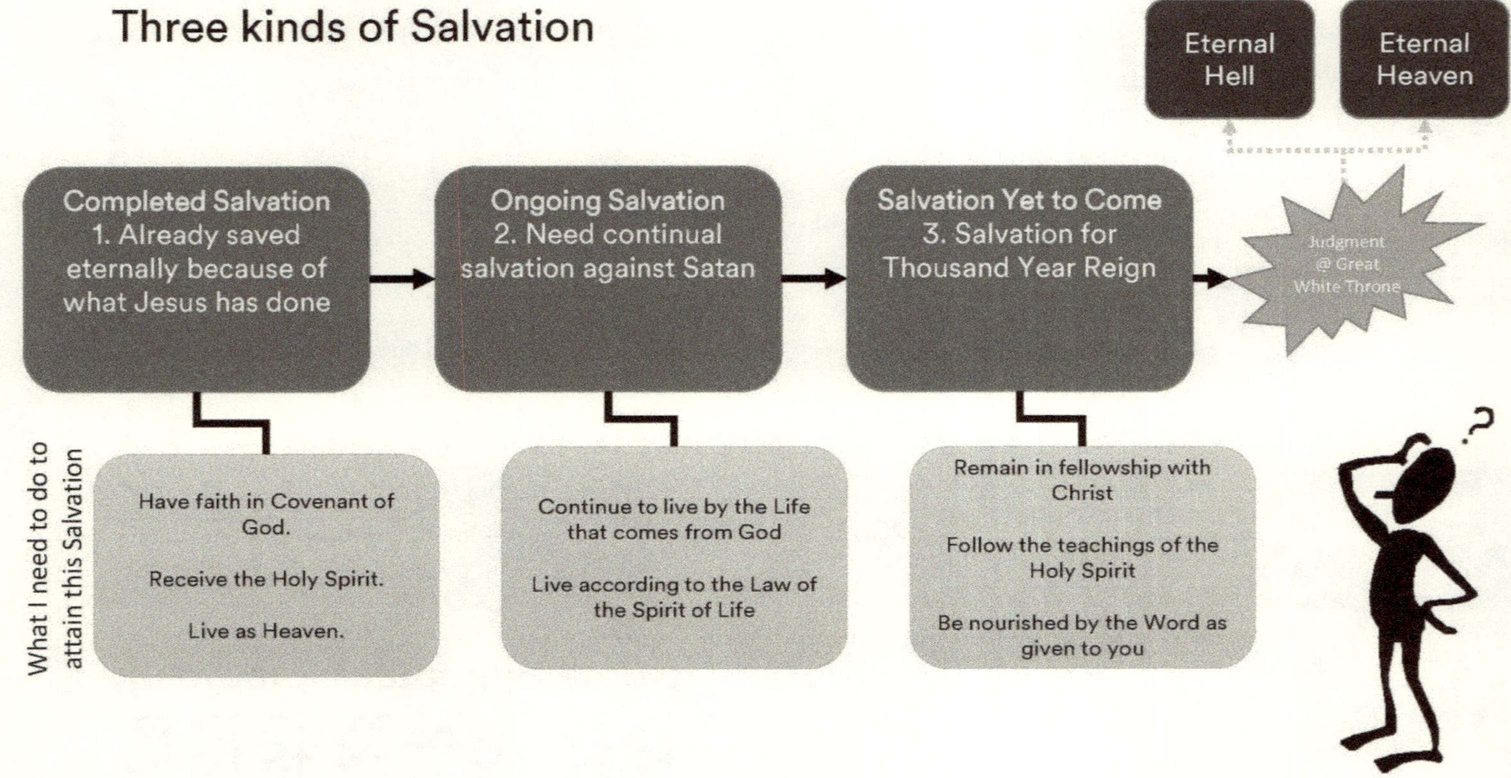
Three kinds of Salvation
Eternal Hell
Eternal Heaven
Completed Salvation
1. Already saved eternally because of what Jesus has done
Ongoing Salvation
2. Need continual salvation against Satan
Salvation Yet to Come
3. Salvation for Thousand Year Reign
Judgment @ Great White Throne
What I need to do to attain this Salvation
Have faith in Covenant of God.
Receive the Holy Spirit.
Live as Heaven.
Continue to live by the Life that comes from God
Live according to the Law of the Spirit of Life
Remain in fellowship with Christ
Follow the teachings of the Holy Spirit
Be nourished by the Word as given to you
?

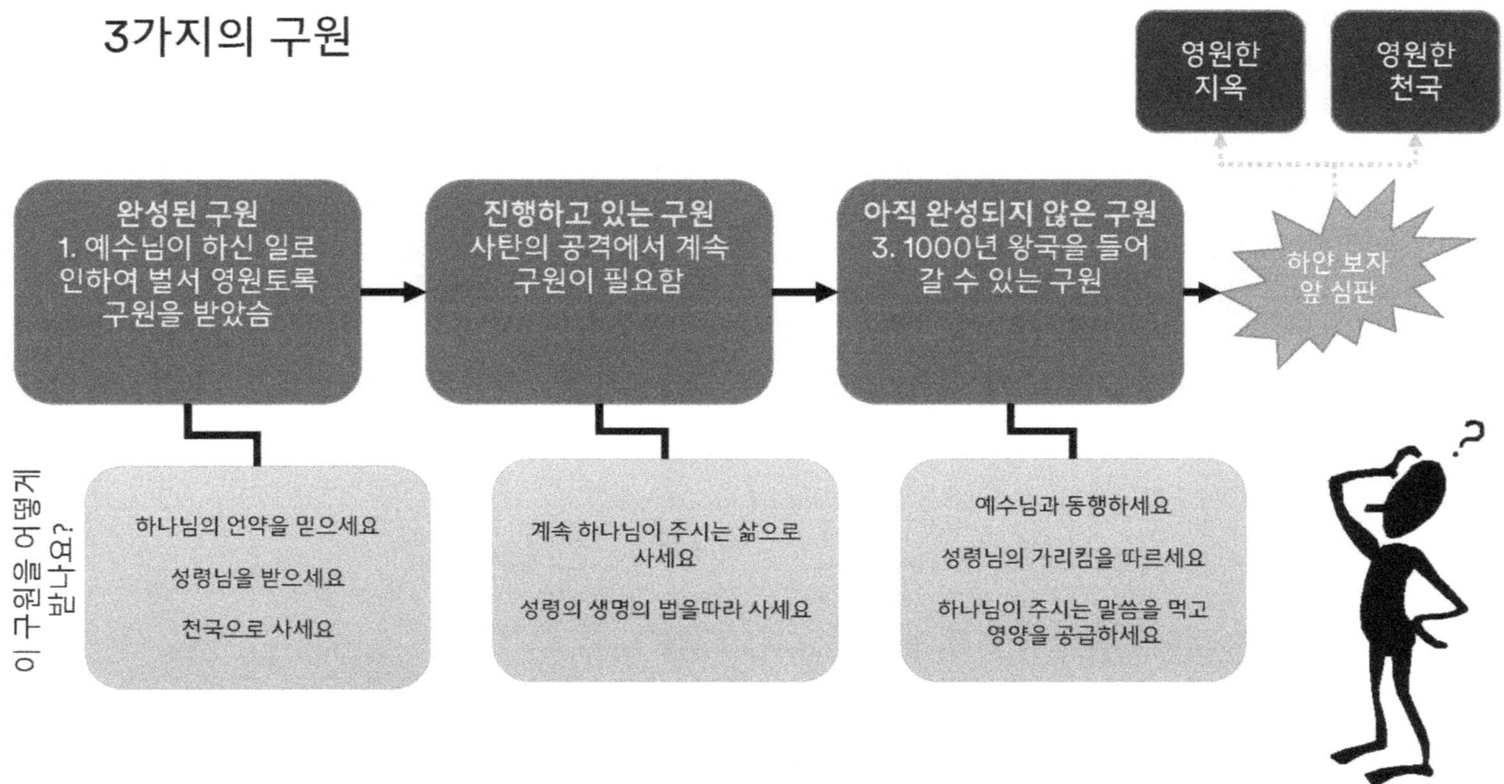
3가지의 구원
완성된 구원
1. 예수님이 하신 일로
인하여 벌서 영원토록
구원을 받았슴
진행하고 있는 구원
사탄의 공격에서 계속
구원이 필요함
아직 완성되지 않은 구원
3. 1000년 왕국을 들어
갈 수 있는 구원
하얀 보자
앞 심판
영원한
지옥
영원한
천국
이 구원을 어떻게
받나요?
하나님의 언약을 믿으세요
성령님을 받으세요
천국으로 사세요
계속 하나님이 주시는 삶으로
사세요
성령의 생명의 법을따라 사세요
예수님과 동행하세요
성령님의 가리킴을 따르세요
하나님이 주시는 말씀을 먹고
영양을 공급하세요
?

You believe in the Covenant that God swore to accomplish

One Covenant of God with different names		
Original Covenant	Given to Adam and Eve	Genesis 3:15, 21
Covenant of Circumcision Everlasting Covenant	Given to Abraham	Genesis 17
New / Second Covenant	Given to Moses @ Moab	Deuteronomy 30:6

We are not people who hear the Word of God through people and try to obey them; rather, we are people who receive teachings from the Holy Spirit. We are people who live with the mind of Christ that is given to us from Him as we live in Him.

당신은 하나님이 이루겠다고 맹새하신 한 언약을 믿습니다

다른 이름들을 갖인 하나님의 한 언약		
원례 언약	아담과 하와에게 주었음	창 3:15, 21
할례 언약 영원한 언약	아브라함에게 주었음	창 17
두번제 / 새 언약	모세에게 모압산에서 주었음	신 30:6

우리는 하나님의 말씀(계명)을 사람에게 듣고 가르침을 받아 순종하려는 자들이 아니라 성령의 가르침을 받아 그리스도 안에서 그리스도께서 주시는 그리스도의 마음으로 사는 자들입니다.

What is wrong with the brief version of the Gospel?

Brief version: Believe in Jesus and you can go to heaven

- There is no next step. As a result, the person is told to go to church, attend services, listen to sermons, and serve in the church. It leads to following and striving to keep the law and be in good standing compared to others. Satan deceives them to stay captive to the Law of Sin and Death.
- Pharisees and Sadducees were very prominent people that were highly respected (c.f. Acts 5:34) that studied the Word of God very carefully. However, Jesus called them snakes (c.f. Matthew 23:33).
- Unfortunately, without knowing the Second/New Covenant and the secrets of heaven, they will be rejected by Jesus on the Day of Judgment.

Satan abbreviates the Gospel so we don't understand the full effects; we must recognize Jesus returned to us as Holy Spirit so that we may live the life He lived, that is as a sanctuary for God (Kingdom, Heaven)

짧은 버전 복음을 전하는 것에 문제가 있나요?

짧은 버전: 예수를 믿으면 천국간다

- 믿은 후에 다음에 단계가 없으며, 이 사람에게 교회를 가서 예배를 드리고, 설교를 듣고, 섬기라고 가리키게 된다. 그래서 이 새로운 믿음을 얻은자는 법을 따르려 힘을 쓸 것이면 다른 사람들 앞에서 양호하게 보이려 노력하게 된다. 사탄이 죄와 사망에 법으로 이 사람을 잡아 논다.
- 바리세인들과 사두개인들도 사람들이 많이 존경했고 (행 5:34) 하나님의 말씀을 열심히 공부하고 따르려 하던 사람들입니다. 그러나 예수님은 그들이 뱀, 곧 사탄의 자녀들이라고 부릅니다 (마 23:33)
- 두번제/새 언약과 천국의 비밀을 모르므로 예수님이 심판날에는 모른다고 할 것입니다.

사탄은 복음을 압축해서 사람들이 하나님의 완벽하신 계획을 못 보게 합니다. 예수님이 우리에게 성령님으로 돌아오셔서 이제는 우리고 예수님 처럼 하나님과 동행하는 하나님의 성전이 되어 살아야 된다는 것은 알아야 됩니다.

A-2. Glossary

Authority of Satan

Satan is the ruler/king of this world. Satan uses the law (the Word of God) to deceive and misuse the intent. He kills people by causing people to "obey" the law and by giving them the mind of Satan, which includes being greedy, blaming, and judging others.

Covenant

Promise. The Gospel. It is conditional. We must first believe in God and His promises, then God fulfills His part, which is to circumcise our hearts. Jesus will put into our hearts the Law of the Spirit of Life that is in Him so that we may live as He did."

First Covenant

This is an old promise that is not valid. It was used solely to show that people cannot fulfill the requirements of the law with our own strength and discipline. It is meant to turn people to God and rely on His Covenant. Satan continues to deceive believers to stay true to this Covenant, which Jesus abolished (c.f. Hebrews 10:9-10)

Fulfillment of the New Covenant Means

We can be the Church (c.f. Acts 20:28)

We can serve God with a clean heart (c.f. Hebrews 9:14)

We can be free from the empty ways of the past (c.f. 1 Peter 1:18)

We can be forgiven and cleansed from our sins (c.f. 1 John 1:7)

We can be completely free from captivity of sin (c.f. Revelations 1:5)

We can live as the Kingdom of God (Heaven) (c.f Revelations 1:6)

We can reign on earth as kings (c.f. Revelations 5:9-10)

Glory of God

In the Life of God is the glory of God, which is filled with God's authority, power, character, wisdom, and knowledge. Only the Holy Spirit can show God's glory to us.

We can display the glory of God when we have the mind of Christ.

How can people go to hell?

As a result of Jesus' removal of all our sins (c.f. Isaiah 53:4-6), no one can go to hell because of their sinfulness; rather, they would go to hell because they do not believe in Jesus that has removed all our sins.

"In Me"

Place as head (e.g. "In Christ" means "place Christ as our head")

Law of Faith

Something God initiated as a Covenant. If we respond to and believe in this Covenant, God will fulfill His end of the Covenant, which is to bring about salvation for us who believe.

Law of Moses

Law given to the life of flesh. See First Covenant.

Law of Sin and Death

Method by which Satan causes people to commit sin and lead them toward death with him.

Law of the Spirit of Life or Law of Christ

Living in Christ through the Holy Spirit with the life that comes from God. Living only by faith and reliance only on the grace of God

Method of How God's Power Revealed

All things submit to Jesus. As God works in us, they will submit before us, who are sanctuaries for the Living God.

Order in which Second Covenant is Fulfilled

Holy Spirit, through Christ, circumcises our and our children's hearts, which

Enables us to truly know the Almighty God and His Son Jesus, which in turn

Enables us to love God with all our hearts and mind so that

We would be born again with the life that comes from God

Enabling us to accept Jesus Christ

We would be able to hear the voice of God as He speaks from within us

Our Purpose in Life

It is sin to not know and live out one's purpose and mission in life. Our purpose is to reveal God to the world; but God cannot be made known or visible by the wisdom of this world; He can only be revealed by His working from within us (miracles, healings, power of prayer)

People who break God's Laws

In reference to Matthew 7:23, these are people that thought they were Christians, but are rejected by Jesus on Day of Judgment. They have been deceived by Satan to follow the First Covenant, which was abolished by Jesus. They may:

- listen to the Law of Moses from others and strives on his/her accord to keep them

- may use the Name of Jesus and perform miracles that may attract many people

These people tend to:

1. Not know the full Gospel (they believe simply believing in Jesus give them eternal life)

2. Not understand the secrets of heaven

3. Not know the Covenant of God (Second/New Covenant)"

Purpose of Listening to Other People

Law of Moses requires us to listen from other people and follow laws.

Rather, those that follow the Law of the Spirit of Life, we listen to the Holy Spirit that speaks directly to us. However, we should listen to the sermons of pastors and still diligently study Scriptures for the sole purpose of growing in Jesus to be led by Him. Our primary focus is to remain in Him and continue to live in Him.

Salvation

Enablement to see the Life that cannot be seen physically with our eyes or hearts

Secret of Heaven

Jesus, who has arrived and is at hands reach. Only through Him are we forgiven

To be in purpose of God

We are to be people that are born again with the life that comes from God. Then we would be in Christ, place Christ as our head, have the heart that Christ gives, live in the Name of Jesus, and then demonstrate the living God through the way we live. Those that do not do this are called sinners.

To Live in Christ and Show God's Life

To live in Christ, place Him as your head, and live with the heart that He gives you. Then Jesus who lives in you will work to show His life through yours.

What does it mean to believe in Jesus?

It means to believe that Jesus will fulfill in you the Covenant that God has promised. When you believe, Jesus will come to your home and fulfill the Covenant in you and your family.

When God fulfills the Second Covenant in us

1. God sends the Holy Spirit (c.f. Romans 2:29) through Christ (c.f. Colossians 2:11)

2. Then circumcises our hearts so that

3. We may love God with all our hearts and soul, which then

4. Enables us to receive the life that comes from God so that

5. We may accept Jesus Christ. This will enable us to

6. Hear the voice of Jesus and live according to His guidance

A-3. Words or Phrases that means the same

Kingdom of God
Kingdom of Heaven
Heaven
Sanctuary for the Living God

Name of Jesus
Jesus
Ark
Jehovah/Yahweh

To live as the Church
To live in Christ
To live with Christ as the head
To listen to and obey the Word of Christ
To live with the heart that comes from Christ
To live in the Name of Jesus

Sin is:
Living according to one's accord
Living with the thoughts and mind of the flesh
Not living with the Spirit of God

To live according to the Law of Moses, or the letter of the law
To live according to the flesh
To live according to the thoughts and minds of the flesh
To live hearing and learning about God's Word from other people

It means the same to say we live:
By God
By the Name of God
By the Name of Jesus
By the Glory of God
By the Life of Jesus
In Christ (c.f. 1 John 5:11-12)
With Christ as our Head
With the heart that Christ provides
With Christ as our covering (clothes)
Revealing Jesus

Seeing the face of God
Seeing the glory of God
Revealing the glory of God
Revealing God
Revealing the Name of God
Revealing the Life of God
Seeing the Heart of God

Glory
Face
Name
Life
Heart

Other Recommended Books by the Publisher

Our Highest Calling

by Dr. Sang Sur
ISBN: 978-1-953167-00-2

ourhighestcalling.com

Become a Disciple of Jesus to Make Disciples

In this book, you will learn:
- How Jesus made disciples, modeling His command for us to do the same
- How the gospel may have been distorted over history, leading to the way we do church today, requiring us to renew our minds
- How to be a disciple of Jesus who makes other disciples by meeting the lost where they are

Scripture Reflections of a Christian Businessman
ISBN for Old Testament: 978-1-953167-97-2
ISBN for New Testament: 978-1-953167-05-7

Gospel that Jesus preached – the Kingdom Gospel

Author: Rev. Sang Kwan Lee

Publisher: Prayer Tents Media

Translation by: Dr. Sang Sur

Published Date: July, 2020

Location of Publishing: Old Tappan, NJ

ISBN 978-1-953167-99-6 (e-book)

ISBN 978-1-953167-98-9 (Softcover)

Visit us:

https://www.prayertents.com

www.ingramcontent.com/pod-product-compliance
Lightning Source LLC
Chambersburg PA
CBHW021354090426
42742CB00009B/853

* 9 7 8 1 9 5 3 1 6 7 9 8 9 *